'*Sowing Seeds* is an invaluable blend of Sharon Moughtin's reflective practice and contemporary thinking about childhood spirituality. The result is an exceptional and inspiring resource for churches working with the very youngest children. A powerful case for seeing why the very young deserve the very best, and this is a well-tested method for doing that.'

Dr Rebecca Nye, Godly Play expert and researcher and consultant in children's spirituality

'I'm excited by *Sowing Seeds*! It's a celebration of Psalm 8.2 and all that babies and toddlers bring to worship. Movement, stories, actions and songs combine in carefully crafted sessions to draw groups into a new way of worshipping that will enrich everyone involved. I can't wait to start using it.'

The Revd Mary Hawes, former National Youth Adviser, The Church of England

'Sowing Seeds is being taken up enthusiastically by a growing number of Helping young children grow into the fullness of Christ through creativ derful journey of adventure and discovery; and this book, which I gladly com nyone starting out on that path.'

The outhwark

'We've loved using the Sowing Seeds material at St Albans Cathedral for our babies and young children as part of our worship on Sunday mornings. The modular format makes it easy to adapt for different ages or lengths of time, and the children really respond to the familiarity of the structure, the singing and interactive storytelling, and the repetition. We've seen steady growth in the number of families who come regularly on Sundays, and the parents are often less ready to move on from this resource than their children! Having such clear material has been great for our volunteer leaders, and we particularly love the fact that even our smallest babies and toddlers can participate in worship, rather than just being in a crèche.'

Beccy Baird, children's worship leader, St Albans Cathedral

'Our young children love joining in with the simple songs and actions, and before we know it they (and I) have a real understanding of the church liturgy. The resources give all types of children a chance to engage in a variety of activities: the chatty ones can sing, the active ones can move, the creative ones can get arty but the highlight of the week is always "What's in the Box?"

'I love preparing as it is all done for me – I just pick up the book and off I go. If I can't remember a tune, I either hum it and it comes back to me or one of the children sings it for me, as they all know the nursery-rhyme tunes. The crafts are all very basic and the children seem to like to be able to "make it their own". Before using this resource I used to spend hours preparing complicated crafts that took the children two minutes to complete, leaving them bored and me frazzled!!'

Charlotte Chappell, Christ Church Aughton, Liverpool

'The *Sowing Seeds* resource has become a crucial part of our worship at Sheffield Cathedral. The careful attention Sharon Moughtin has paid to immersing our very youngest members in the changing seasons and the liturgical rhythm of the Eucharist makes it the perfect resource for our context. Hearing the voices of children and encouraging them as they grow and develop as disciples is absolutely key for us, and it is a very great delight to hear them sing and praise using the Sowing Seeds materials with such joy. Seeing our very youngest members stride into the Cathedral, own the space and join in worship with so much confidence is in a very large part down to this thoughtful and imaginative resource.'

The Very Revd Abi Thompson, Dean of Sheffield Cathedral

'*Sowing Seeds* is an invaluable resource that we use in school to support our collective worship and Religious Education curriculum with the youngest of pupils. It helpfully provides some background knowledge of theological concepts and Bible stories to support the staff leading the sessions. I would highly recommend this to schools as it is unlike any other resource we have found.'

Kate Penfold-Attride, Headteacher, St Matthew's Church of England Primary School, Redhill

'*Sowing Seeds* is a gift to the church. Sharon Moughtin manages to combine sharp biblical insight, creative use of the liturgy, the immersive experience of storytelling, and a great deal of fun in a single resource. What you have here is a way to engage the children in your church, school or home with robust biblical scholarship, the lessons liturgy teaches without words, and an experience of worshipping God in community. Just be warned: you'll be humming the Sowing Seeds songs all week long.'

The Revd Dr Casey Strine, Theological Adviser to the House of Bishops and Secretary for Theology

'I warmly commend *Sowing Seeds*. A church which uses *Sowing Seeds* consistently over time will see its work with children, young people and families transformed. Everything you need is in the book. Commit your hopes to God and let the Lord work with you in sowing seeds.'

The Rt Revd Jane Steen, Bishop of Lynn

'*Sowing Seeds* is a game changer for any church wanting to engage with younger children. This is seriously impressive biblical theology presented in an engaging, fun and accessible way. My own children love it.'

The Revd Michael Robinson, Rector, Holy Trinity, Sloane Square

'Wonderful! We have here a handling of Christian worship and the Bible that embodies a rich and creative imaginative seriousness, a sure understanding of theology and an experienced appreciation of the practicalities of working with young children. I haven't come across anything else nearly as good as this.'

The Revd Professor Walter Moberly, Durham University

'We all think we know that biblical scholarship and Sunday School teaching belong in different worlds. *Sowing Seeds* shows that we are wrong. Sharon Moughtin brings the wisdom of a professional biblical scholar to the task of communicating the essence of the Bible to very young children, unveiling the depths of biblical stories for young disciples. Very user-friendly material from which adults can learn too.'

The Revd John Barton, Emeritus Professor, University of Oxford

'When Jesus taught, he often used a language that was unafraid to hover rather than land. Through imaginative and playful provocation, he was opening up spaces for his listeners to move into. This is exactly what *Diddy Disciples* (now *Sowing Seeds*) does. It takes for granted the fact that young children are intelligent and perceptive, and it therefore doesn't look down on them. Neither does it pretend that Christian faith is anything but a rich, complex and teasing migration towards the love and mystery of God, where questions can be as vital as insights. This is a liberating combination for everyone involved.'

The Very Revd Dr Mark Oakley, Dean of Southwark Cathedral

'This resource approaches worship and storytelling with reverence and joy! Children and leaders alike will learn from the liturgical intelligence, sensitivity and natural language of Sharon Moughtin's approach. An inspirational resource for all on the way of discipleship, including special attention to the new texts for baptism.'

Dr Matthew Salisbury, National Liturgy and Worship, Church of England

'This is a flexible resource that acknowledges the importance and significance of enabling the youngest at church to engage in worship and begin a faith journey. The book not only offers ideas for a range of different settings and of personality and learning styles, but is also clearly built upon a theological and developmental understanding of children and faith. This is a resource that we will be using within our church setting, as we seek to engage and empower children from the youngest age in their understanding of God, faith, themselves and the world.'

Steve Chalke, founder and leader, Oasis Global

'Even though Jesus makes it clear that entering the kingdom of God requires us to become like children, real children are often neglected in the catechetical and formational life of the Church. *Diddy Disciples* (now *Sowing Seeds*) puts that right! Here is a resource to help the children come to Jesus and grow as his disciples.'

The Most Revd and Rt Hon. Stephen Cottrell, Archbishop of York

'This resource is aimed at pedagogy for children, but the author is mindful of Jesus' words, and what she has written is just as relevant for adult education and pedagogy as well. Sharon Moughtin's book stresses that education is "not words alone", and that doesn't just apply to children. What she has produced gives due attention to what it is one is wanting to communicate. What she has given us is based on the importance of movement, repetition, attending to children's own voices and emotions, nurturing what's already there and offering children a space in church that is dedicated to their needs and gifts. We are all in her debt for this insightful mixture of information and method.'

The Revd Professor Christopher Rowland, Emeritus Professor of Exegesis of Holy Scripture, University of Oxford

'Sharon Moughtin has accomplished something marvellously fresh, profound and practical with *Diddy Disciples* (now *Sowing Seeds*). There is a depth of biblical and liturgical understanding here which sets this resource apart, yet that understanding consistently serves the most kinetic and straight-out joyful set of Christian materials for children that one could hope to encounter. The rich array of options on offer within each unit and section means that it is all superbly flexible and adaptable for churches of different sizes, shapes and settings. I cannot recommend it highly enough.'

The Revd Dr David Hilborn, Principal, St John's College, Nottingham

The Revd Dr Sharon Moughtin is the author of Sowing Seeds, which began when her own wriggly and chatty children were 3, 3 and 2, and going to church with them felt impossible! She is now Vicar of St Mary in the Wilderness, created by Lambeth Palace and the Diocese of Southwark (Church of England) to respond to the challenges of climate change and the biodiversity crisis. Sharon is a professional Bible scholar, previously teaching Old Testament at Ripon College Cuddesdon and now Visiting Research Fellow at King's College London. She is passionate about the Bible, the environment, education, creativity and learning how to 'be like a child' from the youngest of children.

Sowing Seeds

Book 1: Bible storytelling and worship with children

Includes Advent, Christmas and Epiphany

Second edition

Sharon Moughtin

First published in Great Britain in 2017

SPCK Publishing
Part of the SPCK Group, Studio 101, The Record Hall, 16–16A Baldwin's Gardens, London EC1N 7RJ
https://spckpublishing.co.uk

Second edition published 2025

Text copyright © Sharon Moughtin 2017, 2025
This edition copyright © Society for Promoting Christian Knowledge 2025

Sharon Moughtin has asserted her right under the Copyright, Designs and Patents Act, 1988, to be identified as Author of this work.

All rights reserved. No part of this book may be reproduced or transmitted in any form or by any means, electronic or mechanical, including photocopying, recording, or by any information storage and retrieval system, without permission in writing from the publisher.

SPCK does not necessarily endorse the individual views contained in its publications.

The author and publisher have made every effort to ensure that the external website and email addresses included in this book are correct and up to date at the time of going to press. The author and publisher are not responsible for the content, quality or continuing accessibility of the sites.

Unless otherwise noted, Scripture quotations are taken from the New Revised Standard Version of the Bible, Anglicized Edition, copyright © 1989, 1995 by the Division of Christian Education of the National Council of the Churches of Christ in the USA. Used by permission. All rights reserved.

Quotations marked NIV are taken from The Holy Bible, New International Version (Anglicized edition). Copyright © 1979, 1984, 2011 by Biblica. Used by permission of Hodder & Stoughton Ltd, an Hachette UK company. All rights reserved.'NIV' is a registered trademark of Biblica. UK trademark number 1448790.

Every effort has been made to seek permission to use copyright material reproduced in this book. The publisher apologizes for those cases where permission might not have been sought and, if notified, will formally seek permission at the earliest opportunity.

Permission is given to photocopy the following, provided that they are for use by the purchaser's organization only and are not for resale: the Bible Storytelling material and Building Blocks, and the music resources and craft templates.

There are supporting web resources at <**www.sowingseeds-online.org**>. The password for the website is **mustard251**

EU GPSR Authorised Representative
LOGOS EUROPE, 9 rue Nicolas Poussin, 17000, La Rochelle, France
Email: Contact@logoseurope.eu

British Library Cataloguing-in-Publication Data
A catalogue record for this book is available from the British Library

ISBN 978–0–281–09089–1
eBook ISBN 978–0–281–09090–7

10 9 8 7 6 5 4 3 2 1

Designed by Melissa Brunelli
Typeset by Fakenham Prepress Solutions, Fakenham, Norfolk NR21 8NL
Printed and bound in Great Britain by Clays Ltd, Elcograf S.p.A.

eBook by Fakenham Prepress Solutions, Fakenham, Norfolk NR21 8NL

Produced on paper from sustainable sources

*For Ross and Jacqui, my wonderful parents,
with thanks for all they taught and gave me.*

CONTENTS

Acknowledgements — xiii

Introduction — 1

Part 1: Interactive Bible storytelling

Introduction — 7

The Light of the World Is Dawning unit (Advent and Christmas) — 10

Storybox 1: Getting Ready for Baby Jesus — 12
- Baby John's Story (Luke 1.5–25, 57–79) — 12
- Mary's Story — 15
  - Option 1: '"Yes!" said Mary' (Luke 1.26–38) — 15
  - Option 2: 'Let's tell Mary's story' (Luke 1.26–38) — 18
- Mary's Song — 22
  - Option 1: 'What can Jesus hear?' (Luke 1.39–55) — 22
  - Option 2: 'My God is a topsy turvy God!' (Luke 1.39–55) — 26
- The Angels' Song (Luke 2.8–16a) — 31
- Christmas — 34
  - Option 1: Meet Baby Jesus! (Luke 2.16–20) — 34
  - Option 2: The Shepherds' Story! (Luke 2.8–20) — 35

Storybox 2: Lighting the Advent Wreath — 39
- **Candle 1:** The Patriarchs and Matriarchs (Abraham and Sarah) (Genesis 12.1–5; 13.14–18; 15.4–6) — 39
- **Candle 2:** Prophets of Old (Isaiah 9.1–7) — 43
- **Candle 3:** John the Baptist (Luke 3.1–6; Isaiah 40.3–5) — 47
- **Candle 4:** Mary, Jesus' Mummy — 50
- **Candle 5:** Jesus, Light of the World — 50

Extra: The Christingle's Story — 51
Extra: Interactive Nativity with Mini Carols — 59

Jesus, Light of the World! unit (Epiphany) — 67

- The Magi's Journey (Matthew 2.1–2) — 68
- The Magi's Gifts (Matthew 2.1–2, 9–11) — 71
- Extra: Baby Jesus, the Refugee (Matthew 2.13–18) — 76
- Anna the Prophet's Story (Luke 2.36–38; Isaiah 40; 60) — 79
- Jesus, Light of the World! (The presentation of Jesus, Luke 2.22–33) — 83

John the Baptist unit (the weeks before Lent) — 88

- Meet John (Matthew 3.1–6) — 88
- John Baptizes Jesus (Matthew 3.13–17) — 92
- Extra: Our Baptism: a baptism roleplaying workshop — 97
- Jesus Is Thrown into the Wilderness (Mark 1.9–12) — 107

Part 2: Bible storytelling for baby and toddler groups

Introduction — 115

Basic Structure — 116

The Light of the World Is Dawning unit (Advent): Getting Ready for Baby Jesus — 119

Getting Ready for Baby Jesus songbox	119
'Busy, busy, busy, getting ready for Christmas!'	119
'"Yes!" said Mary'	121
'My God is a topsy turvy God!'	121
'Little donkey'	122
'The cow by the manger'	122
'Silent night'	123

Jesus, Light of the World! unit (Christmas and Epiphany) — 124

Jesus, Light of the World! songbox	124
'Joy! Joy! Joy! It's Christmas!'	124
'See in the darkness'	125
'Twinkle, twinkle, holy star'	126
'Follow, follow, follow the star'	126
'Giving a present to Jesus'	128
'We are marching in the light of God'	128

John the Baptist and Baptism unit (the weeks before Lent) — 130

John the Baptist and Baptism songbox	130
'Get ready for our God!'	130
'Wash me in the river'	131
'Down, down, down into the water'	131
'The welcome'	133
'Shine like a light in the world!'	133

Part 3: Creative Response starter ideas

Introduction	**137**
The Light of the World Is Dawning unit (Advent and Christmas)	**137**
Story Starter Ideas	138
Sensory Starter Ideas (including for babies and toddlers)	143
Unit Starter Ideas	144
Jesus, Light of the World! unit (Epiphany)	**145**
Story Starter Ideas	146
Sensory Starter Ideas (including for babies and toddlers)	150
Unit Starter Ideas	151
John the Baptist and Baptism unit (the weeks before Lent)	**152**
Story Starter Ideas	152
Sensory Starter Ideas (including for babies and toddlers)	154
Unit Starter Ideas	154

Part 4: The Building Blocks

Introduction	**159**
The Sowing Seeds Website	159
Teaching Your Group New Songs	160
The Building Blocks	**160**
Welcome	160
Getting Ready to Worship	161

Introducing the Unit	162
Gathering Song	165
Getting Ready for Bible Storytelling	178
Interactive Bible Storytelling	179
Saying Sorry to God	179
Saying Sorry Action	181
God Gives Us a New Start	188
Prayers for Other People	190
Prayer Actions	192
Thank You, God	196
Creative Response	200
Sharing God's Peace	200
The Peace	201
Around a Table	202
Taking God's Love into the World	202
Go in Peace to Love and Serve!	203

Sowing Seeds resources

Introduction	207
Imaginative aids	207
Peace cloth	207
Focal table	208
Creative Response resources	208
Collage materials	208
Interesting media	209
Recipes	210
Photocopiable templates	211
Notes	233

ACKNOWLEDGEMENTS

Sowing Seeds would never have happened without the children who have been part of creating it along the way. Many of the words, phrases, actions, symbols and ideas in this book came from them, as well as all the illustrations for the book cover, icons and templates. Thank you, little sisters and brothers, for your energy, insights, playfulness and willingness to share your gifts.

With special thanks to the amazing illustrators: Abigail, Amelia, Anastasia, Bella, Christian, Connie, Daijuan, Darcey, Ebba, Eden, Elijah, Gavin, Grace, Harry, Isabella, Isla, Jessica, Joy, Julia, Kayleigh, Marlon, Michael, Mitchell, Mya, Nancy, Ottie, Pearl, Philip, Rita, Samson, Samuel, Susan, Susannah, Zoe and Zoe.

Thank you also to all who have walked alongside me, advised me, and contributed to Diddy Disciples and Sowing Seeds in other ways over the years. Particular thanks go to Bishop Christopher Chessun, Bishop Jane Steen, Bishop Martin Gainsborough, Betsy Blatchley, Bill McGarvey, Brother Sam SSF, Dan Trott, Eve Bradshaw, Gene Doughlin, Henrietta Hastings, John Barton, Kate Penfold-Attride, Karen Wilson, Kev Smart, Mary Hawes, Michael Robinson, Mike Smith, Niall Sloane, Odette Penwarden, Renate Tulloh, Robert Harris, Rosy Fairhurst, Ruth Martin, Sarah Dawson, Sarah Fielding, Sheridan James, Simon Gates, Sarah Smith, Sister Judi CSF, Tom Hassan, Tracey Messenger and Will Cookson.

Thank you to the children and adults of St Mary in the Wilderness and all the placement students who have passed through there.

Thank you to the team at SPCK for their guidance and experience, especially Deborah Lock and Rima Devereaux.

Thank you to my mum and dad, my sisters, Debs, Beth and Jen, and the wider Moughtin clan.

Most of all, thank you to my daughters, Joy, Ana and Zoe, for your inspiration, love and energy – without you this would never have been written.

INTRODUCTION

Sowing Seeds is a collection of Bible storytelling, prayer and worship materials especially designed for groups of children ranging from babies and toddlers to 8–9 years old. The materials aim to create a space for children to encounter God for themselves. Through movement, imagination, faces and bodies, symbols, creative activities, music and song, Sowing Seeds encourages and enables children to participate fully. Older children and young people also have the opportunity to become leaders with the easy-to-access material.

Parts 1 and 2 contain interactive Bible Storytelling materials. Part 3 has a wealth of creative responses to the storytelling, including art, craft and sensory play. Part 4 has the Building Blocks of worship resources in the form of prayers and songs.

Sowing Seeds is flexible enough to be used in a variety of settings and Christian traditions. Some groups will create a session entirely from the books. Others will find a song or story or creative idea within its pages which will contribute to an established pattern. There's no single 'right way' to use the materials! Instead, explore the books and discover the materials that most resonate with your church setting, and that will support your time with God alongside children.

As Sowing Seeds was developed, seven principles emerged which underpin the resources. It might be helpful to familiarise yourself with these as you explore the materials. It will help you understand the decisions made in their creation (and re-creation) as we learned through trial and error.

Sowing Seeds: seven principles

1 Sowing Seeds celebrates movement

Sowing Seeds celebrates body language as our first language, which we can all share. This includes babies, children who are non-verbal, and those who speak English as an additional language. The materials encourage full body actions so that everyone can join in.

Children are naturally wriggly and chatty, so Sowing Seeds celebrates that. It scoops up children's desire to move and be heard and incorporates it in worship, growing a people of God who are active, vocal and expect to be included from the very beginning.

2 Sowing Seeds celebrates our voices

In Sowing Seeds, almost everything is sung. That's because we've found that singing when worshipping with children helps in all sorts of ways.

- Singing is something we do together. It gives everyone the opportunity to feel what it's like to be part of God's family, whatever their age.
- Singing means the words of the story are not said just once, they're repeated again and again. This can help children whose attention may wander, as well as babies and toddlers, and those who speak English as an additional language. Alongside this, the song's shape, tune, rhythm, pitch and volume provide additional clues to the story's meaning.
- With singing there is no need for shushing! Wriggly and chatty children can make it difficult for others to hear if there's only one voice telling the story. But if the whole room is telling the story together and singing, a chatty child is much less likely to become a distraction and far more likely to actually join in! Singing tends to attract and keep children's attention far more easily than words alone.
- Songs and tunes tend to stay with us much longer than words alone (thanks to Mary Hawes for this insight and all her other contributions).

Through listening and swaying, moving and dancing, and joining in actions and even some of the words, even the youngest present can join in worshipping God through song. Perhaps most importantly, singing allows the

Bible stories to become 'our story and our song' for the children. This is fundamental in Sowing Seeds. It's why everything is sung or said 'my turn', 'your turn'.

Tip: Our story: our song

In Deuteronomy 5.3–4 (NIV), Moses speaks about God's covenant to the people gathered before him. He says:

It was not with **our ancestors** that the Lord made this covenant, but with **US**, with all of us who are **alive here** TODAY. The Lord spoke to YOU **face to face** out of the fire on the mountain.

The words are emphatic. The point is clear. The people that Moses is talking to were there at the mountain when God made the covenant.

The unexpected thing is that a closer look at the story reveals that most of the people present were not there at all. This is the next generation; it **was** their parents who were at the mountain.

Moses hasn't made a mistake here. He's making a vital point about storytelling in God's family. These stories are not just their parents' stories, which happened long ago to be passed on and remembered. These stories are to become **their** story, and – as children adopted into God's family – **our** story too.

Sowing Seeds takes this seriously. When we tell these stories together with children, we're not simply remembering a story that happened to someone else. It's **our** story. We **ourselves** are becoming part of the story. We find ourselves in it in all sorts of different places. And as we tell the story together, it is to **us** that God is speaking.

Tip: Leading Sowing Seeds

Christian philosopher Søren Kierkegaard wrote:

'People have an idea that the preacher is an actor on a stage and they are the critics, blaming or praising the preacher.'

Leading worship and telling Bible stories to groups can feel like this sometimes! Thankfully, Kierkegaard continues:

'What they **don't** know is that **they** are the actors on the stage; the preacher is merely the prompter standing in the wings, reminding them of their lost lines.'[1]

The good news for leaders is that this takes the pressure off. When we tell these stories with the children, the attention is not on us. The quality of our singing voice is not the point.

The **children** and their adults are the actors on the stage, we leaders are simply the prompter, standing in the wings, reminding them of their lost lines – or often, in this case, the lines they haven't even been told yet. And how are they to know if no one tells them?

3 Sowing Seeds celebrates repetition: 'Again! Again!'

Finding a pattern and rhythm is key to Sowing Seeds. Choose the material that resonates best with your context, then keep to that pattern at least for a unit (4–7 sessions). This repetition gives children and their adults confidence. They know what's coming next and are therefore more likely to take part fully and maybe even take a lead, rather than having to wait or watch because they're not sure what's happening.

Sowing Seeds moves between periods of movement and (very short) periods of quieter calm. As the children become familiar with this, it becomes much easier for them to remain quiet for a short time when appropriate. A familiar pattern also takes the pressure off the person leading worship. Once you're in the rhythm, it can be liberating to know that almost all the next week's worship will be familiar to you as well as to others in the group.

4 Sowing Seeds celebrates children's spirituality

Dr Rebecca Nye's work on children's spirituality has been a very important influence on Sowing Seeds.[2] Her research (and that of many others) shows that children possess an innate sense of wonder and an innate sense of God. We do not need to introduce this sense of spirituality to children – it's already there! The challenge is how we make connections so that a child's spirituality resonates with what they see and experience when they enter a church. Sowing Seeds aims to create safe spaces, building what Rebecca Nye calls 'two-way bridges', between children's spirituality and the worship they will experience in church.

5 Sowing Seeds celebrates being part of the Church

Babies and children are full members of the worshipping community and Sowing Seeds celebrates this. By choosing from worship materials laid out in 'Building Blocks' in Part 4, alongside Bible storytelling, your group can create a service that reflects the main Sunday service of your church as closely as possible. This can help to build bridges between Sowing Seeds sessions and the other worship that takes place in your church.

The Building Blocks include plenty of opportunities for children to lead, enabling them to discover their own ministries and what they can offer. Sowing Seeds also recognizes that adults will be present during the sessions – as leaders, parents and carers – and that it's important that these adults are also fed and nourished by your time together, with opportunities to grow too.

> **Tip**
>
> If your church holds all-age or whole church services, encourage the leaders to borrow elements from Sowing Seeds which will already be familiar to the children. The Sorry Song (p. 179) and Prayers for Other People (p. 190) are among the worship elements in Building Blocks which can be incorporated into other worship services.

6 Sowing Seeds celebrates learning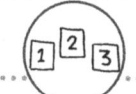

Sowing Seeds seeks to grow a people of God who naturally bring their relationship with God into their home life and work, and their home life and work into their relationship with God. For this reason, the material makes multiple links with the learning that babies, toddlers and children are experiencing at home, school and nursery. There's lots of counting out loud on fingers, naming colours, noticing different kinds of weather, learning how plants grow and exploring different kinds of emotions. Well-known nursery-rhyme tunes also bring a sense of familiarity to the Bible storytelling and worship.

> **Tip: Everyday connections matter**
>
> Throughout the Bible, everyday objects and experiences are used to make connections between our daily lives and God. Jesus used the everyday of Galilee: wildflowers, bread, water, wine, wheat, sparrows, sheep, goats, vineyards. The apostle Paul focussed on the everyday experiences of people living in the Roman empire: architecture, discoveries about the human body, war, Olympic games, trading. Following their examples, Sowing Seeds helps young children make two-way connections between their everyday life and the stories of God's people.

7 Sowing Seeds celebrates our feelings and emotions

God created humans with a wide range of emotions and feelings. All human emotions are explored openly in the Bible: jealousy, rage, anger and fear are acknowledged, as well as joy, peace, love and so on. In countless passages, negative emotions are brought before God and transformed. Moses' deep anger – expressed in murderous rage – is seen by God, transformed and used to set God's people free. Peter's fear and his denial of even knowing Jesus are brought into the open and lead to a new start for Peter not only as a follower of Jesus but as a leader.

Sowing Seeds can help to create safe spaces where human emotions and feelings are named and explored together. Early childhood is a time of big emotions, that can sometimes startle young children (and their parents and carers!). Together, God's people can learn to bring all sorts of feelings before God, growing in hope and trust that even negative emotions can be transformed by God into something beautiful, holy and life-giving. Early childhood is a wonderful place to begin this way of life.

Part 1
Interactive Bible storytelling

Introduction

Sowing Seeds was originally created for babies, toddlers and young children aged around 0–7. As the children in our group grew older, however, we found that most of the material worked with children up to the age of around 9. For the few stories that didn't work, we've created a separate option. Each story now begins with an indication of the age range it has been designed for: either 0–7 or 0–9. When choosing which stories to use for your group it may be helpful to think of the age range currently represented there.

Groups that include no children above the age of two and a half will probably find the material in Part 2 more appropriate.

> **Tip: Including babies in mixed groups**
>
> For babies, Sowing Seeds represents an immersive approach to worship. They're not expected to follow and understand every word, but they're drawn into the experience that is taking place around them, encouraged to participate and lead in their own ways (which usually involves using their bodies). Being actively included from the very beginning is important in itself. As part of God's family, these babies take part in the family's activities, just as at home they spend some time in the melee of family life. By being immersed in activities that are especially designed for the first years of life – alongside children only a little older than they are – these babies are also given the opportunity to gradually develop skills that will deepen their experience over time.
>
> Including babies can also be beneficial for parents and carers, meaning they no longer have to spend the adult sermon either 'shushing' their children or segregated into a crèche area where it can be difficult for them to feel an active part of the church. We've found that many adults themselves find Sowing Seeds worship and Bible storytelling meaningful, and are often moved by the experience of worshipping alongside – and being led by – the youngest of children.

The Building Blocks

Sowing Seeds isn't just Bible storytelling. The Building Blocks in Part 4 (p. 160) provide a wide range of prayer, worship and creative materials to resource and nurture your group's time with God. Once you've chosen your stories from the storyboxes in this section, take a look to see what those Building Blocks might have to offer your group. Find out more in the introduction to the Building Blocks on p. 159.

The website includes an introduction to teaching songs for the first time, which might sometimes also come in useful for the storytelling below.

What's in the Box?

'What's in the Box?' is one of the Building Blocks that is often referred to in the storytelling material below. This option is especially helpful for groups that include babies and toddlers who might need support with some of the vocabulary in the story. Simply find a box for your group that looks inviting. Place within it the items suggested at the beginning of each story and open it with the children each time you meet to discover what's inside, asking 'What's in the box?' and inviting a child to lead the group in responding.

The 'I'm Sorry' and 'New Start' signs

The 'I'm Sorry' and 'New Start' signs that appear throughout the storytelling material are among the very few Sowing Seeds signs and actions that are fixed. Usually, the children are trusted with the responsibility for creating the actions for the songs and storytelling as the hope is that this will become *their* story and *their* song (p. 2). However, the 'I'm Sorry' and 'New Start' signs have been chosen for the resonances they create through the material. Videos of the movement for both signs can be found on the website next to the Sorry Song Building Block in any of the units.

The 'I'm Sorry' sign

The 'I'm Sorry' sign not only conveys sadness. It calls to mind the waters of baptism being splashed over us. The echoes of an 'X' shape not only show that we know that we've got something wrong, but can also call to mind at the same time the cross of Jesus in the background. Start with your hands lightly crossed in front of your forehead, then move them in opposing arcs downwards towards your chest and round in opposing circles, and back just in front of your forehead. This opposing circular motion is the 'I'm Sorry' sign.

The 'New Start' sign

The 'New Start' sign can best be described as the 'winding' action from the nursery rhyme 'Wind the bobbin up'. Repeatedly rotate your arms around each other in front of your body. It shows that we want a chance to 'start again' but it has been chosen to point us also to the rolling away of the stone on Easter Day that brings about that great 'new start' for the whole world. The 'New Start' sign appears and reappears in so many of the stories throughout the Sowing Seeds units. It's the sign for:

- Mary's song about the 'topsy turvy God who turns things upside down' (which is sung in response to John's prophetic somersault).
- 'The first will be last and the last will be first' in God's revolutionary, 'topsy turvy' kingdom.
- Jesus turning the tables 'topsy turvy' in the Temple – 'Look! Jesus is giving the Temple a new start!'
- Jesus washing the disciples' feet, as the longed for king turns everything upside down to become the servant.
- The prayer 'Holy Spirit, come!' as Jesus' friends wait for the Spirit who will turn their lives (and the world) topsy turvy at Pentecost.
- Paul falling 'topsy turvy' off his horse when he meets Jesus and is given his 'new start'.

And more. Keep an eye out for the 'New Start' sign in the storytelling. It creates a golden thread of forgiveness and can appear in the most surprising of places!

Tip: Creative Responses

There are a wealth of suggestions for Creative Responses to the storytelling through art and sensory resources in Part 3. See p. 137 for more information and options.

Tip: Presentation folders

Presentation folders can really help when leading Sowing Seeds. They're much easier to manage than loose sheets, especially when doing actions! We've found that A5 folders are best, and the Bible storytelling has been formatted to slip easily into A5 folders.

Tip: Continuity

Sowing Seeds assumes that children won't be present every week and that new people may join or visit at any time! Units that involve an ongoing story that unfolds over a few weeks therefore tell the whole story from the beginning each week in abbreviated form, as if it hasn't been told before (a little like a recap sequence at the beginning of some TV series). This allows those who weren't there for a previous session to take full part in the storytelling, while giving those who were there the opportunity to strengthen and deepen their knowledge of the story.

Tip: Sowing Seeds and the Lectionary

Some churches use the Lectionary (a set pattern of reading followed each week in worship). It's not exactly child-friendly so, rather than follow it precisely, Sowing Seeds works in units which match the Church's seasons and broader themes. This allows for the rhythm of the liturgical year to be approached in a way specially formed and shaped for young children.

The Light of the World Is Dawning unit (Advent and Christmas)

This unit helps your group prepare for Baby Jesus, the Light of the World whose birth we celebrate at Christmas. There are two choices of storybox for this unit. There is also a mini carol service and Christingle material for groups who would like to create additional services.

Choose a storybox, work out how many times you will be meeting before and during Christmas, then choose which stories will work best in your setting.

Storybox 1: Getting Ready for Baby Jesus

'Getting Ready for Baby Jesus' contains stories from Luke's Gospel that lead up to the birth of Baby Jesus. There is not always time to tell all these stories at Christmas itself! Some of these stories include different options depending on the age range of your group.

Baby John's Story (Luke 1.5–25, 57–79) 12
Appropriate for mixed groups of 0–9 years

Mary's Story

Option 1: '"Yes!" said Mary' (Luke 1.26–38) 15
Appropriate for mixed groups of 0–7 years

Option 2: 'Let's tell Mary's story' (Luke 1.26–38) 18
Appropriate for mixed groups of 0–9 years

Mary's Song

Option 1: 'What can Jesus hear?' (Luke 1.39–55) 22
Appropriate for mixed groups of 0–5 years

Option 2: 'My God is a topsy turvy God!' (Luke 1.39–55) 26
Appropriate for mixed groups of 0–9 years

The Angels' Song (Luke 2.8–16a) 31
Appropriate for mixed groups of 0–9 years

Christmas

Option 1: Meet Baby Jesus! (Luke 2.16–20) 34
Appropriate for mixed groups of 0–9 years
With shorter storytelling to allow for longer creative activity

Option 2: The shepherds' story! (Luke 2.8–20) 35
Appropriate for mixed groups of 0–9 years

Note: The story of the Magi (or Three Kings/Wise Men) can be found in the Jesus, Light of the World! unit on p. 68. Some groups may prefer to use stories from this unit during the lead up to Christmas.

> **Tip**
> Even if you don't use the other Building Blocks, you may find it helpful to use the Gathering Song ('Busy, busy, busy, getting ready for Christmas') just before the storytelling in every session of this unit as it gathers together the themes of the unit as a whole. See p. 165.

Storybox 2: Lighting the Advent Wreath

'Lighting the Advent Wreath' contains stories that are themed around the traditional lighting of five candles over the course of Advent. This storybox is especially helpful for groups that include children age 7+. If your group doesn't include any children age 7+, you might find the first storybox, 'Getting Ready for Baby Jesus' more appropriate. For tips on how to involve babies actively in these mixed groups, see 'Including babies in mixed groups' on p. 7.

There are different traditions about the meaning of the five candles of the Advent wreath. If your church follows a different pattern, feel free to adapt the material accordingly.

Candle 1: The Patriarchs and Matriarchs (Abraham and Sarah)
(Genesis 12.1–5; 13.14–18; 15.4–6) 39
Appropriate for mixed groups of 0–9 years

Candle 2: Prophets of Old (Isaiah 9.1–7) 43
Appropriate for mixed groups of 0–9 years

Candle 3: John the Baptist (Luke 3.1–6; Isaiah 40.3–5) 47
Appropriate for mixed groups of 0–9 years

Candle 4: Mary, Jesus' Mummy 50
Appropriate for mixed groups of 0–9 years

Candle 5: Jesus, Light of the World 50
Appropriate for mixed groups of 0–9 years

> **Tip**
> Even if you don't use the other Building Blocks, you may find it helpful to use 'The Advent Wreath' Song just before the storytelling in every session of this unit as it gathers together the themes of the unit as a whole. See p. 169.

Extra (relevant to both storyboxes)

The Christingle's Story 51
Appropriate for mixed groups of 0–9 years or whole school or all-age services

Interactive Nativity with Mini Carols 59
Appropriate for mixed groups of 0–9 years or whole school or all-age services

Storybox 1: Getting Ready for Baby Jesus

Baby John's Story

→ Luke 1.5–25, 57–79
→ Song: 'Jesus, Light of the World'. Words © Sharon Moughtin.
→ Tune: 'What shall we do with the drunken sailor?' (traditional).

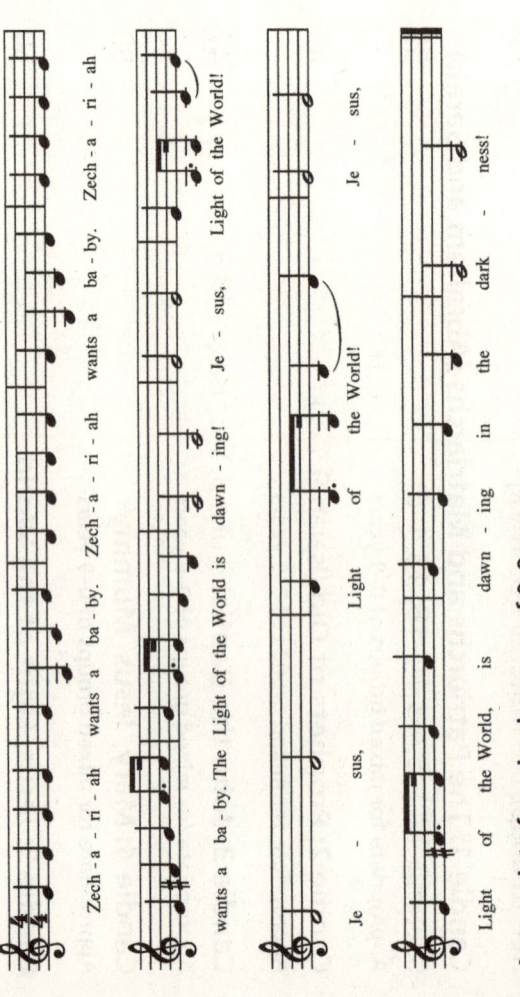

Appropriate for mixed groups of 0–9 years.

The song from Baby John's story provides the basis of the Gathering Song for the whole unit (see p. 165). Even if you are planning to use the Gathering Song for the rest of the unit, skip it for this week.

In this story, the 'New Start' sign (the winding action from 'Wind the bobbin up') is used to show how Baby John will 'get the world ready'. This is among the very few Sowing Seeds signs and actions that are fixed. See p. 8 or the website (www.sowingseeds-online.org) for a description and explanation.

Ask the children to sit for a moment of quiet.

To tell our story today, first we need to learn a song.
It's called 'Jesus, Light of the World'!
Let's close our eyes and feel the dark . . .
Now let's imagine a bright light shining in the darkness!
Wow!
Let's open our eyes again.

In our story, Zechariah sings that Baby Jesus
is like a bright light in the dark,
like the sun rising in the morning.
You might like to show the children a picture of the sun rising at this point.

Let's show the sun 'dawning' with our bodies.
Let's crouch down low . . .
Let's close our eyes . . . it's dark!
Let's show the sun coming up and up and up and out . . .
The sun is 'dawning' in the morning.
Lead the children in showing the sun rising with your hands as you stand up.

Now let's do that as we sing our song,
'Jesus, Light of the World'.

Lead the children in singing quietly.

Je-sus, Light of the World, *Sun dawning action*
Je-sus, Light of the World, *Sun dawning action*
Je-sus, Light of the World, is *Sun dawning action*
dawning in the darkness! *Sun dawning action*

We're ready!

Optional: What's in the Box? (see p. 7)

Invite one of the children to open the box. Inside will be an angel

or a picture of an angel. You might even like to show your group a
photograph of an angel depicted somewhere in your church building.
What's in the box? Ask the child to respond
This is the angel Gabriel.
He's a very special angel.
Gabriel takes messages from God to people:
he's like a post-angel.
Today Gabriel's going to take his first message
to a man called Zechariah!

Let's tell Zechariah's story together.
Zechariah was a very good man!
Let's be Zechariah. Let's sit up straight!
Show me how you look when you're being good.
Zechariah really, really wanted something.
Can you show me how you feel when you really want something?
Zechariah really, really wanted a baby!
Invite the children to rock their arms like rocking a baby.

But everyone said he was too old.
Can you show me how you feel
when you don't get something
you really, really want?
Lead the children in looking sad, cross, fed up.

Let's sing together in a very quiet, sad voice.
Zechariah wants a baby. *Rock arms looking sad, fed up*
Zechariah wants a baby.
Zechariah wants a baby.
[The] Light of the World is dawning! *Sun dawning action*

Lead the children in singing a little more excitedly but still quietly.
Je-sus, Light of the World, *Sun dawning action*
Je-sus, Light of the World, *Sun dawning action*
Je-sus, Light of the World, is *Sun dawning action*
dawning in the darkness! *Sun dawning action*

Now Zechariah had a very special job.
He led the prayers at the 'Temple'.
The Temple was God's house, where people went to pray,
a bit like our church.
Zechariah lit some special candles.
The smoke went up to God.
Let's sway our bodies like smoke going up, up, up!
Crouch down low, then reach up tall as you sway.

The prayers went up with the smoke!
Zechariah didn't say anything
but his secret prayer for a baby went up to God, too.
Let's sing quietly again . . . .
The prayers are going up to God.
The prayers are going up to God.
The prayers are going up to God.
[The] Light of the World is dawning! *Sun dawning action*

Lead the children in singing even more excitedly and a little louder.
Je-sus, Light of the World, *Sun dawning action*
Je-sus, Light of the World, *Sun dawning action*
Je-sus, Light of the World, is *Sun dawning action*
dawning in the darkness! *Sun dawning action*

Suddenly, the Holy Place was filled with light!
Shield eyes with your hand.

The brightest light Zechariah had ever seen!
Zechariah saw an angel standing there!

He fell to the floor!
Invite the children to fall to the floor.

We're going to be the angel Gabriel together.
Let's stand up tall and strong and sing nice and loud . . . .
'Zechariah! *Point strongly* You will have a baby!'

Lead the children in pointing strongly at someone else each time as you sing:
Zechariah, *Point you will have a baby! Rock arms*
Zechariah, *Point you will have a baby! Rock arms*
Zechariah, *Point you will have a baby! Rock arms*
[The] Light of the World is dawning! *Sun dawning action*

Go straight into the following without the refrain.
This baby isn't Jesus. *Shake head*
We're not ready for Baby Jesus yet!
This baby will help us get ready for Jesus.
This is Baby John!
The angel says to Zechariah,
'Baby John will get the world ready!'
'New Start' sign (see p. 8) to show 'getting ready'.

Let's sing together!

Baby John will get the world ready. *'New Start' sign*
Baby John will get the world ready. *'New Start' sign*
Baby John will get the world ready. *'New Start' sign*
[The] Light of the World is dawning! *Sun dawning action*

Je-sus, Light of the World, *Sun dawning action*
Je-sus, Light of the World, *Sun dawning action*
Je-sus, Light of the World, is *Sun dawning action*
dawning in the darkness! *Sun dawning action*

But Zechariah shook his head.
Let's shake our heads and look sad.
'I can't have a baby!' said Zechariah.
'I'm too old!'
Zechariah didn't believe the angel!
Look shocked.

The angel said, 'Because you didn't say yes,
you won't be able to open your mouth!'
Let's zip our mouths shut after three:
1, 2, 3 . . . Zip!
Then the angel leaves. Gone!

Zechariah tries to tell everyone about the angel,
Pretend to speak with your mouth closed,
'Mmmmmm', but he can't speak!
Let's be Zechariah trying to tell people about the angel!
Mmmmmm! Mmmmm! *With frenetic pointing*
Then do you know what happened?
Nine months later, a baby was born!
Lead the children in holding a baby gently.

Let's be Zechariah holding our baby.
Let's sing together really happily and joyfully.

Zechariah has a baby. *Rock arms gently*
Zechariah has a baby. *Rock arms gently*
Zechariah has a baby. *Rock arms gently*
[The] Light of the World is dawning! *Sun dawning action*

Je-sus, Light of the World, *Sun dawning action*
Je-sus, Light of the World, *Sun dawning action*
Je-sus, Light of the World, *Sun dawning action*

14

Je-sus, Light of the World, *Sun dawning action*
dawning in the darkness! *Sun dawning action*

Zechariah's friends ask 'What's his name?'
What do you think Zechariah says?

If appropriate, invite the children to guess.

Trick question!
Zechariah can't say anything!
He still can't open his mouth! Mmmmmm!
But his friends give him something to write on
and Zechariah writes 'John' on it!
Let's write John together . . .

Lead the children in writing letters or squiggling in the air. The children may join in with you in spelling the name out. If you know the phonic sounds, it's best to use those. You could always ask a Year 1 or Reception child to help you out.

j . . . o . . . h . . . n

That moment, Zechariah's mouth was opened up!
Let's unzip our mouth . . . .
1, 2, 3, zip!

Zechariah sang a beautiful song:
the song we've been singing
about the Light of the World
getting ready to shine in the darkness.

Put your hand up if you've seen Christmas lights being put up!
At Christmas, we have Christmas lights to remind us
that Jesus is the 'Light of the World'.

When we see Christmas lights,
let's remember we're getting ready for Baby Jesus.
Let's sing Zechariah's song together,
this time as loud and joyfully as we can!

Je-sus, Light of the World, *Sun dawning action*
Je-sus, Light of the World, *Sun dawning action*
Je-sus, Light of the World, is *Sun dawning action*
dawning in the darkness! *Sun dawning action*

Je-sus, Light of the World, *Sun dawning action*
Je-sus, Light of the World, *Sun dawning action*
Je-sus, Light of the World, is *Sun dawning action*
dawning in the darkness! *Sun dawning action*

Mary's Story: Option 1: '"Yes!" said Mary'

→ Luke 1.26–38
→ '"Yes!" said Mary'. Words © Sharon Moughtin.
→ Tune: '"Pop!" goes the weasel' (traditional).

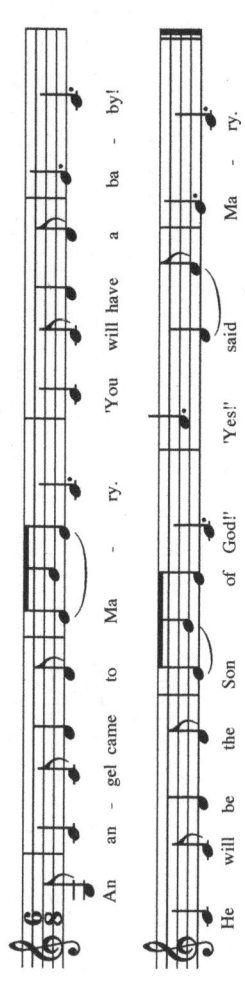

Appropriate for mixed groups of babies, toddlers and children up to the age of 7. Groups that include children up to the age of 9 may prefer to use Option 2. The storytelling is very similar, but the song in Option 1 is more memorable for the youngest children. Choose which version works best in your setting.

Optional: What's in the Box? (see p. 7)

Invite one of the children to open the box. Inside will be an angel or a picture of an angel. Like last week, you might even like to show your group a photograph of an angel depicted somewhere in your church building.

What's in the box? *Ask the child to respond*
This is the angel Gabriel.
He's a very special angel.

Gabriel takes messages from God to people:
he's like a post-angel.
Today Gabriel's going to take a message
to a girl called Mary.

To tell our story today, we need to learn a song.
The actions of this song are designed to mirror a jack-in-the-box, with its lid closing and the puppet bursting out at the 'pop' moment. To teach this song, sing it alone the first time, with the children copying your actions. See if they can join in on the second time around.
Start standing on tiptoes with your hands stretched high. You could make angel wings (like butterfly wings) with your hands.
An angel came to Ma-a-a-ry.
Bring hands down from on high and come down from tiptoes.
'You will have a baby!
Rock baby, standing at normal height.
He will be the Son of God!'
Crouch down on the ground like tiny child.
'Yes!' sa-id Mary.
Jump up and shout 'Yes!'
Repeat.

We're going to tell the story of our song together now.
First we need to practise showing
how we feel with just our faces.
Not opening our mouths at all.
Who can show me . . . .
As you list the following emotions one by one, give the children time to show each emotion with their face. You might like to point out some good examples given by the children:
sad . . . .
happy . . . .
confused (when you don't understand) . . . .
amazed! . . . .
scared.

We're ready to tell our story.
Mary was at home, sweeping.
Let's be Mary and sweep the floor.
Lead the group in sweeping like Mary.

Hum the tune of 'Pop goes the weasel' quietly as you sweep.
Suddenly, the room was filled with light!
Shield eyes with hand.

The brightest light Mary had ever seen!
Mary saw an angel standing there!
She fell to the floor!
Lead the children in falling to the floor.

Now we're going to be the angel Gabriel together.
These words are very important.
Let's kneel up high on our knees for a moment
to say the angel's words together.

Lead the children in kneeling.
It's 'my turn' *Point to self* 'your turn' *Leader's hands out to group.*

Lead the children in saying the following words.
Hello Mary. *Wave*
Hello Mary. *Wave*
Don't be frightened. *Hands out*
Don't be frightened. *Hands out*
God is very happy with you! *Draw smile on face*
God is very happy with you! *Draw smile on face*
You're going to have a baby. *Rock arms*
You're going to have a baby: *Rock arms*

a little boy called Jesus. *Rock arms*
a little boy called Jesus. *Rock arms*
He's going to be king! *Place imaginary crown on head*
He's going to be king! *Place imaginary crown on head*

Wow! These words are very special words.
Shall we say them again together?
Hello Mary. *Wave*
Hello Mary. *Wave*
Don't be frightened. *Hands out*
Don't be frightened. *Hands out*
God is very happy with you! *Draw smile on face*
God is very happy with you! *Draw smile on face*
You're going to have a baby: *Rock arms*
You're going to have a baby: *Rock arms*
a little boy called Jesus. *Rock arms*
a little boy called Jesus. *Rock arms*
He's going to be king! *Place crown on head*
He's going to be king! *Place crown on head*

I wonder how Mary's feeling now?

*Invite the children to explore their feelings or use the following.
As you list these emotions one by one, give the children time to show each emotion with their face. You might like to pick out some examples given by the children.*
  Can you show me amazed?
  Show me scared!
  Show me happy!
  Show me excited!

Mary is feeling lots of things!
Mary's also feeling confused.
Show me confused! Mary doesn't understand.

Can you show me how you look
when you don't understand – when you're confused?
Lead the children in looking confused.

Mary says, 'How? I'm not meant to have a baby yet!
I'm just a girl.'
Let's put our hands out like a question and say 'How?' . . . '

The angel says, 'The Holy Spirit will come on you . . .'
Let's all raise our hands in the air
and bring them down in front of us
to show the Holy Spirit coming down.
The angel says,
'The Holy Spirit will come down.
Your baby will be very special,
he will be the Son of God!'
Mary's baby isn't going to just be a king,
He's going to be God!
I wonder how Mary is feeling now?
Can you show me?

One last special action! . . . .
And then, do you know what Mary says?
She says, 'Yes!' Can you nod your head in a big 'Yes'?
Lead the children in nodding: **'Yes!'**

Mary says, 'I am God's servant.
YES. I will do this!'
Then the angel leaves.
I wonder how Mary is feeling now?
How would you feel,
if an angel came to your home?!
Can you show me?
Accept any responses.

Mary's Story: Option 2: 'Let's tell Mary's story'

→ Luke 1.26–38
→ 'Let's tell Mary's story'. Words © Sharon Moughtin.
→ Tune: 'Mary had a baby' (traditional).

Appropriate for mixed groups of babies, toddlers and children up to the age of 9.
Groups that only include children up to the age of 7 may prefer to use Option 1.
The storytelling is very similar, but the song in Option 2 is slightly more developed.
Choose which version works best in your setting.

If you're using the What's in the Box? option (p. 7), invite one of the children to open the box. Inside will be an angel or a picture of an angel. You might even like to show your group a photograph of an angel depicted somewhere in your church building.

What's in the box? *Ask the child to respond*
This is the angel Gabriel.
He's a very special angel.
Gabriel takes messages from God to people:
he's like a post-angel.
Today Gabriel's going to take a message
to a girl called Mary.

To tell our story today, we need to learn a song.
The last words of the song are the hardest.
They go like this

Let's sing our song about Mary's story.
Start standing on tiptoes with your hands stretched high. You could make angel wings (like butterfly wings) with your hands.
An angel came to Ma-a-a-ry.
Bring hands down from on high and come down from tiptoes.
'You will have a baby!
Rock baby, standing at normal height.
He will be the Son of God!'
Crouch down on the ground like a tiny child.
'Yes!' sa-id Mary.
Jump up and shout 'Yes!'

Mary said 'yes' to God!
I wonder how easy you find it to say 'yes'?
I wonder what would have happened if Mary had said 'no!'?
Accept any responses.

Thankfully, Mary said 'yes!'
After three, let's all nod and say 'yes!' together like Mary.
Let's imagine saying 'yes' to God like Mary.
1, 2, 3 . . . **Yes!**
Let's sing our song one last time to finish
and sing our 'yes' especially loud and clear.

Start by standing on tiptoes with your hands stretched high.
An angel came to Ma-a-a-ry.
Bring hands down from on high and come down from tiptoes.
'You will have a baby!
Rock baby, standing at normal height.
He will be the Son of God!'
Crouch down on the ground like a tiny child.
'Yes!' sa-id Mary.
Jump up and shout 'Yes!'

Singing slowly: 'Let's celebrate the story *Jazz hands* of Love *Cross arms on chest* come down'. *Touch floor*

Can you sing that?

Lead the group in singing, with jazz hands:
Let's celebrate the story *Jazz hands*
of Love *Cross arms* **come down!** *Touch floor*

And again?
Lead the group in singing, with jazz hands:
Let's celebrate the story *Jazz hands*
of Love *Cross arms* **come down!** *Touch floor*

Okay. Then the first bit goes like this.
See if you can join in. . . .
Lead the group in singing:
Let's tell Mary's story. Glory! *Jazz hands*
Let's tell Mary's story. Glory! *Jazz hands*
Let's tell Mary's story. Glory! *Jazz hands*
Let's celebrate the story *Jazz hands*
of Love *Cross arms* **come down** *Touch floor*

So we've got our song.
Now we need to practise showing
how we feel with just our faces.
Not opening our mouths at all.
 Who can show me . . . .

 As you list the following emotions one by one, give the children time to show each emotion with their face. You might like to point out some good examples given by the children:
 sad . . . .
 happy . . . .
 confused (when you don't understand) . . . .
 amazed! . . .
 scared.

We're ready to tell our story.
Mary was at home, sweeping.
Let's be Mary and sweep the floor.
Lead the group in sweeping like Mary.

Suddenly, the room was filled with light!
Shield eyes with hand.

The brightest light Mary had ever seen!
Look! There's an angel standing there!
Mary fell to the floor!
Lead the children in falling to the floor.

Now we're going to be the angel Gabriel together.
Let's stand up tall and be the angel Gabriel!
Lead the children in standing.
Let's show the angel's wings.
Lead the group in standing tall with slowly flapping wings. This will become the angel action.

Let's sing: God sent an angel! Glory!
Remember your jazz hands for 'Glory!'

Lead the group in singing:
God sent an angel. *Angel action* **Glory!** *Jazz hands*
God sent an angel. *Angel action* **Glory!** *Jazz hands*
God sent an angel. *Angel action* **Glory!** *Jazz hands*
Let's celebrate the story *Jazz hands*
of Love *Cross arms* **come down** *Touch floor*

How do you think Mary's feeling?

 Invite the children to explore their feelings or use the following.

You *Point* **will have a baby!** *Rock baby* **Glory!** *Jazz hands*
You *Point* **will have a baby!** *Rock baby* **Glory!** *Jazz hands*
You *Point* **will have a baby!** *Rock baby* **Glory!** *Jazz hands*
Let's celebrate the story *Jazz hands*
of Love *Cross arms* **come down!** *Touch floor*

And the angel kept on speaking.
The angel said: 'His name will be Jesus!' *Rock baby*
And THEN, the angel said. . . . .
'He'll be king for ever!' *Crown on head*
Let's sing the angel's words together!

He'll be king for ever! *Crown on head* **Glory!** *Jazz hands*
He'll be king for ever! *Crown on head* **Glory!** *Jazz hands*
He'll be king for ever! *Crown on head* **Glory!** *Jazz hands*
Let's celebrate the story *Jazz hands*
of Love *Cross arms* **come down!** *Touch floor*

Mary's baby is going to be king! Forever!
How do you think Mary's feeling now?
Can you show me?
Accept the group's responses.

Mary is feeling lots of things!
Mary's also feeling confused.
Show me confused! Mary doesn't understand.
Can you show me how you look
when you don't understand – when you're confused?
Lead the children in looking confused.

Mary says, 'How? I'm not meant to have a baby yet!
I'm just a girl.'
Let's put our hands out like a question and say 'How?'
Let's sing 'How can this be?' with our confused faces.

As you list these emotions one by one, give the children time to
show each emotion with their face. You might like to pick out some
examples given by the children.
Can you show me amazed?
Show me scared!
Show me happy!
Show me excited!

How do YOU think Mary's feeling?
With the angel standing just there! *Point at the group*
Can you show me?
Accept the group's responses.
Then the angel spoke!
With the biggest voice!
The angel said. . . . .
Booming: 'Do not be afraid!' *Cupped hands round mouth*
Oh my goodness!
It's hard not to be afraid when angels talk!
Let's sing the angel's words together!

Lead the group in singing with a booming voice:
Do not be afraid! *Cupped hands round mouth* **Glory!** *Jazz hands*
Do not be afraid! *Cupped hands round mouth* **Glory!** *Jazz hands*
Do not be afraid! *Cupped hands round mouth* **Glory!** *Jazz hands*
Let's celebrate the story *Jazz hands*
of Love *Cross arms* **come down!** *Touch floor*

How do you think Mary's feeling now?
Can you show me?
Accept the group's responses.
Then the angel spoke again!
The angel said: 'You *Point* will have a baby!' *Rock baby*
Let's sing the angel's words together!

And let's make our Glory *Jazz hands* into a big question *Hands out in question*
How can this be? Glory?! *Hands out in question*
How can this be? Glory?! *Hands out in question*
How can this be? Glory?! *Hands out in question*
Let's celebrate the story *Jazz hands*
of Love *Cross arms* **come down!** *Touch floor*

The angel says, 'The Holy Spirit will come on you . . .'
Let's all raise our hands in the air
and bring them down in front of us
to show the Holy Spirit coming down on Mary.
Lead the group in raising then lowering arms.

The angel says,
'The Holy Spirit will come down. *Arms raised then lowered*
Your baby will be very special,
he will be the Son of God!'
Mary's baby isn't going to just be a king,
He's going to be GOD!
I wonder how Mary is feeling now?
Can you show me?
Accept responses.

Then Mary says words that have become very important!
Mary says: 'I am God's Servant!'
'Let it be to me'.
That means 'yes!' I will do this *Thumbs up*
Let's sing together Mary's words: 'Let it be to me!'
Let's show our thumbs up high over our head for 'Yes!' as we sing.
And don't forget the jazz hands for Glory!

Let it be to me! Glory! *Thumbs up followed by jazz hands*
Let it be to me! Glory! *Thumbs up followed by jazz hands*
Let it be to me! Glory! *Thumbs up followed by jazz hands*
Let's celebrate the story *Jazz hands*
of Love *Cross arms* **come down!** *Touch floor*

Then the angel leaves.
I wonder how Mary is feeling now?
Can you show me?
Accept any responses.

Let's sit down for a moment.
When the group is ready.
Mary says to God 'Let it be to me!'
Mary says 'Yes!' to God.
Let's close our eyes for a moment.
Lead the group in closing eyes.

God had a special job for Mary.
God has a special job for all of us!
Will we say 'yes' to God?
Let's practice saying 'yes' now.
Let's make Mary's song our song.
Let's sing quietly to God:
'Let it be to me! Me too!'
And point at ourselves.
Let's make our song into a prayer.

Lead the group in singing reflectively:
Let it be to me! Me too!
Let it be to me! Me too!
Let it be to me! Me too!
Let's celebrate the story *Jazz hands*
of Love *Cross arms* **come down!** *Touch floor*

Mary's Song: Option 1: 'What can Jesus hear?'

→ Luke 1.39–55
→ Poem: 'What can Jesus hear?' © Sharon Moughtin.
→ Song: 'My God is a topsy turvy God!' Words © Sharon Moughtin.
→ Tune: 'O the grand old Duke of York' (traditional).

To tell our story today,
we need to practise making shapes with our body.
Can you show me the biggest shape
you can make with your body?

Now show me the smallest, tiniest shape
you can make with your body.
Now show me the highest you can reach!
And the lowest you can be!

We need to learn a song.
This is Mary's song.

Talk the children through the song ('my turn', 'your turn') then add the tune.

My God is very BIG!
Make the biggest shape you can with your whole body.
And I am very small!
Make the smallest shape you can.
My God is a topsy turvy God,
'New Start' sign.
who turns things upside down!
And those who are low will be high!
Start low and end up high.
And those who are high will be low!
Start high and end up low.
My God is a topsy turvy God,
'New Start' sign.
who turns things upside down.

We're ready to tell our story.

Optional: What's in the Box? (see p. 7).
Invite one of the children to open the box. Inside will be two baby dolls or pictures of babies.

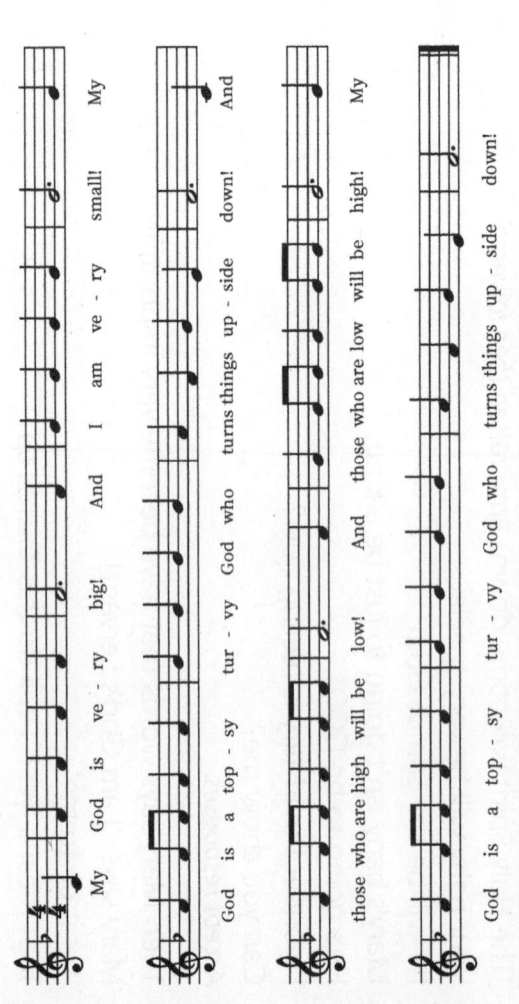

Appropriate for mixed groups of babies, toddlers and children up to the age of 5. This option is especially appropriate for groups where there are very young children. It focuses on the journey that Mary and Baby Jesus in her tummy take to visit Elizabeth. Groups with children over the age of 5 present may find the version in Option 2 more suitable. This focuses instead on the opposites celebrated in Mary's song. Choose which version works best in your setting.

The 'New Start' sign (the winding action from 'Wind the bobbin up') used here to show both Baby John turning upside down in Elizabeth's womb and the 'topsy turvy God who turns things upside down' is among the very few Sowing Seeds signs and actions that are fixed. See p. 8 or the website (www.sowingseeds-online.org) for a description and explanation.

What's in the box? *Ask the child to respond*

Our story today is about two babies.
Baby Jesus and Baby John.
But Baby Jesus and Baby John aren't born yet.
They're still inside their mummies' tummies.

If appropriate, if there is an expectant mum present:
Like *Name* has a baby inside her tummy.

Let's put our hands on our tummy.
Baby Jesus is inside Mary.
And Baby John is inside Elizabeth.

Recap the story from last week by saying these words alone. If the children join in that's great.
An angel came to Mary.
Hands high in the sky and bring them down like angel wings.
[And said,] 'You will have a baby!'
Rock arms as if holding a baby.
'He will be the Son of God!'
'Yes!' said Mary!
After three, let's all shout 'yes!' together.
1, 2, 3 . . . Yes!

Now Mary has Baby Jesus, God, growing inside her! *Hands on tummy*
Mary wants to tell someone!
Her cousin Elizabeth has a baby inside her, too.
Her baby is called Baby John.
So Mary goes on a journey to see Elizabeth.

We're going to imagine Mary's journey together now.
Someone is travelling with Mary, inside her.
Who's inside Mary? *Hands on tummy*
Baby Jesus is inside Mary!

Baby Jesus can't see anything, but he can hear. *Hands behind ears*
Let's imagine together what Baby Jesus hears on Mary's special journey.

Let's stand up together.
Let's walk on the spot. Ssssh! Be gentle!

We're going to say this 'my turn' *Point to self*, 'your turn' *Leader's hands out to group.*
Start with a whisper.
We're on the way to Elizabeth's house.
We're on the way to Elizabeth's house. *Walk gently on spot*
What can Jesus hear? *Hands behind ears*
What can Jesus hear? *Hands behind ears*
Sssh! Sssh! Sssh! *Finger on lips*
Sssh! Sssh! Sssh! *Finger on lips*
What can Jesus hear? *Walk gently on spot*
What can Jesus hear? *Walk gently on spot*

Lead the children in swaying like trees.
Trees are swaying in the breeze:
Trees are swaying in the breeze:
Wishy, washy, wishy, washy . . .
Wishy, washy, wishy, washy . . .

We're on the way to Elizabeth's house. *Walk gently on spot*
We're on the way to Elizabeth's house. *Walk gently on spot*
What can Jesus hear? *Hands behind ears*
What can Jesus hear? *Hands behind ears*
Sssh! Sssh! Sssh! *Finger on lips*
Sssh! Sssh! Sssh! *Finger on lips*
What can Jesus hear? *Walk gently on spot*
What can Jesus hear? *Walk gently on spot*

Ask the children for a sign for sheep.
Lead the children in the sheep action.
Sheep are baaing in the fields:
Baa! Baa! Baa! Baa!
Baa! Baa! Baa! Baa!

Lead the children in swaying like trees.
Trees are swaying in the breeze:
Trees are swaying in the breeze:
Wishy, washy, wishy, washy.

We're on the way to Elizabeth's house. *Walk gently on spot*
We're on the way to Elizabeth's house. *Walk gently on spot*
What can Jesus hear? *Hands behind ears*
What can Jesus hear? *Hands behind ears*
Sssh! Sssh! Sssh! Sssh! *Finger on lips*
Sssh! Sssh! Sssh! Sssh! *Finger on lips*
What can Jesus hear? *Walk gently on spot*
What can Jesus hear? *Walk gently on spot*

Lead the children in showing birds tweeting with their hands.
Birds are singing in the trees:
Birds are singing in the trees:
Twitter, tweet, twitter, tweet.
Twitter, tweet, twitter, tweet.

Lead the children in the sheep action.
Sheep are baaing in the fields:
Sheep are baaing in the fields:
Baa! Baa! Baa! Baa!

Lead the children in swaying like trees.
Trees are swaying in the breeze:
Trees are swaying in the breeze:
Wishy, washy, wishy, washy.

We're on the way to Elizabeth's . . .
Interrupt yourself!
Look! We're HERE!
Mary calls Elizabeth.
After three, let's call Elizabeth. 1, 2, 3 . . . .
Elizabeth! Elizabeth!
Elizabeth hears Mary.
Someone else can hear Mary, too! *Hands on tummy*
Baby John inside Elizabeth!
After three, let's call Elizabeth again with our hands over our mouth.
A bit quieter, like Baby John can hear Mary inside his Mummy's tummy. 1, 2, 3 . . . .
Elizabeth! Elizabeth!

Baby John hears Mary calling.
Baby John knows that Baby Jesus is here!
And Baby John jumps head over heels for joy inside his mummy. *'New Start' sign*

Let's show baby John with our arms, jumping head over heels, topsy turvy with joy! *'New Start' sign*

If some of your group are familiar with the Sorry Song:
Look, it's our 'New Start' sign from our Sorry Song!
Baby John knows that Baby Jesus is going to bring a new start when he's born!
So he's jumping head over heels! *'New Start' sign* Amazing!
Let's show the new start that Baby Jesus will bring like Baby John.
Lead the children in the 'New Start' sign.

Elizabeth feels Baby John jumping inside her. *'New Start' sign*
Hold hands on tummy.

She says, 'My baby is jumping for joy!'
And Mary bursts with joy! *Fling arms outwards*
And she sings an amazing song
about God who turns the world upside down. *'New Start' sign*
Like John turning upside down,
head over heels, in his Mummy's tummy! *'New Start' sign*

Let's sing Mary's song
about our topsy turvy God together.

My God is very BIG!
Make the biggest shape you can with your body.
And I am very small!
Make the smallest shape you can.
My God is a topsy turvy God,
'New Start' sign.
who turns things upside down!

And those who are low will be high!
Start low and end up high.
And those who are high will be low!
Start high and end up low.
My God is a topsy turvy God, *'New Start' sign*
who turns things upside down!

Repeat.
Ask the children to sit down for a moment of quiet.
Let's close our eyes.
I wonder if there are times when you feel small?
So small you don't matter?

To God the smallest people
are the most important people of all!

Let's open our eyes.
God came to us as a tiny baby.
Let's put our hands on our tummies to remember Baby Jesus.

And the first person to recognize Jesus
was another tiny baby, not born yet –
not even able to see yet!
Baby John, inside his mummy's tummy!
Baby Jesus came to Baby John first!
Small people are very, very important to Jesus.
Next time you feel small remember that!

Let's sing our song one last time.
Let's sing 'My God is very big and I am very small'.
This time, let's not sing as Mary,
Let's sing as ourselves:
Mary's song is going to become our song!

My God is very BIG!
Make the biggest shape you can.
And I am very small!
Make the smallest shape you can.
My God is a topsy turvy God,
'New Start' sign.
who turns things upside down!

And those who are low will be high!
Start low and end up high.
And those who are high will be low!
Start high and end up low.
My God is a topsy turvy God,

'New Start' sign.
who turns things upside down!

Mary's Song: Option 2: 'My God is a topsy turvy God'

→ Luke 1.39–55
→ Song: 'My God is a topsy turvy God!' Words © Sharon Moughtin.
→ Tune: 'O the grand old Duke of York' (traditional).

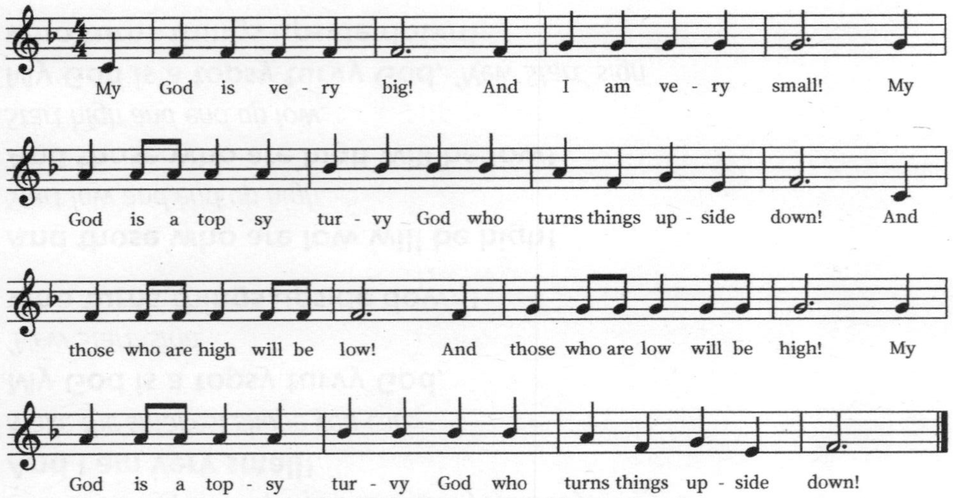

My God is ve-ry big! And I am ve-ry small!

God is a top-sy tur-vy God who turns things up-side down!

those who are high will be low! And those who are low will be high!

God is a top-sy tur-vy God who turns things up-side down!

Appropriate for mixed groups of babies, toddlers and children up to the age of 9. This version focuses on the song that Mary sings and its celebration of opposites. Groups that only include children up to the age of 7 may prefer to use Option 1.

In this story, the 'New Start' sign (the winding action from 'Wind the bobbin up') is used to show both Baby John turning upside down in Elizabeth's womb and the 'topsy turvy God who turns things upside down'. This is among the very few Sowing Seeds signs and actions that are fixed. See p. 8 or the website (www.sowingseeds-online.org) for a description and explanation.

To tell our story today,
we need to practise making shapes with our body.
Can you show me the biggest shape
you can make with your body?

Now show me the smallest, tiniest shape
you can make with your body.
Now show me the highest you can reach!
And the lowest you can be!

We need to learn a song.
This is Mary's song.

Talk the children through the song ('my turn', 'your turn') then add the tune.
My God is very BIG!
Make the biggest shape you can with your whole body.
And I am very small!
Make the smallest shape you can.
My God is a topsy turvy God,
'New Start' sign (see p. 8).
who turns things upside down!
And those who are low will be high!
Start low and end up high.
And those who are high will be low!
Start high and end up low.
My God is a topsy turvy God,
'New Start' sign.
who turns things upside down.

We're ready to tell our story.

Optional: What's in the Box? (see p. 7).

Invite one of the children to open the box. Inside will be two baby dolls or pictures of babies.

What's in the box? *Ask the child to respond*

Our story today is about two babies.
Baby Jesus and Baby John.
Baby Jesus and Baby John aren't born yet.
They're still inside their mummies' tummies.

If appropriate, if there is an expectant mum present:
Like *Name* has a baby inside her tummy.

Let's put our hands on our tummy.
Baby Jesus is inside Mary.
And Baby John is inside Elizabeth.
They're both very special babies!

Recap of story: this can be helpful whether you've told this story with the group or not. If you have previously told the story with them, some of the children may well join in!

Either said or sung (see p. 18):

An angel came to Mary.
Hands high in the sky and bring them down like angel wings.
[And said,] 'You will have a baby!'
Rock arms as if holding a baby.
'He will be the Son of God!'
'Yes!' said Mary!
After three, let's all shout 'yes!' together.

1, 2, 3 . . . Yes!

Now Mary has Baby Jesus, God, growing inside her! *Hands on tummy*
Mary wants to tell someone!
Her cousin Elizabeth has a baby inside her, too.
Her baby is called Baby John.
So Mary goes to visit her cousin Elizabeth.

It's a long journey!
Let's be Mary.
Can you show me how you feel
when you've been on a long journey?
Accept the different responses.

We've just arrived at Elizabeth's house.
Can you show me how you feel when you've arrived?
And you're going to see your cousin – your family!
Accept the different responses.

Mary calls Elizabeth.
After three, let's call Elizabeth. 1, 2, 3 . . .
Elizabeth! Elizabeth!

Elizabeth hears Mary.
Someone else can hear Mary, too! *Hands on tummy*
Baby John in Elizabeth's tummy!
After three, let's call Elizabeth again with our hands over our mouth.
A bit quieter, like Baby John can hear Mary
inside his Mummy's tummy. 1, 2, 3 . . .
Elizabeth! Elizabeth!

Baby John hears Mary calling.
Baby John knows that Baby Jesus is here!
And Baby John jumps head over heels for joy
inside his mummy. *'New Start' sign*

Let's show baby John with our arms, jumping head over heels,
topsy turvy with joy! *'New Start' sign*

If some of your group are familiar with the Sorry Song:
Look, it's our 'New Start' sign from our Sorry Song!
Baby John knows that Baby Jesus
is going to bring a new start when he's born!

27

So he's jumping head over heels! *'New Start' sign*
Amazing!
Let's show the new start that Baby Jesus will bring like Baby John.
Lead the children in the 'New Start' sign.

Elizabeth feels Baby John jumping topsy turvy inside her. *'New Start' sign*
Hold hands on tummy.
She says, 'My baby is jumping for joy!'
And Mary bursts with joy! *Fling arms outwards*
And she sings an amazing song
about God who turns the world upside down. *'New Start' sign*
Like John turning upside down,
head over heels, in his Mummy's tummy! *'New Start' sign*

Let's sing Mary's song
about our topsy turvy God together.

My God is very BIG!
Make the biggest shape you can with your body.
And I am very small!
Make the smallest shape you can.
My God is a topsy turvy God,
'New Start' sign.
who turns things upside down!

And those who are low will be high!
Start low and end up high.
And those who are high will be low!
Start high and end up low.
My God is a topsy turvy God,
'New Start' sign.
who turns things upside down!

Baby John helped Mary see
that God is the one who turns everything upside down!
Topsy turvy!
God makes the low high! And the high low!
But that's not all!
Mary saw other ways God will turn everything upside down.
Can you show me hungry?
Really, really hungry!
Lead the group in showing hungry.

Mary sang that those who are hungry will be full!
Can you show me how you feel when you've had the best dinner!
And you're all full up!
Lead the group in showing full.

Let's sing our song again.
This time after 'upside down' let's sing
'those who are hungry will be full!'
AND 'those who are full will be. . . . .hungry
Encourage the children to join in: . . .hungry
Let's go!

My God is very BIG!
Make the biggest shape you can with your body.
And I am very small!
Make the smallest shape you can.
My God is a topsy turvy God,
'New Start' sign.
who turns things upside down!

And those who are hungry will be full!
Hungry action followed by full action.
And those who are full will be hungry!
Full action followed by hungry action.

My God is a topsy turvy God,
'New Start' sign.
who turns things upside down!

So the low will be high *Start low and end up high*
and the high will be low! *Start high and end up low*
The hungry will be full *Hungry action followed by full action*
and the full will be hungry! *Full action followed by hungry action*

But that's not all!
Can you show me poor?
When you have no money!
Choose one of the actions. This will become the 'poor action'.

Mary saw that the poor *Poor action* will be. . . .
Encourage the group to join in.
If necessary add 'What's the opposite of poor?. . .'
. . .rich! The poor will be rich.
Can you show me an action for rich!
When you have lots and lots of money!
Choose one of the actions. This will become the 'rich action'.

And the rich *Rich action* will be. . . .
Encourage the group to join in.
. . . poor!
The rich will be poor! *Rich action followed by poor action*

Let's sing Mary's song with those words!

My God is very BIG!
Make the biggest shape you can with your body.
And I am very small!
Make the smallest shape you can.
My God is a topsy turvy God,
'New Start' sign.
who turns things upside down!

And those who are poor will be rich!
Poor action followed by rich action.
And those who are rich will be poor!
Rich action followed by poor action.
My God is a topsy turvy God,
'New Start' sign.
who turns things upside down!

Encourage the group to join in with this recap using the actions to remind them.

So the low will be. . . **high** *Low action followed by high action*
and the high will be **low**! *High action followed by low action*

The hungry will be. . . **full** *Hungry action followed by full action*
and the full will be. . . **hungry!** *Full action followed by hungry action*

The poor will be. . . **rich** *Poor action followed by rich action*
and the rich will be. . . **poor!** *Rich action followed by poor action*

Baby John helped Mary see all of that!
And when Jesus was a grown up,
Jesus really did turn things upside down!
For instance, Jesus said,
The first will be. . . *Point ahead for 'first action'*
Encourage the group to join in.
. . .last *Point behind for 'last action'*
And the last will be. . . **first!** *'Last action' followed by 'first action'*
Jesus is the one who turns things upside down![1]

If appropriate:
Mary's song is one of the oldest songs in the Church!
It's become really important for lots of people.
Some churches sing it every day!

Ask the children to sit down for a moment of quiet.
Let's close our eyes.
I wonder if there are times when you feel small?
So small you don't matter?
To God the smallest people
are the most important people of all!

Let's open our eyes.
God came to us as a tiny baby.
Let's put our hands on our tummies to remember Baby Jesus.

And the first person to recognize Jesus
was another tiny baby, not born yet –
not even able to see yet!
Baby John, inside his mummy's tummy!
Baby Jesus came to Baby John first!
Small people are very, very important to Jesus.
Next time you feel small remember that!

Let's sing our song one last time.
Let's sing 'My God is very big and I am very small'.
This time, let's not sing as Mary,
Let's sing as ourselves:
Mary's song is going to become our song!
Let's get up and get ready!

Either: Let's sing 'those who are high will be low'!

My God is very BIG!
Make the biggest shape you can.
And I am very small!
Make the smallest shape you can.
My God is a topsy turvy God,
'New Start' sign.
who turns things upside down!

And those who are low will be high!
Start low and end up high.
And those who are high will be low!
Start high and end up low.
My God is a topsy turvy God,
'New Start' sign.
who turns things upside down!

Or (for groups that are up for the challenge!):
And let's see if we can bring in all our opposites
All of them at the same time!
Encourage the group to join in with this recap using the actions to remind them before you sing.

So. . .
The low will be. . . **high** *Low action followed by high action*
and the high will be **low**! *High action followed by low action*
The hungry will be. . . **full** *Hungry action followed by full action*
and the full will be. . . **hungry!** *Full action followed by hungry action*
The poor will be. . . **rich** *Poor action followed by rich action*
and the rich will be. . . **poor!** *Rich action followed by poor action*
The first will be. . . **last** *First action followed by last action*
and the last will be. . . **first!** *Last action followed by first action*

Let's go! Let's use our bodies to help us remember the words!

My God is very BIG!
Make the biggest shape you can.
And I am very small!
Make the smallest shape you can.

The Angels' Song

→ Luke 2.8–16a
→ Song: The angels' song.
→ Tune: a 'Gloria'.

Appropriate for mixed groups of babies, toddlers and children up to the age of 9.

Tip

The material below uses the 'Clapping Gloria' by Mike Anderson © 1999 Kevin Mayhew Ltd (p. 964 in *Complete Anglican: Hymns Old and New*). Other options include the first line of the Peruvian Gloria adapted: 'Glory to God! Glory to God! Glory in the highest!' or another straightforward Gloria or 'Glory to God' song that you're familiar with. Alternatively, you could speak the words 'Gloria! Gloria! In excelsis Deo!' or 'Glory! Glory! Glory to God in the highest!' without a tune. Adapt the material below accordingly. This is a good opportunity to familiarize the children with words that they will hear repeatedly not only on Christmas cards and in Christmas carols, but also in a communion service.

Recent scholarship by Amy Lindeman Allen has shown that it's most likely the shepherds in Luke's story were children: boys and girls, looking after their family's sheep.[2]

If appropriate, before the story begins, ask an adult to stand by the light switch and be ready to turn the light off, then later turn it on again (or even flash the light on and off a few times).

Optional: What's in the Box? (see p. 7).

My God is a topsy turvy God,
'New Start' sign.
who turns things upside down!

Interrupt: Are you ready?
We're going to sing all of them!
Lead the group in singing, repeating the line to the same tune with different words four times, using the actions to help you all remember. You will almost certainly need to slow down!

And those who are low will be high!
Start low and end up high.

And those who are high will be low!
Start high and end up low.

And those who are hungry will be full!
Hungry action followed by full action.

And those who are full will be hungry!
Full action followed by hungry action.

And those who are rich will be poor!
Rich action followed by poor action.

And those who are poor will be rich!
Poor action followed by rich action.

And those who are first will be last!
First action followed by last action.

And those who are last will be first!
Last action followed by first action.

Sing extra loud and slow:
My God is a topsy turvy God,
'New Start' sign.
who turns things upside down!

Invite one of the children to open the box. Inside will be the angel Gabriel (or a picture of the angel Gabriel) and lots of other angels. As in previous weeks, you might like to show your group a photograph of angels depicted somewhere in your church building. Or, if you are providing paper angels that fold out like paper dolls for one of your Creative Response starter ideas, you could use these.

What's in the box? *Ask the child to respond*
It's the angel Gabriel.
He's a very special angel who takes messages
from God to people, like a post-angel.
But look! Today's Gabriel's not the only angel!
There are lots and lots and lots of angels!
A whole sky full of angels!
Shall we tell the story of the night
when the whole sky was full of angels?

If appropriate:
It's nearly Christmas!
Baby Jesus, the Light of the World, is about to come.
And our story today is all about light:
darkness and light!

If appropriate (different parts of the world get dark at different times of the year!)
Has anyone noticed how dark
it's getting at the moment?
Before we go to bed, it's already dark!
When people decided what day Christmas should be on,
they chose it because it was the darkest time of the year.
Jesus, the Light of the World, is born
in the deep, deepest dark.
Our story today is all about darkness and light.

All groups:
For our story today, we need to practise two things.
First, we need to learn a song:
the angels' song!

At this point, teach the children the Gloria words as follows, or the version you would like to use:

So 'my turn' *Point to self,* 'your turn' *Leader's hands out to group.*
Gloria! *Clap, clap* Gloria! *Clap, clap*
Gloria! *Clap, clap* **Gloria!** *Clap, clap*
In excelsis Deo! *Palms up, raise arms heavenwards*
In excelsis Deo! *Palms up, raise arms heavenwards*
That means Glory to God!
Glory in the highest! *Show the raising arms action*
The Gloria is really important.
It's the song of the angels.

If you're using a tune, teach it to the children at this point.
Let's sing it (*or say it*) together:

Quietly. . . .
Gloria! *Clap, clap* **Gloria!** *Clap, clap*
In excelsis Deo! *Palms up, raise arms heavenwards*

Loudly. . . .
Gloria! *Clap, clap* **Gloria!** *Clap, clap*
In excelsis Deo! *Palms up, raise arms heavenwards*

Really loudly! . . . .
Gloria! *Clap, clap* **Gloria!** *Clap, clap*
In excelsis Deo! *Palms up, raise arms heavenwards*

Second, we need to practise 'freeze frames'.
Freeze frames are when you show an action . . . *Demonstrate* then freeze! *Demonstrate* Keeping absolutely still!

Let's have a go at freeze-framing. Can you show me . . .
Scared . . .
Ready to run . . . .
Amazed . . . .
Happy! Full of joy and excited . . . .
Asleep . . . .

We're ready to tell our story.
Ask an adult or older child to turn the light off.
Our story begins in the dark.
Outside, up in the cold, dark hills.

We're shepherd children – girls and boys –
looking after our family's sheep.
Let's all be the shepherd children!
It's cold outside. Can you show me cold!
Lead the group in rubbing hands or arms.
Really, really cold!
We're watching for wolves and other dangers of the night.
Look! Is there a wolf over there?! *Point*
Or over there?! *Point*

So we're shepherd children and we're looking for wolves and bears.
Can you show me a 'looking out for wolves' freeze-frame?
And another one, looking that way?
Suddenly, the skies are filled with light!
The brightest light the shepherd children have ever seen!
Shield eyes with hand.

Then the light of God's glory began to flash all around.
Ask the adult to turn the light on, or even flash it on and off.

The shepherd children were terrified. Very, very scared!
Can you show me terrified and scared?

They looked into the light.
Let's hold our hand over our eyes to see.
An angel was standing there!

Let's stand up tall and strong and be the angel Gabriel.
Can you say after me?
'My turn' *Point to self,* 'your turn' *Leader's hands out to group.*
Don't be frightened! *Hold hands out and smile*
Don't be frightened! *Hold hands out and smile*
I have Good News. *Thumbs up*
I have Good News. *Thumbs up*
There's a new baby king! *Place imaginary crown on head*
There's a new baby king! *Place imaginary crown on head*
Go! *Point*
Go! *Point*
Find him!
Find him!

Suddenly the skies were filled with noise.
It was all God's armies of angels singing!
We're going to be the angels.
Not pretty, baby angels, but soldiers of light,
warriors in an army! Super-powerful!
Can you show me a super-powerful pose and freeze!
We're super-powerful angels.
We're far away at the moment, so let's sing really quietly.

Gloria! *Clap, clap* Gloria! *Clap, clap*
In excelsis Deo! *Palms up, raise arms heavenwards*

We're getting a bit closer so let's sing a little louder . . . .
Gloria! *Clap, clap* Gloria! *Clap, clap*
In excelsis Deo! *Palms up, raise arms heavenwards*

If your group includes children who are unsettled by loud noises, you could keep to clapping at this point.
And even louder. This time let's stamp our feet!
Gloria! *Stamp, stamp* **Gloria!** *Stamp, stamp*
In excelsis Deo! *Palms up, raise arms heavenwards*

Then the angels came right up to the child shepherds!
It was the loudest noise of praise and joy
the children had ever heard!

If appropriate:
   Let's sing as loud as we have ever sung.
   Let's use our whole bodies to sing!

Gloria! *Stamp, stamp.* **Gloria!** *Stamp, stamp*
In excelsis Deo! *Palms up, raise arms heavenwards*
And again! Louder!
Gloria! *Stamp, stamp.* **Gloria!** *Stamp, stamp*
In excelsis Deo! *Palms up, raise arms heavenwards*

Then all of a sudden . . . the angels had gone.
Silence!
The shepherds were amazed!
Let's crouch down and be the shepherd children, amazed!
The shepherds looked at each other.
Let's look right, then left. *Lead the children in looking side to side*
What shall we do?
What did the angel say to do?
Can anyone remember?

Accept the children's responses.
Go! *Point away.* Find him!
So what are we waiting for?
After three, let's get up and run like the child shepherds
And find the baby king!
Let's run as fast as we can on the spot.
1, 2, 3 . . . Run!
Faster! Faster!
Freeze!
We'll find out what the child shepherds found in Bethlehem on Christmas Day!

Christmas: Option 1: Meet Baby Jesus!

→ Christmas, Luke 2.16–20

Appropriate for mixed groups of babies, toddlers and children up to the age of 9. This story is much shorter than other stories in the storybox, to open up the opportunity for a longer Creative Response time. For a longer version of the story see Option 2. You may wish to use this time for the children to make their own presents for Baby Jesus. Choose a Creative Response to accompany this story that best suits your group from p. 138 or beyond.

Tip

During the Christmas period, we keep a Baby Jesus doll in a manger in the centre of our circle from the beginning of the session. If your group includes toddlers, you may find that they take him out every now and then for a cuddle. We place paper stars in the manger throughout to remind us that Jesus is the Light of the World.

Recent scholarship by Amy Lindeman Allen has shown that it's most likely the shepherds in Luke's story were children: boys and girls, looking after their family's sheep. See note 2 on p. 233.

The shepherd children are running!
After three, let's jump up and run on the spot as fast as we can.
1, 2, 3 . . . Run! Faster! Faster!
Freeze!

Let's sit down for a minute.
The shepherd children are running to find a very special baby!
Which baby has been born at Christmas?
Give the children the chance to answer.
Baby Jesus!

The shepherds want to see Baby Jesus.
They want to see Jesus with their own eyes.
After three, let's jump up again and run on the spot.
As fast as we can to find Baby Jesus.
1, 2, 3 . . . Run! Faster! Faster!
Freeze!

Look! It's a manger!
Who do you think is inside?
Give the children the chance to say who they think is inside.

Look! It's a little baby! Baby Jesus!
Shall we tiptoe on the spot
like we're getting close to the manger?
Ssssh! Let's be quiet. As quiet as we can.
Tiptoe, tiptoe, tiptoe . . . Ssssh!

Look! It's Baby Jesus! *Point to Baby Jesus*
The shepherd children see Baby Jesus.
And they kneel down and they worship him.
Let's kneel down. Let's worship Baby Jesus.
Let's sing Baby Jesus a song,
Like a lullaby, ever so gently.

Lead the children in singing 'Away in a manger' or another appropriate song that they can sing together or listen to.

Christmas: Option 2: The Shepherds' Story!

↱ Christmas, Luke 2.16–20
↱ Song: 'Come, see!' Words © Sharon Moughtin.
↱ Tune: 'My bonnie lies over the ocean' (traditional).

The sky was filled with an-gels! The sky was filled with light!
We ran and we ran to the man-ger! And, oh, what a glo-ri-ous sight!
Come, see! Come, see! The Light of the World is here is
here! Come, see! Come, see! The Light of the World is here!

Appropriate for mixed groups of babies, toddlers and children up to the age of 9. Groups that only include children up to the age of 7 may prefer to tell the shorter story, 'Meet Baby Jesus' on p. 34.

35

> Recent scholarship by Amy Lindeman Allen has shown that it's most likely the shepherds in Luke's story were children: boys and girls, looking after their family's sheep. See note 2 on p. 233.

The shepherds' story is designed to be told at or just after Christmas. It provides the children with an opportunity to meet with Baby Jesus.

What's in the box? *Ask the child to respond*
Inside will be a picture of shepherd children.
We're going to tell the shepherds' story!
They're boys and girls: children like you!
Looking after their family's sheep on the hills at night.

To tell our story, we need to learn a song.
Can you sing after me?
'My turn' *Point to self,* 'your turn' *Leader's hands out to group.*

Come, see! Come, see! *Beckon on 'come' and point on 'see'*
The Light of the World is here! *Point downwards to show 'here'*
Come, see! Come, see! *Beckon on 'come' and point on 'see'*
The Light of the World is here! *Point downwards*

Come, see! Come, see! *Beckon on 'come' and point on 'see'*
The Light of the World is here! *Point downwards to show 'here'*
Come, see! Come, see! *Beckon on 'come' and point on 'see'*
The Light of the World is here! *Point downwards*

Shall we sing that together?
That's the important part!

Lead the group in singing:

Come, see! Come, see! *Beckon on 'come' and point on 'see'*
The Light of the World is here! *Point downwards*
Come, see! Come, see! *Beckon on 'come' and point on 'see'*
The Light of the World is here! *Point downwards*

That's our chorus. Now for the verse.
'My turn' *Point to self* 'your turn' *Leader's hands out to group again.*

The sky was filled with angels! *Throw hands up*
The sky was filled with light! *Shield eyes with hands*
The sky was filled with angels! *Throw hands up*
The sky was filled with light! *Shield eyes with hands*

We ran and we ran like they told us *Running on the spot*
and, oh, what a marvelous sight! *Throw hands out*
We ran and we ran to the manger *Running on the spot*
and, oh, what a glorious sight! *Throw hands out*

And our chorus. . .
Come, see! Come, see! *Beckon on 'come' and point on 'see'*
The Light of the World is here! *Point downwards*
Come, see! Come, see! *Beckon on 'come' and point on 'see'*
The Light of the World is here! *Point downwards*

Let's sing that all together.
And if you're not sure about the words,
join in the actions even bigger!

Lead the group in singing:
The sky was filled with angels! *Throw hands up*
The sky was filled with light! *Shield eyes with hands*
We ran and we ran to the manger *Running on the spot*
and, oh, what a glorious sight! *Throw hands out*

Come, see! Come, see! *Beckon on 'come' and point on 'see'*
The Light of the World is here, is here! *Point downwards*
Come, see! Come, see! *Beckon on 'come' and point on 'see'*
The Light of the World is here, is here! *Point downwards*

Repeat until the children are confident at least with the actions of the song.

We're ready to tell our story.
It's a story of hope.
Not just for us, but for the whole world!

We're children! We're shepherds!
And we're running!
After three, let's jump up and run on the spot
as fast as we can.
1, 2, 3 . . . Run! Faster! Faster!
Freeze!
Let's sit down for a minute.

When the group are ready:
We're running! Running fast!
We want to see the new King!

Excitedly:
There were angels! Hundreds, thousands of them!
They told us there's a new king in a manger!
So we're running to find him!
We want to see him with our own eyes. *Point to eyes*

After three, let's jump up again and run on the spot.
As fast as we can to find the new king!
1, 2, 3 . . . Run!
Faster! Faster!
Freeze!

We're here! Let's look through the window.
Lead the children in pretending to peer through a window.
Look! There's the manger!
Can you see him?
I can't see him! *Shake head*

Let's go inside!
First let's get ourselves ready!
We've been running very fast and we look a bit scruffy.
Let's make sure our clothes are straight.
We're going to meet a king!
Lead the children in straightening your clothes.

We're ready!
Let's tiptoe on the spot and go inside.
Ssssh! Let's be quiet. I think the baby King's asleep!
Tiptoe, tiptoe, tiptoe . . . Ssssh!

Place the manger with Baby Jesus inside in the centre of the group.

The child shepherds saw Baby Jesus. *Point to the manger*
They knew what the angels said was true.
And they were filled with hope.
Hope not just for themselves but for the whole world!
And they knelt down and worshipped him.

Let's kneel down. Let's worship Baby Jesus.
If there is silence, hold it for a moment.

Optional
We're going to pass Baby Jesus, around the circle now.
Everyone's going to have a turn, so it will just be for a moment.

As we pass Baby Jesus around, let's imagine we're the child shepherds
meeting this tiny baby and knowing he's the new king!
Knowing that we're holding the Light of the whole world
that will shine in the dark and bring **hope** to everyone.
As we pass Baby Jesus around, let's sing our 'Come, see!' song: just the chorus.

Lead the children in singing quietly and with awe as you pass Baby Jesus around. You or another leader may need to be ready to help the children remember to pass him on and to skip over children who don't wish to hold Baby Jesus.

Come, see! Come, see! *Beckon on 'come' and point on 'see'*
The Light of the World is here, is here! *Point to Baby Jesus*
Come, see! Come, see! *Beckon on 'come' and point on 'see'*
The Light of the World is here, is here! *Point to Baby Jesus*

Repeat until all the children have had the opportunity to hold Baby Jesus.

It's time to go.
Lead the children in standing.
But the child shepherds in our story didn't go back to the fields.
Shake head.
They went home! And told EVERYONE what had happened!
So everyone in their place heard the good news.
Let's be the child shepherds.
Can you show me excited?
Lead the children in looking excited.

Let's sing our song to everyone around.
Let's tell everyone the Good News!
The story of what happened to us!

We should always tell an adult when something important has happened!

Lead the group in singing:
The sky was filled with angels! *Throw hands up*
The sky was filled with light! *Shield eyes with hands*
We ran and we ran to the manger *Running on the spot*
and, oh, what a glorious sight! *Throw hands out*

Come, see! Come, see! *Beckon on 'come' and point on 'see'*
The Light of the World is here, is here! *Point downwards to show 'here'*
Come, see! Come, see! *Beckon on 'come' and point on 'see'*
The Light of the World is here, is here! *Point downwards*

38

Storybox 2: Lighting the Advent Wreath

There are different traditions about the meaning of the five candles of the Advent wreath. If your church follows a different pattern, feel free to adapt the material accordingly.

Candle 1: The Patriarchs and Matriarchs (Abraham and Sarah)

→ Genesis 12.1–5; 13.14–18; 15.4–6
→ Song: 'Come on now, Abraham! Get up and go!' © Sharon Moughtin.
→ Tune: 'Father Abraham' (traditional).

Appropriate for mixed groups of babies, toddlers and children up to the age of 9. If your group doesn't include children age 7+, you might find the first storybox, 'Getting Ready for Baby Jesus', more appropriate. Choose what's most appropriate for your group.

Our story today is about Abraham and Sarah.[3]
They're two very important people in the story of God's family.
Abraham was the first father of God's People!
Sarah was the first mother of God's People!
What does that mean?
We'll find out in our story.

One day, God spoke to Abraham.
Abraham had never spoken with God before. *Shake head*
I wonder how Abraham felt when God spoke to him?
Can you show me!
Accept the children's responses.

God said to Abraham:
'Get up and go! *Point*
Leave your home and your family.
You're going on a journey!'

Let's be God and point at Abraham and sing 'My turn', 'your turn':

Come on now Abraham! Get up and go! *Point*
God calls you on a journey! *Come action*
Come on now Abraham! Get up and go! *Point*
God calls you on a journey! *Come action*

And then the same words but a different tune. Listen!
Come on now Abraham! Get up and go! *Point*
God calls you on a journey! *Come action*
Come on now Abraham! Get up and go! *Point*
God calls you on a journey! *Come action*

'Leave your home! Leave your family!'
How do you think Abraham is feeling?
Accept responses and point some of them out.
And what do you think Abraham did?
Accept responses.
Abraham got up! And he went! *Look very surprised*
What a brave thing to do!

Let's be Abraham.
Let's get up.

Lead the group in standing.
Let's pack all our things.
Lead the group in packing.
Don't forget your tent!

And Abraham went!
Let's be Abraham and set off on our journey.
Let's walk on the spot as we sing.

Lead the group in walking on the spot and singing.
Come on now Abraham! Get up and go!
God calls you on a journey!
Come on now Abraham! Get up and go!
God calls you on a journey!

And not only Abraham went, but Sarah went too!
Let's be Sarah on her journey with God.

Lead the group in walking on the spot and singing.
Come on now Sarah! Get up and go!
God calls you on a journey!
Come on now Sarah! Get up and go!
God calls you on a journey!

Who's feeling tired?
Abraham and Sarah did a lot of walking!
And a lot of putting tents up and putting tents down again!

Then one day, God spoke again.
God said, 'Come here Abraham!'
So what do you think Abraham did?
Accept responses.
Abraham came.

Abraham came to a very dusty place.

So dusty, it was like walking on sand on the beach.
Who has walked on sand on the beach?
Can you show me how to walk on sand?
Choose one of the actions and copy it.

Then God said, 'Look up! Look around!'
What do you think Abraham did?
Accept responses.
Abraham looked up and looked around.
Let's look up and look around.
Lead the group in looking around.
All this land, all around you.
Let's point in a circle all around us.
Lead the group in turning on the spot pointing.
I give it to you!

Then God told Abraham to look at the dust.
What do you think Abraham did?
Accept responses.
Abraham looked at the dust.
Let's pick up a handful of dust.
And look carefully at it.
God said, 'Count the dust!'
'That's how many children you will have!'

Count the dust!
How can we count the dust?
Shall we try?
Lead the group in miming counting the dust.
1, 2, 3, 4, 5. . . .
I can't count even a handful of dust! *Look shocked*
I can't count the dust of all that land!
Let's show all the land around again. . .

Abraham went outside.
God told Abraham to look up at the stars. *Point upwards*
God said, 'Count the stars!'
'That's how many children you will have!'

Count the stars!
How can we count the stars!
Shall we try?
Lead the group in miming counting the stars.
1, 2, 3, 4, 5 . . .
I can't count even the stars I can see!
And there are stars I can't even see all around our planet!
I can't count the stars of all the sky!
Let's sing, 'Come on now Abraham count the stars!'
Mime counting stars.
'You will have that many children!' *Turn on spot and point*

Are you ready? Go!
Come on now Abraham count the stars! *Mime counting stars*
You will have that many children! *Turn on spot and point*
Come on now Abraham count the stars! *Mime counting stars*
You will have that many children! *Turn on spot and point*

I'm feeling even more dizzy! Are you?
But Abraham looked at the stars.
Let's look at the stars.
Abraham knew he couldn't count the stars or the dust. *Shake head*
But Abraham trusted God.

Let's sit down for a moment.
When the group is ready:
Abraham trusted God.
And you know what?
Abraham did have children!

Lead the group in turning on the spot pointing.
Let's sing, 'Come on now Abraham count the dust!'
Mime counting dust.
'You will have that many children!' *Turn on spot and point*

Are you ready? Go!
Come on now Abraham count the dust! *Mime counting dust*
You will have that many children! *Turn on spot and point*
Come on now Abraham count the dust! *Mime counting dust*
You will have that many children! *Turn on spot and point*

I'm feeling dizzy! Are you?
How many children do you think Abraham is going to have?
Oh my goodness!
How do you think Abraham is feeling now?
Can you show me?
I think Abraham was feeling dizzy too!

Abraham went back to his tent,
feeling very confused.
Can you show me confused?
Lead the group in looking confused.

Then one night, God spoke to Abraham again!
Uh oh! What's God going to say this time?
This time, before God finished speaking,
Abraham spoke to GOD!
Abraham said, 'How? I haven't even got one baby yet!
And I'm an old man!' *Lead the children in looking confused*
Let's put our hands out like a question and say 'How?'

God said, 'Come on now Abraham, come outside!'
What do you think Abraham did?
Accept responses.

41

Show counting on fingers as you speak.
And those children had children
and those children had children
and those children had children
and this kept on going.
And the family didn't even stop there!

Because after Jesus was born, lots more children
were adopted into Abraham's family,
Show counting on fingers as you speak.
and they had children and they had children
and they had children and they had children
and this kept on going too!
So today all of us in the Church
are part of the family of Abraham and Sarah!

So our first candle on our Advent wreath
reminds us of Abraham and Sarah!
The first father and mother of God's People!
Let's remember again how our story started.
Let's sing 'Come on now Abraham! Get up and go!
God calls you on a journey.'

Lead the group in walking on the spot and singing.
Come on now Abraham! Get up and go!
God calls you on a journey!
Come on now Abraham! Get up and go!
God calls you on a journey!

And Sarah!
Lead the group in walking on the spot and singing.
Come on now Sarah! Get up and go!
God calls you on a journey!
Come on now Sarah! Get up and go!
God calls you on a journey!

And all God's people!
Abraham and Sarah's children
and children's children
and children's children!
Let's sing:
Come on, God's People! Get up and go!
God calls you on a journey!
And remember! We're part of God's people too!
God calls US on a journey this Advent!
That's what our Advent wreath wants us to remember!

Lead the group in walking on the spot and singing.
Come on God's People! Get up and go!
God calls you on a journey!
Come on God's People! Get up and go!
God calls you on a journey!

Candle 2: Prophets of Old (Isaiah)

→ Isaiah 9.1–7
→ Song: 'Isaiah 9' © Sharon Moughtin.
→ Tune: 'I ain't gonna grieve my Lord no more' (traditional).

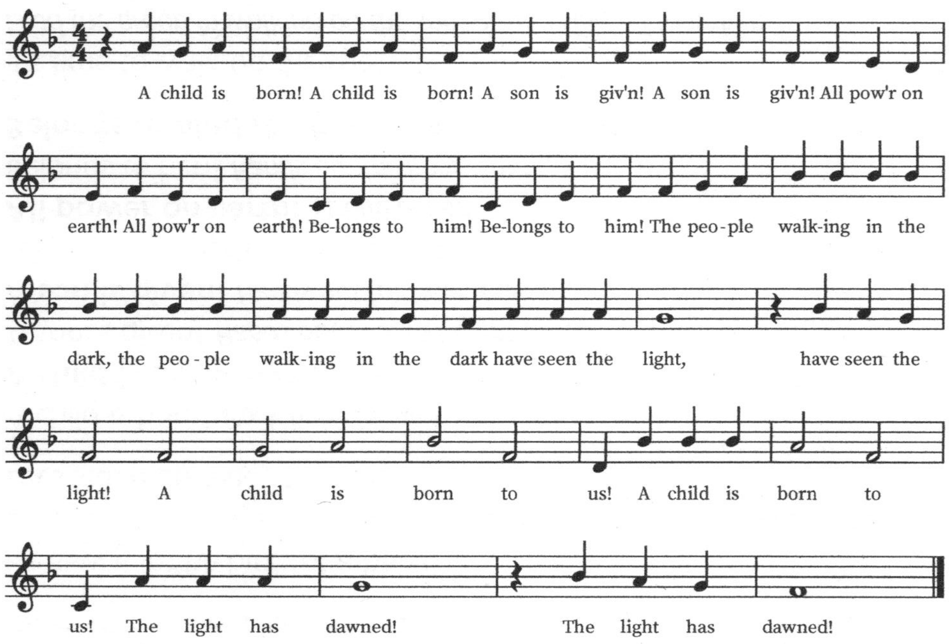

Appropriate for mixed groups of babies, toddlers and children up to the age of 9. If your group doesn't include any children age 7+, you might find the first storybox, 'Getting Ready for Baby Jesus', more appropriate.

Our story today is about the 'prophets of old'.
In the Bible, a prophet is someone
who learns to see with God's eyes.
Let's imagine for a moment we can see with God's eyes!
Let's close our eyes. . .
Lead the group in closing eyes.

And open them. Imagine we're seeing with God's eyes!
The world looks different!
Everything looks different!

The Bible has so many prophets!
One of the prophets that we hear about most near Christmas
is Isaiah!
Can you say: 'Isaiah'?

Isaiah

If appropriate:
Isaiah means 'to save'.
It's from the same word as 'Jesus'!
'Jesus' means 'to save' too!
And our story today is all about special names!

The book of Isaiah is very long!
Can you show me long.
Lead the group in reaching out arms wide.
It's one of the longest books in the Bible!
Today we're not going to try and read all of Isaiah's words!
Just a few of them: about a special child.

It's time to learn a song: it's Isaiah's song.
Let's learn it 'my turn' *Point to self*, 'your turn' *Leader's hands out*

The people walking in the dark,
the people walking in the dark!
Have seen the light, have seen the light! *Jazz hands*

**The people walking in the dark,
the people walking in the dark!
Have seen the light, have seen the light!** *Jazz hands*

A child is born to us! A child is born to us! *Rock baby*
The light has dawned! The light has dawned! *Arms up and out*

A child is born to us! A child is born to us! *Rock baby*

A child is born to us! A child is born to us! *Rock baby*
The light has dawned! The light has dawned! *Arms up and out*

And this special child has SO many names!
Are you ready?

Name number one... *Show one finger*
'Wonderful Guide!'
A guide is someone who walks with us and knows the way.

We're going to point ahead as we sing. *Point ahead*
But we're not going to just sing the names to one place.
These names are special!
We're going to shout each of them to the four corners of the world
so that everyone can hear!
Let's start with that corner.
Choose a corner, point to it, and face it.
Are you ready?
'My turn' *Point to self*, 'your turn' *Leader's hands out to group.*

As you sing turn in a circle so that you are singing one line to each corner of the room.
Wonderful Guide! *Point ahead* **Wonderful Guide!** *Point ahead*
Wonderful Guide! *Point ahead* **Wonderful Guide!** *Point ahead*
Wonderful Guide! *Point ahead* **Wonderful Guide!** *Point ahead*
Wonderful Guide! *Point ahead* **Wonderful Guide!** *Point ahead*

Lead the group in walking on the spot as you sing all together:
The people walking in the dark,
the people walking in the dark!
Have seen the light, have seen the light! *Jazz hands*
A child is born to us! A child is born to us! *Rock baby*
The light has dawned! The light has dawned! *Arms up and out*

Name number two! *Show two fingers*

The light has dawned! The light has dawned! *Arms up and out*
Let's sing that together:

The people walking in the dark,
the people walking in the dark!
Have seen the light, have seen the light! *Jazz hands*
A child is born to us! A child is born to us! *Rock baby*
The light has dawned! The light has dawned! *Arms up and out*

Isaiah lived at a time when everything felt so dark.
Let's cover our eyes to show the darkness.
Lead group in covering eyes.
But Isaiah the prophet could see with God's eyes!
Isaiah the prophet saw the light dawning! *Jazz hands*

He saw it in the birth of a baby!
Let's tell the story 'my turn' *Point to self*, 'your turn' *Leader's hands out.*
Let's stand up ready to sing!

A child is born! *Rock baby in arms*
A child is born! *Rock baby in arms*
A son is given! *Hands out to show a gift*
A son is given! *Hands out to show a gift*
All power on earth! *Strong action*
All power on earth! *Strong action*
Belongs to him! *Hands out to show a gift*
Belongs to him! *Hands out to show a gift*

It's time to walk on the spot!
Lead the group in walking on the spot as you sing all together.
The people walking in the dark,
the people walking in the dark!
Have seen the light, have seen the light! *Jazz hands*

44

'Almighty. . . .' That means mighty all of the time *Strong action*
God!
We need an action for God.
Who can show me an action for God?
Choose one of the actions. This will become the 'God action'.
Let's sing that name to the four corners of the earth!
Are you ready?
'My turn' *Point to self,* 'your turn' *Leader's hands out to group.*

As you sing turn in a circle so that you are singing one line to each corner of the room.

Almighty God! *Strong then God action*
Almighty God! *Strong then God action*
Almighty God! *Strong then God action*
Almighty God! *Strong then God action*
Almighty God! *Strong then God action*
Almighty God! *Strong then God action*
Almighty God! *Strong then God action*

Lead the group in walking on the spot as you sing:
The people walking in the dark,
the people walking in the dark!
Have seen the light, have seen the light! *Jazz hands*
A child is born to us! A child is born to us! *Rock baby*
The light has dawned! The light has dawned! *Arms up and out*

Name number three! *Show three fingers*
'Father. . .' Who can show us an action for Father?
Choose one of the actions. This will become the 'Father action'.
'. . .forever': not just Father for now and for some of us.
But for ALL of us and for EVER!

Let's show our more and more and more sign to show 'for ever'.
'New Start' sign
Are you ready to sing to the four corners of the earth!
'My turn' *Point to self,* 'your turn' *Leader's hands out to group.*

As you sing turn in a circle so that you are singing one line to each corner of the room.

Father for ever! *Father action then 'New Start' sign*
Father for ever! *Father action then 'New Start' sign*
Father for ever! *Father action then 'New Start' sign*
Father for ever! *Father action then 'New Start' sign*
Father for ever! *Father action then 'New Start' sign*
Father for ever! *Father action then 'New Start' sign*
Father for ever! *Father action then 'New Start' sign*

Lead the group in walking on the spot as you sing:
The people walking in the dark,
the people walking in the dark!
Have seen the light, have seen the light! *Jazz hands*
A child is born to us! A child is born to us! *Rock baby*
The light has dawned! The light has dawned! *Arms up and out*

Name number four! *Show four fingers*
How many names does a child need?
Just one more!
'Prince. . .' *Crown on head*
A prince is someone born to be king!
'. . .of Peace!' *Clasp hands together*
Peace isn't just when there's no fighting.
It's when everyone can take part and be together. *Clasp hands*

If appropriate:
 That's why we sometimes shake hands to show Peace.

So name number four. Show four fingers
Prince of Peace! *Crown action then clasp hands*
Let's sing to the four corners of the earth!

The Prince of Peace! *Crown action then clasp hands*
The Prince of Peace! *Crown action then clasp hands*
The Prince of Peace! *Crown action then clasp hands*
The Prince of Peace! *Crown action then clasp hands*
The Prince of Peace! *Crown action then clasp hands*
The Prince of Peace! *Crown action then clasp hands*
The Prince of Peace! *Crown action then clasp hands*
The Prince of Peace! *Crown action then clasp hands*

Lead the group in walking on the spot as you sing:
The people walking in the dark,
the people walking in the dark!
Have seen the light, have seen the light! *Jazz hands*
A child is born to us! A child is born to us! *Rock baby*
The light has dawned! The light has dawned! *Arms up and out*

Let's sit down for a moment.
When the group is ready:
That's Isaiah's song!

In Advent, as we wait for Jesus, Light of the World, to come,
 If appropriate: we light our second candle.
we remember Isaiah the Prophet's words
about the people walking in the dark seeing the light.

At this point, you could finish by singing the refrain one more time:

Let's sing Isaiah's song one more time.

This time let's sing it quietly as a prayer.
Lead the group in singing reflectively:
The people walking in the dark,
the people walking in the dark!
Have seen the light, have seen the light! *Jazz hands*
A child is born to us! A child is born to us! *Rock baby*
The light has dawned! The light has dawned! *Arms up and out*

Or you can close with a reprise of the song as follows:

Let's sing the beginning of Isaiah's words again.
'My turn' *Point to self*, 'your turn' *Leader's hands out to group.*

A child is born! *Rock baby in arms*
A child is born! *Rock baby in arms*
A son is given! *Hands out to show a gift*
A son is given! *Hands out to show a gift*
All power on earth! *Strong action*
All power on earth! *Strong action*
Belongs to him! *Hands out to show a gift*
Belongs to him! *Hands out to show a gift*

Let's stand up!

Lead the group in walking on the spot as you sing:
The people walking in the dark,
the people walking in the dark!
Have seen the light, have seen the light! *Jazz hands*
A child is born to us! A child is born to us! *Rock baby*
The light has dawned! The light has dawned!
Arms up and out.

This time try and do all the names in one verse!
Then we can all join in at the end!

46

Candle 3: John the Baptist

→ Luke 3.1–6; Isaiah 40.3–5
→ Song: 'Get ready for our God!' © Sharon Moughtin.
→ Tune: 'She'll be coming round the mountain' (traditional).

Get rea-dy, get rea-dy for our God! Get rea-dy, get rea-dy for our God!

It's time for a new start, time for a

new start! Get rea-dy, get rea-dy for our God!

Appropriate for mixed groups of babies, toddlers and children up to the age of 9.
Alternatives to this story include 'Baby John's Story' from Storybox 1 (p. 12) above.

For today's session, you may like to use a 'wilderness tray': a tray filled with sand (or brown sugar) with a few rocks and stones placed around so that it looks desolate.

Our story today is about the John the Baptist.
Let's stand up and be John the Baptist together.
Lead the children in standing.

John wore clothes made from camel hair!
Let's put our camel-hair coat on!
Lead the children in putting on a coat and scratching.
It's very itchy!

John's job was to get the world ready for God!
John called out,
'Get ready for God!' *Cup hands around mouth*

Are you ready?
'My turn' *Point to self*, 'your turn' *Leader's hands out to group!*

Wonderful Guide! *Point ahead*
Wonderful Guide! *Point ahead*
Almighty God! *Strong then God action*
Almighty God! *Strong then God action*
Father for ever! *Father action then 'New Start' sign*
Father for ever! *Father action then 'New Start' sign*
The Prince of Peace! *Crown action then clasp hands*
The Prince of Peace! *Crown action then clasp hands*

Lead the group in walking on the spot as you sing:
The people walking in the dark,
the people walking in the dark!
Have seen the light, have seen the light! *Jazz hands*
A child is born to us! A child is born to us! *Rock baby*
The light has dawned! The light has dawned!
Arms up and out.

The 'New Start' sign (the winding action from 'Wind the bobbin up') is used in this story to show 'getting ready' is among the very few Sowing Seeds signs and actions that are fixed. See p. 8 or the website (www.sowingseeds-online.org) for a description and explanation.

After 3, let's shout, 'Get ready for God!'
1, 2, 3 . . . Get ready for God! *Cup hands around mouth*

It's time to learn a song.
It's an important song!
Long before it was John the Baptist's song,
it was Isaiah the Prophet's song!

Isaiah was one of the 'prophets of old'!
In the Bible, a prophet is someone
who learns to see with God's eyes.
Let's imagine for a moment we can see with God's eyes!
Let's close our eyes. . . .
Lead the group in closing eyes.

And open them. Imagine we're seeing with God's eyes!
The world looks different!
Everything looks different!

Our second candle *Point to second candle*
reminds us of prophets like Isaiah!

If appropriate:
We sang some of Isaiah's words last week!
About a special child.
Today we're going to sing more of Isaiah's words.

It's time to learn a song.
It's Isaiah's song.
Let's learn it 'my turn', 'your turn'.

Get ready, get ready for our God!
Get ready, get ready for our God!
It's time for a new start, time for a new start! *'New Start' sign*
Get ready, get ready for our God!

This song of Isaiah starts in the wilderness.

If you're using a wilderness tray:
This is like the 'wilderness'.
Place your wilderness tray in front of the children. If you're using the
What's in the Box? option (p. 7), this can become this week's object.
You may like to have a cloth over it, in which case invite a child to
remove the cloth at this point.

What do you see? *Invite a child to respond*

Sand, rocks and sky and nothing else. *Shake head*

Let's imagine we're in the wilderness.
Look over here! *Point one way*
All we can see is sand and rocks and sky!

Look over there! *Point opposite way*
Encourage the group to join in after the dots.
All we can see is sand and rocks . . . **and sky!**

And look behind us! *Point behind*
Encourage the group to join in after the dots.
All we can see is . . . **sand and rocks and sky!**

In the wilderness there isn't much to hear.
Just sand and rocks and sky. *Shake head*
So it's a good place to hear God.

Isaiah the prophet said:
'A voice is calling in the wilderness'.
Let's sing that and cup our hands round our mouth
to make our voice big and echoing!

A voice is calling in the wilderness!
A voice is calling in the wilderness!

It's time for a new start, time for a new start! *'New Start' sign*
A voice is calling in the wilderness!

God is coming!
We need to get the road ready!
Use your hands to show the road as you describe it.
It's a road with valleys and mountains. *Low then high*
And it's winding with so many bends and turns. *Snaking hands*
It will take so long for God to come! *Hands out in concern*

But Isaiah was a prophet.
And Isaiah saw with God's eyes!
Isaiah saw every valley being lifted up high!

Let's bend down low to show the low, low valley. *Low action*
Then let's stand up high to show the valley lifting up! *High action*

Let's sing 'Lift up every valley high!' *Low action then high action*

Lift up every valley high! *Low action then high action*
Lift up every valley high! *Low action then high action*
It's time for a new start, time for a new start! *'New Start' sign*
Lift up every valley high! *Low action then high action*

And Isaiah the prophet saw
every mountain being brought down low!

Let's reach up high to show the high, high mountain. *High action*
Then let's bend down low to show the mountain becoming low! *High action*

Let's sing 'Bring down every mountain low!' *High action then low action*

Bring down every mountain low!
Bring down every mountain low!
It's time for a new start, time for a new start! *'New Start' sign*
Bring down every mountain low!

And Isaiah the prophet saw all the winding roads *Snaking road action*
going in a straight line! *Both arms straight in front*

Let's show the winding roads *Snaking road action*
going in a straight line: going direct! *Both arms straight in front*

Let's sing 'Make all the winding roads direct!' *Snaking action then arms straight*

Make all the winding roads direct! *Snaking action then arms straight*
Make all the winding roads direct! *Snaking action then arms straight*
It's time for a new start, time for a new start! *'New Start' sign*
Make all the winding roads direct! *Snaking action then arms straight*

And Isaiah the prophet could see with God's eyes.
This wasn't just for some people.
This was for everyone! For all God's creation! *Arms out wide*

Let's sing 'Everyone will see God come to save!' *Arms wide then arms crossed on chest.*

Everyone will see God come to save! *Arms wide then arms crossed*
Everyone will see God come to save! *Arms wide then arms crossed*
It's time for a new start, time for a new start! *'New Start' sign*
Everyone will see God come to save! *Arms wide then arms crossed*

John the Baptist knew Isaiah's song.
And Isaiah's song became John the Baptist's song too.

If appropriate:
God is good at giving everything a new start.
Making them more and more and more. *'New Start' sign*
Even words!

John the Baptist went out into the wilderness!

With sand and rocks and sky and nothing else.
And John the Baptist became the voice calling in the wilderness!
Let's be John the Baptist.
Let's put our camel-hair coat on!
Lead the group in in putting on a coat and scratching.
It's very itchy!

After 3, let's shout, 'Get ready for God!'
1, 2, 3 . . . Get ready for God! *Cup hands around mouth*

It's time to sing our song:
Get ready, get ready for our God! *'New Start' sign*

Lead the group in singing:
Get ready, get ready for our God! *'New Start' sign*
Get ready, get ready for our God! *'New Start' sign*
It's time for a new start, time for a new start! *'New Start' sign*
Get ready, get ready for our God! *'New Start' sign*

Let's sit down for a moment.
When the group is ready:

When we light our third candle on our Advent wreath
we remember John the Baptist.
John the Baptist, who heard the prophet Isaiah's song
and became a prophet himself.
Who learned to see with God's eyes.
And helps **us** get ready, get ready for our God.

It's time to get ready! Not just OUTside with all our decorations. But INside.

Let's sing our 'get ready' song one more time!
This time let's sing it quietly as a prayer.
Let's ask God to help **us** get ready to meet with God.

Lead the group in singing:
Get ready, get ready for our God! *'New Start' sign*
Get ready, get ready for our God! *'New Start' sign*
It's time for a new start, time for a new start! *'New Start' sign*
Get ready, get ready for our God! *'New Start' sign*

Candle 4: Mary, Jesus' Mummy

Choose one of the stories from 'Mary's Story' (p. 15 and p. 18) or 'Mary's Song' (p. 22 and p. 26).

Our story today is about Mary, Jesus' mummy.
Continue with your choice of story.

Candle 5: Jesus, Light of the World

Choose one of the stories from 'Christmas' (pp. 34 and 35).

Today is our last candle!
Our white candle!
Today we celebrate Baby Jesus being born!

Continue with your choice of story.

Tip

As the song is strongly related, it probably makes sense to leave out the 'Jesus, Light of the World!' Gathering Song for this session even if you have used it throughout the unit. This will also leave more time for Creative Responses.

Extra: The Christingle's Story

→ Song: 'The Christingle song' Words © Sharon Moughtin.
→ Tune: 'What shall we do with the drunken sailor?' (traditional).

This round o-range is the world!_ This round o-range is the world!_ This round o-range
is the world! For this is our Chris-tin-gle! Je - sus, Light of the World!_
Je - sus, Light of the World! - Je - sus, Light of the World is shi-ning in the dark - ness!

The Christingle's Story was originally commissioned by the Children's Society and a version can also be found on the Children's Society website (www.childrenssociety.org.uk). It can take place in your group as normal or in a main Christingle service. If you aren't holding a special service, it is particularly appropriate as an alternative to 'Jesus, Light of the World!' (the climax of the Jesus, Light of the World! unit on p. 83).

If you're collecting money for the Children's Society, remember to inform parents and carers beforehand so the children can be prepared.

For this story you will need at least one Christingle for the leader. There is also an option for the children to make their own. A guide to making a Christingle can be found on the Children's Society website (www.childrenssociety.org.uk). A guide to making Christingles with younger children and alternative Creative Responses to the story can be found on p. 142.

For groups that have been singing the 'Jesus, Light of the World!' song from the 'Getting Ready for Baby Jesus' (Advent) Building Blocks as a Gathering Song.

We've been singing a song as we get ready for Baby Jesus coming at Christmas.
It's our 'busy, busy, busy' song about
Say these words in way that invites the children to join in:
Jesus, Light of the World . . . **DAWNING** in the darkness.

But in our story today Jesus isn't DAWNING in the darkness!
Action for the rising sun
Jesus is SHINING in the darkness! *Jazz hands*
Can you show me your jazz hands for 'shining'? *Jazz hands*

Let's try singing our song
with Jesus SHINING in the darkness at the end.
Lead the children in singing:

Jesus, Light of the World, *Action for the rising sun*
Jesus, Light of the World, *Action for the rising sun*
Jesus, Light of the World . . . *Action for the rising sun*
Interrupt the singing Remember Jesus is SHINING!
is SHINING in the darkness! *Jazz hands*

For groups that are not familiar with the 'Jesus, Light of the World!' song:

We're going to learn a song today.
It's about Jesus being the Light of the World, like the sun.

Let's crouch down and show the sun hiding before it comes up in the morning.
Lead the children in crouching down.
Now let's show the sun rising with our bodies . . .

51

Up, up, up and out!
Raise hands upwards and outwards as you stand up.

We're going to use that action for our song.
And then because Jesus is SHINING bright, *Jazz hands*
we're going to finish with jazz hands! *Jazz hands*

Let's try that.
Lead the children in singing with the actions of the rising sun:
Jesus, Light of the World, *Action for the rising sun*
Jesus, Light of the World, *Action for the rising sun*
Jesus, Light of the World . . . *Action for the rising sun*
is SHINING in the darkness! *Jazz hands*
Repeat if necessary until the children are basically familiar with the tune. Continue with material for all groups below.

All groups:

We're ready to tell our story.

Place a Christingle in front of you where the children can see it and so you can still use your hands. You might find it helpful to place it on a small cup.

This is a Christingle!
Can you say 'Christingle'?
Christingle!
Today we're going to tell the story of the Christingle!

First, who can tell me what fruit this is?
Accept responses.
This is an orange.
What shape is this orange?
Accept responses. If older children suggest sphere, accept this impressive answer and ask what 2D shape a little child would say it is!

The orange is round. *Make a round shape with both your hands.*

It reminds us of the world.
The world is round like an orange.
Let's make a round shape with our hands.
Lead the group in making a round shape with both your hands.
Let's sing 'This round orange is the world!'

This round orange is the world! *Make a round shape*
This round orange is the world! *Make a round shape*
This round orange is the world! *Make a round shape*
Interrupt the singing: "Wait! Listen!"
Continue singing: For this is our Christingle! *Hold cupped hands out as if holding a Christingle*
Can you sing that last line?
Lead the group in singing:
For this is our Christingle! *Hold cupped hands out*

Let's sing that again.

This round orange is the world! *Make a round shape*
This round orange is the world! *Make a round shape*
This round orange is the world! *Make a round shape*
For this is our Christingle! *Hold cupped hands out*

Jesus, Light of the World, *Action for the rising sun*
Jesus, Light of the World, *Action for the rising sun*
Jesus, Light of the World . . . *Action for the rising sun*
is SHINING in the darkness! *Jazz hands*

Indicate the Christingle in front of you.
There's a ribbon around the orange.
After 3, who can tell me what colour the ribbon is?
1, 2, 3. . . RED!
There's a RED ribbon around our orange in a big circle. *Above the orange trace a horizontal circle with your finger*
This red ribbon is the love of Jesus! *Continue tracing the circle*

It goes all around the world!
No one's left out! *Shake head*
Let's sing 'This red ribbon is the love of Jesus!'
Trace a circle with your finger, this time around an imaginary orange so the group can copy the action.

This red ribbon is the love of Jesus. *Trace a circle*
This red ribbon is the love of Jesus. *Trace a circle*
This red ribbon is the love of Jesus. *Trace a circle*
For this is our Christingle! *Hold cupped hands out*

Jesus, Light of the World, *Action for the rising sun*
Jesus, Light of the World, *Action for the rising sun*
Jesus, Light of the World . . . *Action for the rising sun*
is SHINING in the darkness! *Jazz hands*

And look!
There are fruits and sweets on our Christingle!
Say slowly as these will be the words of the song.
the world is filled with all good things!
Mime scooping generously and showing the group.
All sorts of different good things!

Let's imagine we're scooping up all the good things in the world:
Fruits and vegetables and treats and sweet things!
Lead the group in miming scooping generously and showing each other your cupped hands.
Let's sing: The world is filled with all good things! *Scoop and show*

The world is filled with all good things! *Scoop and show*
The world is filled with all good things! *Scoop and show*
The world is filled with all good things! *Scoop and show*
For this is our Christingle! *Hold cupped hands out*

Jesus, Light of the World, *Action for the rising sun*
Jesus, Light of the World, *Action for the rising sun*
Jesus, Light of the World . . . *Action for the rising sun*
is SHINING in the darkness! *Jazz hands*

Optional:
Indicate the sticks on the Christingle.
Our fruits and sweets are on sticks.
Let's count how many sticks there are.
Lead the group in counting as you point to the sticks one at a time.
1, 2, 3, 4!
Point to the sticks one at a time again as you say:
Autumn, winter, spring, and summer!
The four sticks remind us of the four seasons!
Count to four with your fingers as you say:
Autumn, winter, spring, and summer!

Let's sing 'Autumn, winter, spring, and summer!'
Let's count on our fingers as we sing.
Lead the children in counting to four with your fingers and singing:
Autumn, winter, spring, and summer!
Autumn, winter, spring, and summer!
Autumn, winter, spring, and summer!
For this is our Christingle! *Hold cupped hands out*

Jesus, Light of the World, *Action for the rising sun*
Jesus, Light of the World, *Action for the rising sun*
Jesus, Light of the World . . . *Action for the rising sun*
is SHINING in the darkness! *Jazz hands*

Indicate the candle in the Christingle in front of you.

And most important of all, what's this?
Accept responses.
This is a tall candle!
Let's light our candle!
Move the Christingle to a safe place to light it, or hand it to an adult standing in a safe place to hold it.

When the candle is lit.
This candle reminds us of Jesus, Light of the World!
Let's look at our candle for a moment.
Watch the light dancing on the candle!
Let's hold our finger out like a candle.
Lead the children in holding fingers out.
After 3, let's light our finger candles.
1, 2, 3 . . Tsssss
Lead the children in miming striking a match and lighting your finger candles.

Let's stand tall like the candle
and show the light dancing and swaying above our heads.
Lead the group in standing holding your arms above your head to make a flame, then move your arms around like a candle flame dancing in the breeze. This will become the 'flame action'.
Slowly (these words will become the words of the song):
This tall candle is the Light of the World!

Let's sing 'This tall candle is the Light of the World!'
And make our arms dance like the light.

This tall candle is the Light of the World! *Flame action*
This tall candle is the Light of the World! *Flame action*
This tall candle is the Light of the World! *Flame action*
For this is our Christingle! *Hold cupped hands out*

Jesus, Light of the World, *Action for the rising sun*
Jesus, Light of the World, *Action for the rising sun*
is SHINING in the darkness! *Jazz hands*

Look at those beautiful candles shining and dancing!
Let's sit down for a moment.

Let's sit down for a moment.
When the group is ready:
Jesus, Light of the World,
is shining in the darkness! *Jazz hands*

But let me tell you something important.
The Light of the World isn't just shining in Jesus. *Shake head*

Jesus said that you *Point to a child*
and you . . . and you . . . and you . . . *Point to three more children*
All of us . . . *Point in a circle to everyone in the room and back to yourself*
WE are the Light of the World!

When God looks at us, God can see a little light of love shining!
When we share Jesus' light with other people,
It's like a little light is dancing on our head
like the light shining on the Christingles!
Let's imagine we're like the Christingles now!
Let's show our fiery light shining and dancing!
Lead the group in moving hands above head like a flame.

Let's close our eyes for a moment.
When the group is ready:
Let's imagine Jesus' light shining brighter and brighter.
Let's imagine all of us here shining and sharing that light
Until Jesus' light fills up our church/school/name of place,
and shines out across the whole world! *Jazz hands*

54

Let's show our little lights dancing on our heads now
as we sing 'Share the light, let's share the light!'

Share the light, let's share the light!
Share the light, let's share the light!
Share the light, let's share the light!
The Light of the World is shining! *Jazz hands*

Jesus, Light of the World, *Action for the rising sun*
Jesus, Light of the World, *Action for the rising sun*
Jesus, Light of the World *Action for the rising sun*
is shining in the darkness! *Jazz hands*

Optional collection for the work of the Children's Society

If you're collecting money for the Children's Society, this is a good opportunity to mention this, while the children are not distracted by Christingles in their hands. The collection is optional and of course entirely voluntary. Remember to inform parents and carers beforehand, so the children can be prepared.

Adapt according to your setting:

One of the ways we're sharing Jesus' light with other people today is by collecting money for the Children's Society.
The Children's Society help children who are lonely and have no one to talk to.
They make sure those children FIND someone to talk to.
They share Jesus' light with them.

Either:

Some of us have been collecting our money at home.
There'll be a time to give our money to the Children's Society later so they can carry on helping children who are lonely.

Describe simply and clearly how and when this will take place.
When we take our money forward,
we're sharing Jesus' light with other people.

Or:

Some of us have been collecting our money at home.
Let's give our money to the Children's Society now
so they can carry on helping children who are lonely.
Let's shine with Jesus' love like this Christingle!
Let's share Jesus' light with other people.
Let's sing quietly as we bring our money forward.

Share the light, let's share the light!
Share the light, let's share the light!
Share the light, let's share the light!
The Light of the World is shining! *Jazz hands*

End with:

Jesus, Light of the World, *Action for the rising sun*
Jesus, Light of the World, *Action for the rising sun*
Jesus, Light of the World *Action for the rising sun*
is shining in the darkness! *Jazz hands*

The Lighting of the Christingles

Optional. If your group have made Christingles you may like to take the opportunity to light them together. If you normally use a Prayer Building Block (Saying Sorry to God, Prayers for Other People, Thank You God) the 'Lighting of the Christingles' can take the place of this.

Invite the children to sit in a circle. If they've made a Christingle that can be lit, or if you have premade Christingles, invite the children to hold these in their hands (unlit).

Look at these beautiful Christingles!
Our Christingles tell us a story!
We're going to light them in a moment.
But first, let's tell the story of the Christingles again.
Lead the children in singing the song again, this time without the refrain, until the end.
Indicate the orange: First, the orange.
This round orange is the world! *Point to the orange*
This round orange is the world! *Point to the orange*
This round orange is the world! *Point to the orange*
For this is our Christingle! *Hold up Christingle*

Indicate the ribbon: Then the ribbon.
This red ribbon is the love of Jesus. *Trace around the ribbon*
This red ribbon is the love of Jesus. *Trace around the ribbon*
This red ribbon is the love of Jesus. *Trace around the ribbon*
For this is our Christingle! *Hold up Christingle*

Indicate the fruits and sweets. And the sweet treats?
The world is filled with all good things!
Point to each of the fruits/sweets.
The world is filled with all good things!
Point to each of the fruits/sweets.
The world is filled with all good things!
Point to each of the fruits/sweets.
For this is our Christingle! *Hold up Christingle*

Optional:
Indicate the sticks. And the four sticks?
Autumn, winter, spring, and summer!
Point to each of the sticks in turn.
Autumn, winter, spring, and summer!
Point to each of the sticks in turn.
Autumn, winter, spring, and summer!
Point to each of the sticks in turn.
For this is our Christingle! *Hold up Christingle*

And most important of all, the candle!
This tall candle is the Light of the World! *Point to the candle*
This tall candle is the Light of the World! *Point to the candle*
This tall candle is the Light of the World! *Point to the candle*
For this is our Christingle! *Hold up Christingle*

It's time to light our Christingles!
We're going to do this in a special way.

Lighting Christingles with large numbers of very young children can be challenging. Choose from the following two options according to your context. Option 1 is designed for groups where adults can partner with children to keep everyone safe. Option 2 is designed for groups where it is not possible for every child to sit with a designated adult. The muffin trays mean that the Christingles can be placed down without toppling over. If the trays are unsightly, you could wrap them in tinfoil beforehand. For both options you will need designated adults who have been briefed beforehand to keep everyone safe. The Children's Society suggests that these could be the Christingle Organizers.

Ask the designated adults to come to the front.

First, let's turn the lights off and feel the dark.
Pause, as the lights are turned off.

Name, Name and Name have been letting their little lights shine
If appropriate, or adapt accordingly:
in all the work they've done to help us get ready for today!
We're going to light their Christingles now
to show the little light of love that's been shining bright in them.
1, 2, 3. . . . *Strike a match and light the Christingles.*

Look at their little lights, shining in the dark!
Now, let's watch what happens
when we SHARE that light with other people!
When we pass it forward!

Option 1:
In this option, the light is passed from Christingle to Christingle, in the traditional way, as the children stay in their places.

Name, Name and Name are going to share their light with the people sitting next to them.
Indicate to the group. Use names if possible.
Then THEY'RE going to share the light with the people next to them!
Then THEY'RE going to share the light with the people next to them!
And so on!
And the light is going to move out and out and out until EVERYONE is shining with the light of Jesus!

Let's sing, 'Share the light! Let's share the light!'
And watch the room get brighter and brighter
as we share the light of Jesus' love!

Share the light! Let's share the light!
Share the light! Let's share the light!
Share the light! Let's share the light!
The Light of the World is shining! *Jazz hands*

Alternative song: if there are large numbers of people present so that the lighting of the Christingles may take a while, you could sing 'See in the darkness' (to the tune of 'Incy, wincy spider') instead. See the music resources on p. 125.

Option 2:
In this option, the children take turns to come forward and have their Christingles lit. This way, there are only ever two lit Christingles being held at the same time at the front of the group: one by the child doing the lighting, and one by the child whose Christingle is being lit. Each child should be supported by an adult.

Each child:

- comes and stands on one of two designated spots with their Christingle in their hands
- continues to hold their Christingle as the previous child lights it with her/ his Christingle (the first child's Christingle is lit by a Christingle Organizer)
- stays on their spot as the next child comes forward to stand on the other of the two designated spots.
- lights the Christingle of the next child from their own Christingle
- places their Christingle in muffin tray
- returns to their place

For this option, you need four responsible adults to support the children and keep them safe.

- one designated adult to tap the children on the shoulder to let them know when it is their turn to stand on one of the two spots
- two designated adults to stand next to the two designated spots to support the children as one child lights the other child's Christingle
- one designated adult to help the children place the Christingle safely in the muffin tray and return to their place

Place muffin trays in the centre of the circle.
Let's stay sitting down!
We're going to take turns to light our Christingle.
When *Name* taps you on the shoulder, it will be your turn!
You can come and stand here!
Stand on one of the designated spots with your Christingle.
When you're here, hold your Christingle in your hands like this.
Show Christingle.

And a friend will share Jesus' light with you
and light your Christingle like this!
Invite one of the Christingle Organizers to light your candle from the other designated spot with their Christingle.
Then it will be your turn to share Jesus' light with the next person!
When you've shared Jesus' light,
you can put your Christingle down here
Put your Christingle in the muffin tray to model how it's done.
and go back to your seat!

Let's sing, 'Share the light! Share the light!'
and watch Jesus' light shining brighter and brighter
as we share it with each other!

Share the light! Let's share the light!
Share the light! Let's share the light!
Share the light! Let's share the light!
The Light of the World is shining! *Jazz hands*

All groups:
When all the Christingles are lit, you may like to hum the song you have been singing one more time.
When the group is ready:
Look at those beautiful lights!
We started off with just *three* little lights!
But then we shared Jesus' light and look what happened!
The room is full of Jesus' light and love!

But we don't just want to share Jesus' light HERE in this building!
The light of Jesus belongs OUTSIDE in the world!
Jesus asks us to share the light everywhere!

So now it's time for US to become little Christingles!
Sharing Jesus' light out there! *Point outside*

In a moment (not yet!) we're going to blow THESE Christingles out.
Indicate Christingles
But when we blow them out,
the light doesn't disappear!
The light goes inside US!
WE become walking [or crawling] Christingles.
We become part of shining light outside in the world for Jesus!
Sharing light with everyone!

So after 3, let's stay in our places
and with a big *PUFF* blow out our candles
and imagine the light shining in us!

1, 2, 3 . . . Blow!
Lead the children in blowing out the candles, either in their hands or on the muffin trays. If they are on the muffin trays, they'll need a bit of extra help from adults standing a little closer. Make sure enthusiastic children don't run towards the candles!

Now Jesus' light is shining and dancing in us! *Point around the circle*
We're ready to go out and share that light with the world!

The Eating of the Christingles (optional)

If food poverty is an issue in your local area, it is best practice to avoid using food in worship or creative activities that will not be eaten. If the children are not holding their Christingles at this point, you may like to sing the song you have been singing as you return them to the children.

Now it's time to eat our tasty Christingles!
Because WE'VE become little, walking Christingles
like the Christingles here!

Extra: Interactive Nativity with Mini Carols

- Carol: 'O little town of Bethlehem'. Words: Philips Brooks (1868). Tune: St Louis (Redner).
- Song: '"Yes!" said Mary'. Words © Sharon Moughtin. Tune: 'Pop goes the weasel' (traditional) (see p. 15).
- Carol: 'Little donkey'. Tune and words: Eric Boswell © Warner Chappell Music, 1959.
- Carol: 'Once in royal David's city'.
- Carol: 'Hark the herald angels sing'.
- Carol: 'We three kings'.
- Carol: 'O come all ye faithful'.
- Carol: 'We wish you a Merry Christmas'.

This material is designed as a special service where adults are also present. It provides families with the youngest children with an opportunity to take part in a carol service that's designed especially for them, with just one verse of each carol, and no shushing! If your group isn't too big, the material will work best gathered standing around a manger, but it can equally be used in a school or church setting with rows of seating. Adapt the material according to your setting.

You will need a manger (or cardboard box), hay, a baby doll for Baby Jesus wrapped in a white sheet or pillowcase.

There are also options to use paper stars, handfuls of white/silver/gold confetti (biodegradable if possible) or confetti cannons (biodegradable if possible) during the singing of 'O come all ye faithful' depending on your context. See the website for examples and further guidance, particularly for using confetti cannons safely!

Words for the carols will need to be provided either on simple carol sheets or via a projector or TV screen so that hands can be free as you sing (simple white font on black background works best as it doesn't distract).

Recent scholarship by Amy Lindeman Allen has shown that it's most likely the shepherds in Luke's story were children: boys and girls, looking after their family's sheep. See note 2 on p. 233.

You may like to invite the children and adults to come wearing nativity outfits of their choice, or you could provide a range of options (perhaps borrowed from a local school) for everyone (children and adults!) to choose from and put on as they arrive.

When the group is ready to start:
It's time! Time to go to Bethlehem!
Look! Bethlehem is this way!

Our story begins in the dark. Let's close our eyes and feel the dark.
Lead the group in closing their eyes for a moment.
We're waiting in the dark for the light…
But now the waiting is over. Let's open our eyes!

If appropriate (different parts of the world get dark at different times of the year!): It's the darkest time of the year: time to tell our story.

As we sing 'O little town of Bethlehem',
let's watch the light getting brighter and brighter
as we get ready for Jesus, the Light of the World.
Let's imagine a night sky full of stars all around us. *Point upwards*
Let's make twinkle hands to show the stars shining.
Open and shut hands with fingers spread.
Let's hold our hands up high to show the stars shining over Bethlehem!
Lead the group in opening and closing hands in a 'twinkle' action as you sing.

O little town of Bethlehem, how still we see thee lie!

59

Above thy deep and dreamless sleep, the silent stars go by.
Yet in thy dark streets shineth the everlasting light.
The hopes and fears of all the years are met in thee tonight.

We're here in Bethlehem.
But our story starts a long way from Bethlehem.

> *If appropriate:*
> Let's remember together!

Can you sing after me?
'My turn' *Point to self,* 'your turn' *Leader's hands out to group.*

The actions of this song are designed to mirror a jack-in-the-box, with its lid closing and the puppet bursting out at the 'pop' moment. Start standing on tiptoes with your hands stretched high. You could make angel wings (like butterfly wings) with your hands.

An angel came to Ma-a-a-ry.
Bring hands down from on high and come down from tiptoes.
An angel came to Ma-a-a-ry.
Bring hands down from on high and come down from tiptoes.
'You will have a baby!
Rock baby, standing at normal height.
'You will have a baby!
Rock baby, standing at normal height.

Spoken: Now let's crouch down so we're small like a toddler . . .

Singing:
He will be the Son of God!
Crouch down on the ground like tiny child.
He will be the Son of God!'
Crouch down on the ground like tiny child.

'Yes!' sa-id Mary.
Jump up and shout 'Yes!'
'Yes!' sa-id Mary.
Jump up and shout 'Yes!'
Let's sing that together!
Lead the group in singing.

An angel came to Ma-a-a-ry.
Bring hands down from on high and come down from tiptoes.
'You will have a baby!
Rock baby, standing at normal height.
He will be the Son of God!'
Crouch down on the ground like tiny child.
'Yes!' sa-id Mary.
Jump up and shout 'Yes!'

Now Mary has a baby inside her tummy!
Let's be Mary.

> *If appropriate:* Let's hold our tummies and show the baby inside us: Baby Jesus.

But first Mary and Joseph have to go back
to their family home in Bethlehem.
It's a long way to Bethlehem!
Six whole days of walking!

> *If appropriate:*
> Shall we count to 6 on our fingers?
> *Lead the children in counting on their fingers.* **1, 2, 3, 4, 5, 6. . .**

That's a long time to walk! Especially with a baby in your tummy!
I wonder how they did it?
Maybe a donkey helped them carry their bags?
Let's make a cup shape with our hands.
Let's use our hands to make the clop of the donkey's hooves .
Lead the children in making a 'clip clop' sound by clapping cupped hands.

Let's sing as Mary and Joseph go on their long journey.

Lead the group in singing Eric Boswell's 'Little donkey'. This song is under copyright so can't be reproduced here but can be found in many hymn and carol books. Lead the children in continuing to make the 'clip clop' sound with your hands as you sing.

Little donkey, little donkey . . .

When 'Little Donkey' has finished:
Bethlehem is busy, busy, busy!
There's no room in Joseph's family home
for Baby Jesus, the Light of the World.
No special place there, or anywhere else.
Instead, Jesus is born where the animals shelter.
There's no bed for Jesus, no cot.
So Mary lies him in the manger,
the animal's foodbox,
which is warm with hay.

As we sing 'Once in royal David's city',
let's show jazz hands
to show that Baby Jesus,
Light of the World, is here!

Lead the group in jazz hands as you sing:
**Once in royal David's city
stood a lowly cattle shed,
where a mother laid her baby
in a manger for his bed.
Mary was that mother mild,
Jesus Christ, her little child.**
Place Baby Jesus in the manger.

Let's show our jazz hands coming from way up high *Jazz hands high* to way down low *Jazz hands low*
like Baby Jesus came down at Christmas.

Lead the group in moving jazz hands from high to low as you sing.
**He came down to earth from heaven
who is God and Lord of all,
and his shelter was a stable
and his cradle was a stall.
with the needy, poor, and lowly,
lived on earth our Saviour holy.**

Outside busy Bethlehem, up in the cold, dark hills,
shepherd children – girls and boys – are watching their sheep.
Let's all be the shepherd children!
It's cold outside. Can you show me cold?
Lead the people by rubbing hands or arms.
Really, really cold!
We're watching for wolves and other dangers of the night.
Look! Is there a wolf over there?! *Point*
Or over there? *Point*

Suddenly, the skies are filled with light!
The brightest light the shepherd children have ever seen!
Shield eyes with hand.
The light of God's glory begins to flash all around.
The shepherd children are terrified. Very, very scared!
Can you show me terrified and scared?
Lead the group in looking terrified.
They look into the light.
Let's hold our hand over our eyes to see.
Lead the children in shielding eyes with hand.

An angel's standing there!
Let's stand up tall and strong and be the angel Gabriel.

Lead the people in standing up tall.

Can you say after me?
'My turn' *Point to self,* 'your turn' *Leader's hands out to group.*
Don't be frightened! *Hold hands out and smile*
Don't be frightened! *Hold hands out and smile*
I have Good News! *Jazz hands*
I have Good News! *Jazz hands*
There's a new baby king! *Place imaginary crown on head*
There's a new baby king! *Place imaginary crown on head*
Go! *Point*
Go! *Point*
Find him! *Point*
Find him! *Point*
Suddenly the skies are filled with noise.
Let's make a noise!
Lead the group in stamping feet on ground or make a noise another way.
It's all God's armies of angels singing!
We're going to be the angels.
Not pretty, baby angels, but soldiers of light,
but angel warriors in an army! Super-powerful!
Can you show me super-powerful? *Lead the group in a strong pose*
And they're marching!
Let's imagine we're the armies of angels.
Let's march on the spot!
Lead the people in marching:
1, 2, 3, 4, 1, 2, 3, 4 . . .
But these angel warriors haven't come to bring war!
They've come to announce peace!
Peace to the whole world!
Let's continue marching as we sing . . .

Continue marching in time to the carol as you sing:
Hark, the herald angels sing,
'Glory to the new-born King!
Peace on earth, and mercy mild,
God and sinners reconciled!'
Joyful, all ye nations, rise,
join the triumph of the skies.
With th'angelic hosts proclaim,
'Christ is born in Bethlehem!'
Hark! the herald angels sing,
'Glory to the new-born King!'

. . . Then, just as suddenly,
the skies are silent and dark again.
The angels have gone!
The shepherd children looked one way. *Point*
Aside: Let's all look that way. *Point and lead the group in looking*
Then they looked the other way! *Point and lead the group in looking*
What did the angel tell us to do?
Can anyone remember? *Accept any responses*
'Go!' *Point* Find him! *Point*
So what are we waiting for?
After 3, let's run on the spot to find Baby Jesus.
1, 2, 3: Run! *Lead the people in running fast on the spot*
And freeze!

Far, far from Bethlehem, in the East,
there were some people called 'Magi'.
Let's be the Magi.
Now, some people call the Magi 'the Wise Men'
because they were very clever.
Can you show me clever? *Lead the children in looking 'clever'*

Some people call the Magi the 'Three Kings' because they were very important.
Can you show me very important! *Lead the children in looking important*
So the Magi were very important and very clever.
They knew all about the stars in the sky.

One night, they were looking up to the sky. . . .
Let's look up to the sky with our telescope to see the stars like the Magi.
Lead the children in looking up to the sky through an imaginary telescope.
Look at all those stars!
But look! *Point upwards towards an imaginary star*
Look! What's that! That wasn't there before!

One of the Magi noticed a new star.
'That star means there's a new king!' they said.
So the Magi decided to go and meet this new king.
We're going on a journey!
Let's get on our camels.
Lead the people in miming sitting on the back of a camel.
Has anyone been on a camel before? Hold on tight!
Because they sway this way and that way, this way and that way. . .
Lead the children in miming rocking side to side as the camel walks.
As we ride on our camels, let's sing 'We three kings . . .'

Lead the group in swaying on the camel and singing:
We three kings of Orient are,
bearing gifts, we travel afar.
Field and fountain, moor and mountain,
following yonder star.
O, star of wonder, star of night,
star with royal beauty bright.
Westward leading, still proceeding,
guide us to thy perfect light.

Look! The star's stopped! *Point*
The new king must be there.
Let's go and see!

First let's get ourselves ready!
That was a long journey and we look a bit scruffy!
Let's make sure our crown and robe are straight.
Lead the children in straightening your crowns and robes.

Remember! We're very clever.
Let's look very clever! *Lead the children in looking 'clever'*
And we're very important!
We need to look important so the new king knows how important we are!
Let's look very important! Lead the children in looking important

Are we ready to meet the king?
Let's hold our heads high and march in on the spot.
March, march, march, march . . .
Lead the children in marching on the spot.

Stop in surprise and confusion, looking around.
But look! What's this?
This isn't a palace!
And look! What's that? *Point to the manger with Baby Jesus in it*
It's a baby! A tiny baby!
This can't be the new king . . . can it?

But the Magi looked and saw that new king WAS a tiny, tiny baby.
And they looked even closer . . .
Optional: draw closer to the manger, but be aware that children will do the same!
and they knelt down.

Let's kneel down together now.
Lead the people in kneeling, if possible around the manger.

And the Magi forgot about being clever.
And the Magi forgot about being important
because they saw that this wasn't just a new KING.
This baby was the KING OF KINGS!
This baby was GOD!
And the Magi bowed their heads.
Let's bow our heads . . . and worshipped.
Lead the people in bowing heads.

If there is silence, hold it for a moment. Then lead the people in singing 'Away in a manger'.

Away in a manger, no crib for a bed,
the little Lord Jesus
laid down his sweet head.
The stars in the night sky
looked down where he lay,
the little Lord Jesus, asleep on the hay.

So many journeys to find one baby.
Make 'clip clop' sound with cupped hands.
Mary and Joseph walking with their donkey!
March on the spot:
The armies of angels marching through the skies!
Mime running with arms:
The shepherd children running as fast as they can from the hills!
Mime riding a camel:
And the Magi travelling for days and days and days on their camels.
And now us. We've all come on our own journey here!
All for a tiny baby: Jesus, Light of the World. *Point towards the manger*

Choose from one of the three options to end, according to your context.

Option 1: Walking on the spot

Let's join together in singing 'O come, all ye faithful' and walk on the spot as we sing.

Lead the group in singing:
O come all ye faithful,
joyful and triumphant,
O come ye, O come ye to Bethlehem.
Come and behold him,
born the king of angels.

O come, let us adore him,
O come, let us adore him,
O come, let us adore him,
Christ, the Lord.

Option 2: Hay and bling

In a moment, we're all going to find our place around the manger. But first... There's something missing? What's missing from this manger?

Hold hay Hay! Now hay is important in this story!
It reminds us that Jesus came to this world with nothing.
Jesus was king. *Crown on head*
He could have had anything he wanted!
But Jesus came with no home and no bed. Just hay.
Hay reminds us that
we don't have to be feeling special or important
or even tidy inside
to ask Jesus to be with us.
Jesus wants to be with us
in the ordinary and messy bits of our lives too!

64

Jesus loves hay!
We're going to bring hay to the manger as we sing.
And as we bring it, let's imagine we're bringing ourselves, even our messy parts to Jesus!

Lead the group in singing as the children take handfuls of hay to lay in the manger. Baby Jesus may need to be picked up temporarily!

**O come all ye faithful,
joyful and triumphant,
O come ye, O come ye to Bethlehem.
Come and behold him,
born the king of angels.**

**O come, let us adore him,
O come, let us adore him,
O come, let us adore him,
Christ, the Lord.**

But wait! There's something else missing!
Show handful of silver/gold and white confetti.
Bling!
When Jesus came to be with us in the hay
Jesus brought God's glory, God's bling, with him!
It's time to celebrate!

To the children:
In a minute this bling is going to fall down.
Your job is to mix the bling with the hay.
Heaven and earth:
God's glory mixed with our humanity!
So it can NEVER be taken apart again.
That's what happens when Baby Jesus is born.
You have an important job to do!
Are you ready?

If you're using confetti cannons you may like to have a countdown at this point:
If you don't like loud noises, cover your ears!
10, 9, 8, 7, 6, 5, 4, 3, 2, 1…

As the confetti falls from the cannons or from the hands of adults or older children throwing it into the air above the group, lead the group in singing as the confetti falls and the hay is mixed with the confetti.

**Sing, choirs of angels,
Sing in exultation,
Sing, all ye citizens of heaven above!
Glory to God in the highest!**

**O come, let us adore him.
O come, let us adore him.
O come, let us adore him,
Christ, the Lord.**

Repeat 'O come, let us adore him' as appropriate.

Option 3: Stars

It's time for us to come and see Baby Jesus.
If you like,
you could bring a star to welcome him:
Baby Jesus, Light of the World.

Lead the group in singing as anyone who wishes to comes to see Baby Jesus and places a star in the manger:

**O come all ye faithful,
joyful and triumphant,
O come ye, O come ye to Bethlehem.
Come and behold him,
born the king of angels.**

O come, let us adore him,
O come, let us adore him,
O come, let us adore him,
Christ, the Lord.

Sing, choirs of angels,
Sing in exultation,
Sing, all ye citizens of heaven above!
Glory to God in the highest!

O come, let us adore him.
O come, let us adore him.
O come, let us adore him,
Christ, the Lord.

Repeat 'O come, let us adore him' until all who wish to have come to see Baby Jesus and placed a star in the manger.

All groups

End with an appropriate prayer or blessing. Depending on who is present, you may like to end with 'We wish you a Merry Christmas' or a favourite carol.

We wish you a Merry Christmas!
We wish you a Merry Christmas!
We wish you a Merry Christmas
and a Happy New Year!

Good tidings we bring
to you and your kin.
We wish you a Merry Christmas
and a Happy New Year!

Jesus, Light of the World! unit (Epiphany)

The Jesus, Light of the World! unit continues the Christmas celebrations of Jesus' birth. Rather than leaving Christmas behind immediately, the children are invited to join the Magi (Wise Men/Three Kings) in reflecting on the gifts they'd like to bring to Baby Jesus now that all the excitement of the present-giving/receiving in homes is generally over. Some groups may like to use this material in the weeks leading up to Christmas instead. For groups that follow the church seasons, it's designed for the Epiphany season (the weeks immediately after Christmas).

The unit culminates with the joyful presentation of Jesus at the Temple, where Simeon (like Zechariah before him) recognizes Jesus as the Light: this time the Light not just *dawning* in Israel (Luke 1.78) but *shining* through the whole world (Luke 2.32)!

Tip

For groups that follow the Lectionary (a set pattern of reading followed each week in worship): In practice, we've found the Lectionary's move from Jesus being a baby (the Magi) to being an adult (baptism of Jesus and the wedding of Cana) then back to being a baby (presentation of Jesus) can be confusing for young children. The story of the baptism of Jesus therefore follows at the beginning of the next unit, 'Meet John' (p. 88), where groups are invited to meet John the Baptist and experience Jesus' baptism, ending up with Jesus in the wilderness (where the Spirit throws him after the baptism).

Jesus, Light of the World! storybox

Choose from the stories according to your own context.

The Magi's Journey (Matthew 2.1–2) 68
Appropriate for mixed groups of 0–7 years

The Magi's Gifts (Matthew 2.1–2, 9–11) 71
Appropriate for mixed groups of 0–9 years

Extra: Baby Jesus, the Refugee (Matthew 2.13–18) 76
Appropriate for mixed groups of 0–9 years

Anna the Prophet's Story (Luke 2.36–38; Isaiah 40; 60) 79
Appropriate for mixed groups of 0–9 years

Jesus, Light of the World! (Candlemas, Luke 2.22–33) 83
Appropriate for mixed groups of 0–9 years
The presentation of Jesus/Candlemas

Tip

Even if you don't use the other Building Blocks, you may find it helpful to use one of the Gathering Songs ('We are marching in the light of God' or 'Epiphany: O let us see!') just before the storytelling in every session of this unit as they gather together the themes of the unit as a whole. See pp. 172 and 175.

The Magi's Journey

→ Matthew 2.1–2
→ Song: 'Follow the star to Bethlehem'. Words: © Sharon Moughtin.
→ Tune: 'Here we go round the mulberry bush' (traditional).

Let's fol-low, fol-low, fol-low the star, fol-low the star, fol-low the star. Let's fol-low, fol-low, fol-low the star, to meet the spe-cial king!

Appropriate for mixed groups of babies, toddlers and children up to the age of 7. Groups that include children up to the age of 9 may prefer to start the unit with the story of 'The Magi's Gifts' (p. 71).

For the storytelling today, you will need a doll to represent Baby Jesus lying in a manger or on white/gold cloth on your focal table.

Tip

If the children in your group are more familiar with other names for the Magi, adapt the song and material accordingly, for instance to: 'the Three Kings', 'the Wise Men' or 'the Wise Ones'.

Optional: 'What's in the Box? (see p. 7):
Invite a child to open the box.
Inside is a star.

What's in the box?
Accept the child's response.

Today we're going to tell the story of 'the Magi' and the star.

To get ready for today's story, we need to practise using our faces to show how we're feeling.
We're not going to use any sound at all!
Can you show me: sad . . . happy . . . important . . . shocked!
We're ready to tell our story.

In the time that Jesus was born
there were some people called 'Magi'.
Let's get ready to be Magi.

Some people call the Magi 'the Wise Men'
because they were very clever.
Can you show me very clever? *Lead the children in looking clever*

Some people call the Magi 'the Three Kings'
because they were very important in their countries.
Can you show me very important?
And let's put on some important clothes . . .
a robe and a crown.
Lead the children in putting on imaginary robes and crowns.

So the Magi were very important and very clever.
They knew all about the stars in the sky.
One night, they were looking up to the sky . . .
Let's look up to the sky to see the stars like the Magi.
Lead the children in looking up to the sky through an imaginary telescope or with hand over eyes.

Look at all those stars!
Yes, we know all about them! *Look clever*

But look!
Point upwards in surprise towards an imaginary star.
Look! What's that?
That star wasn't there before!
The Magi were amazed!

Can you show me shocked and amazed?
Lead the children in looking shocked and amazed.

'That star means there's a new king!' they said.
'And he looks special . . . really special!'
We need to meet this new king!'
So the Magi decided to follow the star on a very long journey.

Let's get up and get ready to go.
Don't forget your treasure chest – full of special gifts for the king!
Lead the children in picking up an imaginary, very heavy treasure chest.
Phew, that's heavy! Let's put it on our camel.
Lead the children in putting the treasure chest onto an imaginary camel.
Let's walk on the spot together and follow that star!

Lead the children in walking on the spot throughout.
**Let's follow, follow, follow the star,
follow the star, follow the star.
Let's follow, follow, follow the star,
to meet the special king!** *Crown on head*

Uh oh! *Point* Desert!
We can't walk through the sandy desert! *Shake head*
Let's climb on our camels.
Lead the children in climbing onto the imaginary camel.

Now when you ride a camel,
the camel doesn't go up and down like a donkey
Mime *trotting on a donkey.*
The camel goes from side to side:
Lead the children in swaying jerkily from side to side as if on a camel.
This way, that way, this way, that way . . .

Continue the camel riding action as you sing.
**Let's follow, follow, follow the star,
follow the star, follow the star.
Let's follow, follow, follow the star
to meet the special king!** *Crown on head*

Goodness! That was a long way through the desert.
Let's get off our camels.
Lead the children in getting down off the camels.

Uh oh! *Point* It's the sea! *Sound worried*
But look! *Point* There's a boat!
Let's get into our boat to cross the sea.
Lead the children in sitting down on the floor as if in a boat.
Don't forget your camel!
Lead the children in helping a camel into the boat.
Let's row!
Row to the rhythm of the song.
Row and row and row and row . . .

Continue rowing in time as you sing.
**Let's follow, follow, follow the star,
follow the star, follow the star.
Let's follow, follow, follow the star
to meet the special king!** *Crown on head*

Phew! We've reached the shore.
This is a long journey . . . .
Let's get out of our boats . . . .
Lead the children in climbing out of the boat and standing up.
Don't forget your camel!
Lead the children in helping the camel out of the boat.

Uh oh! Look! *Point upwards* Look at that mountain!
Time for some climbing!
Can camels climb? Let's find out . . . .

69

Lead the children in pretending to rock climb a very steep mountain.
**Let's follow, follow, follow the star,
follow the star, follow the star.
Let's follow, follow, follow the star
to meet the special king!** *Crown on head*

Goodness me, this is a hard journey!
And now look! A dark valley!
It's bit scary! Ssssh!
Whisper We don't want to wake any scary animals up.
Let's tiptoe, tiptoe, tiptoe . . .
And whisper our song . . . Ssssssh!

**Let's follow, follow, follow the star,
follow the star, follow the star.
Let's follow, follow, follow the star
to meet the special king!** *Crown on head*

Look! The star's stopped! *Point*
The new king must be there.
Shall we go and see?
Accept the children's responses.

First let's get ourselves ready!
That was a long journey and we look a bit scruffy.
Let's make sure our crown and robe are straight.
Lead the children in straightening your crowns and robes.

Remember! We're very clever!
Let's look very clever!
And we're very important!
We need to look important so the new king
knows how important we are!
Lead the children in looking clever and important.

Are we ready to meet the king?
Let's hold our heads high and march in on the spot.
March, march, march, march . . .
Lead the children in marching on the spot.

Stop in surprise and confusion, looking around.
But look! What's this?
This isn't a palace!
And look! What's this?
Pick the Baby Jesus doll up in your arms.
It's a baby! A tiny baby!
This can't be the new king . . . can it?

But the Magi looked and saw
that the new king WAS a tiny, tiny baby.
And they looked even closer . . .
and they knelt down.
Let's kneel down together now.

Lower your voice.
And the Magi forgot about being clever.
They forgot about being important
because they saw that this wasn't just a new KING.
This baby was the KING OF KINGS.
This baby was GOD!
And the Magi bowed their heads.
Let's bow our heads . . . and worshipped.
If there is silence, hold it for a moment.

The Magi were amazed to see Baby Jesus.
We're going to pass Baby Jesus around the circle now.
Everyone's going to have a turn
so it will just be for a moment.

The Magi's Gifts

→ Matthew 2.1–2, 9–11
→ Song: 'Three special gifts'. Words: © Sharon Moughtin.
→ Tune: 'The farmer's in his den' (traditional).

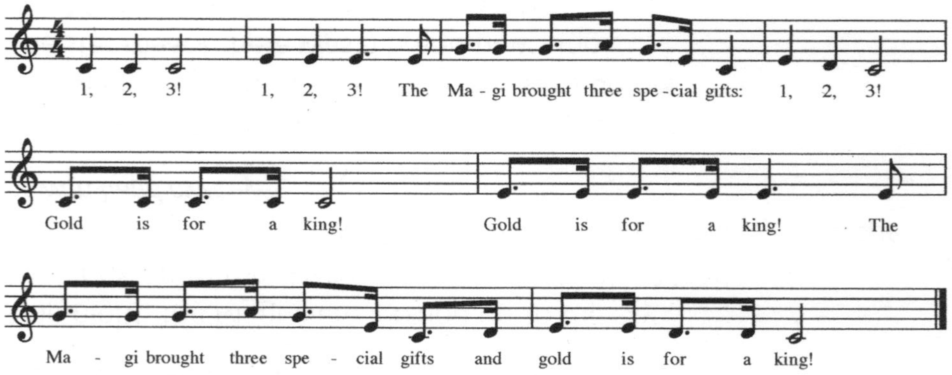

As we pass Baby Jesus around
let's imagine we're the Magi
meeting this tiny baby
and seeing that he's GOD!

Let's sing:

'Look! This is the King of Kings!
We've met the King of Kings!'

Lead the children in singing quietly and with awe as you pass Baby Jesus around. You or another leader may need to be ready to help the children remember to pass him on and to skip over children who don't wish to hold Baby Jesus.

**Look! This is the King of Kings,
the King of Kings, the King of Kings!
Look! This is the King of Kings!
We've met the King of Kings!**

Repeat until all the children have had the opportunity to hold Baby Jesus.

Appropriate for mixed groups of babies, toddlers and children up to the age of 9. This story continues from the previous story that introduced the Magi. It can stand alone for groups that include children up to the age of 9, who might find the previous story too young for them.

For the storytelling today, you will need a doll to represent Baby Jesus, in a manger or on a gold/white cloth on a focal table.

Your group may also like to use items representing the three gifts as visual aids for this story for instance:

1 gold-coloured items such as jewellery (check these are safe for your group) or a picture of gold;
2 cloth soaked in essential oil (frankincense or other) or a bowl filled with incense from your church, or a picture of frankincense;
3 child-safe perfume bottle, essential oil bottle, myrrh resin (if your church has some) or a picture of myrrh;

If you're using the What's in the Box? option (p. 7), these three gifts can be placed inside your usual box.

> **Tip**
> If the children in your group are more familiar with other names for the Magi, adapt the song and material accordingly, for instance to: 'the Three Kings', 'the Wise Men' or 'the Wise Ones'.

Today we're going to tell the story of when the Magi gave 'gifts' – presents – to Baby Jesus.

If your group is using items to represent the gifts, show them at this point.

Let's count our 'gifts'.
How many gifts are there?
Lead the children in counting on their fingers **1, 2, 3!**
If appropriate, invite the children to name the three gifts: gold, frankincense and myrrh. Place the three gifts on the focal table.

If you are going to imagine the gifts:
The Magi gave three 'gifts'.
Let's count to 3 . . .
Lead the children in counting on their fingers **1, 2, 3!**

All groups:
To tell our story about the Magi's gifts we need to learn a song.
It starts with counting . . .
Lead the children in counting on their fingers again **1, 2, 3!**

Now can you say: 'The Magi brought three special gifts'?
Lead the children in saying these words to the rhythm that will be in the song.

The Magi brought three special gifts.
That's quite a tongue twister, isn't it!
Shall we try it again?

The Magi brought three special gifts.
Sing the Magi's gifts song to the children and encourage them to join in as you go.

1, 2, 3! *Count on fingers*
1, 2, 3! *Count on fingers*
The Magi brought three special gifts: *Three fingers*
1, 2, 3! *Count on fingers*
Repeat to give the group confidence in the song.

We're ready to tell our story!
In the time that Jesus was born,
there were some people called Magi.
Now the Magi were very clever and VERY important.
Can you show me clever and important?
Lead the children in looking clever and important.

Let's put on some important clothes . . . .
a robe and a crown.
Lead the children in putting on imaginary robes and crowns.

One night, the Magi were looking up to the sky . . . .
Let's look up to the sky to see the stars like the Magi!
Lead the children in looking up to the sky through an imaginary telescope or with hand over eyes.

Look! *Point with excitement*
The Magi saw a star that no one had seen before.
The star meant there was a brand new king!
The Magi decided to find the new king!
They followed the star on a long, long journey.
Let's walk together on a long journey.
Lead the children in walking on the spot.

Look! The star has stopped over that house!

72

Shall we go in?
The Magi tiptoed into the house.
Can you tiptoe on the spot with me?
Lead the children in tiptoeing on the spot.

They saw Baby Jesus with Mary.
Place the Baby Jesus doll in the centre of the circle in a manger or on gold/white cloth.

The Magi knelt before Jesus to worship him.
Invite the children to kneel with you.
Then the Magi gave the new king three special gifts.

> *If you think that some of the children might know the names of the gifts and you haven't done so already, ask:*
> Can anyone tell us what ONE of the gifts was?
> *Ask for the names of the three gifts one by one, from different children if possible.*

The three gifts were chosen very carefully by the clever Magi.
They show us what kind of king Jesus is going to be!
Shall we open them together?

Let's get our treasure chest with our gifts in.
Lead the children in reaching to the side and each taking an imaginary, very heavy treasure chest with a lot of effort.
Goodness! This is heavy! *Lift the chest and place it in front of you*

What's inside?
Shall we open our chests?
Lead the children in opening your chests in front of you.

Wow! This chest is bright inside!
Lead the children in shielding your eyes from the brightness of this chest.
It's shining, dazzling *Jazz hands* and bright like the sun!

Reach into the chest and take out an imaginary handful or two of gold.
This is gold! The treasure of kings!
The gold shows that Jesus is born to be king!
Can you show me an action for 'king'?
Choose one of the suggested actions for 'king' and use it for the song.

Let's sing our song.
Let's sing 'Gold *Jazz hands* is for a king'. *King action*

Lead the children in singing to the same tune as you learned earlier:
Gold *Jazz hands* is for a king! *King action*
Gold *Jazz hands* is for a king! *King action*
The Magi brought three special gifts *Three fingers*
and gold *Jazz hands* is for a king! *King action*

If appropriate, encourage the children to respond with the word in bold.
So, gold *Jazz hands* is for a . . . **king**. *King action*
King Jesus!

What else are we going to take out of our treasure chest?
Let's reach in and take it out.
Lead the children in taking an imaginary handful of something out of the chest.

Mmmm! This smells nice . . . .
Invite the children to sniff with you.

Goodness! *Rub bottom of nose* Atchoo!
After 3, let's all sneeze, 1, 2, 3 . . .
Atchoo!
This is frankincense! *Sniff again*
Atchoo!

> *Either:* It smells like the incense that people light in the Temple

73

to show that their prayers are going up to God.
Sway hands upwards to show incense going up.

Or, for groups from churches that use incense:
It smells like the incense we use in our church
to show we're in a holy place.

Let's stand up and show
the smoke of the incense
going up to God with our bodies.
Lead the children in standing up and swaying your body and arms like smoke going upwards to God.

Frankincense shows Jesus is born to be 'holy' and special.
Jesus is born to be God!
Let's sing 'Frankincense is holy'.

Lead the children in swaying your body and arms like smoke as you sing.

Frankincense is holy!
Frankincense is holy!
The Magi brought three special gifts *Three fingers*
and frankincense is holy!

Let's sit down again.
  If appropriate, encourage the children to respond with the words in bold.

So gold *Jazz hands* is for a . . . **king** *King action*
Frankincense *Sway arms* is . . . **holy** *Sway arms*
I wonder what our third gift will be?
Let's reach into our treasure chest and see . . .
Lead the children in taking a handful from the chest.
That's strange! What's this? Let's taste it.
Lead the children in imagining to eat something from the chest. Screw your face up as you taste.

Ugh! It tastes bitter: like lemons!
Can you show me what something bitter tastes like with your face?
Lead the children in screwing your face up.

This is myrrh! Myrrh means 'bitter' (in Hebrew).
Normally we bring myrrh when someone dies!
Has someone died here?!
Point to the baby. Invite the children to respond and accept their responses.

No! Someone has been born!
But this gift of myrrh shows that Baby Jesus will die.
God's Son will die! *Sound confused*
What a strange thing.
What a bitter thing! *Lead the children in screwing your face up*
That could be our action for bitter – for myrrh.

Invite the children to sing with you, screwing your face up on 'very bitter' as you sing.

Myrrh is very bitter! *Screw face up*
Myrrh is very bitter! *Screw face up*
The Magi brought three special gifts: *Three fingers*
and myrrh is very bitter! *Screw face up*

  If appropriate, encourage the children to respond with the words in bold.

So gold *Jazz hands* is for a . . . **king** *King action*
Frankincense *Sway arms* is . . . **holy** *Sway arms*
and myrrh *Screw face up* is . . . **very bitter** *Screw face up*
The Magi brought three special gifts
that tell us all about King Jesus.

  If your group has chosen the Prayer Building Block for this unit, today you might like to use the following material in the place of your prayers.

74

When we come to King Jesus,
sometimes WE want to give a 'gift', a present too!
Let's think – what could we give?

Let's stand up. *Lead the children in standing*
In this room, we have so many different gifts for Jesus:
all the things we're good at!
I wonder what our gifts are? Let's see . . . .

Can you show me your best smile?
Maybe you have the gift of smiling!

Can you listen to this and clap/stamp the same back?
Do a couple of simple clapping rhythms of three beats, or more advanced depending on your group. If they haven't done this before, you may need to remind them of the importance of listening well first!

Wow! Some of you are really good!
Maybe you have the gift of music or listening!
Who's good at throwing and catching?
Let's throw . . . .
Lead the children in throwing a ball in the air and catching it.
. . . and catch!
Maybe you have a gift for using your body!

We all have all sorts of gifts,
all sorts of things that we are good at.
But there's one gift we can all give to Jesus:
the gift of love. *Cross hands on chest*
Let's all wave at each other to show our love.
Lead the children in waving to one another.

So there's another treasure chest to open today: ours!
Bend down and pick up an imaginary, very heavy treasure chest.
Encourage the children to do the same.

Let's pick up our treasure chest.

This treasure chest is full of all of OUR gifts:
our smiling and moving and listening and loving,
all the things we're good at!

Let's imagine we're coming to Baby Jesus like the Magi.
Let's tiptoe on the spot into Baby Jesus' room.
Lead the children in tiptoeing on the spot carrying the imaginary chest.
Sssssh! Tiptoe, tiptoe, tiptoe . . . .

In a hushed tone Let's kneel down.
Now let's open the treasure chest and show Jesus what's inside.
Lead the children in opening the chest and showing the contents to Jesus.

Look! Wow!
Look how beautiful your gifts are!
Lead the children in reaching into the chest and taking big handfuls of the treasure out and holding it up high.
Amazing!

Let's sing our song one more time.
This time let's give our gifts to Jesus.
Let's sing 'Jesus, take my gifts.'
Let's make our song into a prayer.

Lead the children in holding out their hands full of their 'treasure' to Baby Jesus as they sing:
Jesus take my gifts!
Jesus take my gifts!
The Magi brought three special gifts:
and Jesus take my gifts!

Extra: Baby Jesus, the Refugee

→ Matthew 2.13–18

Appropriate for mixed groups of babies, toddlers and children up to the age of 9.

Today's material can involve an extended activity. To make time for it, you may like to omit some of your usual Building Blocks (for instance, the Prayer Building Block you've chosen).

For this week's story, you will need:

- figures or pictures of Mary, Joseph and Baby Jesus
- one of the following:
  - body templates (see p. 218)
  - 'small world' people (see p. 153)
  - recent pictures of refugees from newspapers.

Optional: What's in the Box? (see p. 7).

Show the children a suitcase or a form of travel bag. If you think the children would like to open it, you could put some clothes inside. If you have any baby clothes, include these.

We're going to need this suitcase for today's story.

What's this?
Invite the child to respond.

Today's story starts with running!
After 3, we're going to stand up,
we're going to throw our things into a bag as quickly as we can.
Mime throwing things into a bag.
We're going to pick up our baby ever so carefully . . .
Mime picking a baby up.

and we're going to run on the spot!
Are you ready?

1, 2, 3 . . .
Stand up . . . *Lead the children in standing*
Pack, pack, pack, pack . . .
Lead the children in throwing clothes into an imaginary case.
Pick up our baby. *Lead the children in picking up an imaginary baby*
Gentle, careful . . .
And run! *Lead the children in running on the spot holding the baby*
Faster! Faster! Faster!
And freeze!

Let's sit down for a moment.
When the group is ready:
The king's found out about Baby Jesus!
The king knows that people are calling Jesus the new king!
And he's angry!
The king's coming to FIND Baby Jesus!
He wants to get rid of him!

In a serious but calm voice:
We're Joseph and we need to leave . . . fast!
We need to go to another country,
where the king can't hurt us. *Shake head*
You know what we need to do.

After 3, we're going to stand up,
We're going to throw our things into a bag as quickly as we can.
Briefly mime throwing things into a bag.
We're going to pick up Baby Jesus ever so carefully.
Briefly mime picking Baby Jesus up.
And – with Mary – we're going to run on the spot!

76

Are you ready?

1, 2, 3 . . .

Stand up . . . *Lead the children in standing*
Pack, pack, pack, pack . . .
Lead the children in throwing clothes into an imaginary case.
Pick up our baby. *Lead the children in picking up an imaginary baby*
Gentle, careful . . .
And run! *Lead the children in running on the spot holding the baby*
Faster! Faster! Faster!
And freeze!

Let's sit down again.

When the group is ready:
Phew! It's going to be all right. *Smile*
Joseph's found a safe place for Mary and Baby Jesus.
Rock baby gently in arms.
The king won't find him. *Shake head*
Jesus will grow up safe with his mummy and foster daddy.
Rock baby gently in arms.

But not every baby in our story stayed safe.
Lead the children in crossing arms on chest.
Let's bow our heads and cross our arms on our chest
and remember for a moment
the babies that were hurt by the king.
Lead the children in bowing head and keeping arms crossed on chest. Keep a moment of silence – as long as is appropriate for your group.

Let's show tears on our face for the babies that were hurt.
Lead the group in running fingers down face to show tears.

Place figures or pictures of Mary, Joseph and Baby Jesus in the centre of the circle.

Today we're remembering people
who've had to leave their country.
People who've had to pack *Briefly mime packing*
and run very fast *Briefly move arms as if running*
like Mary and Joseph and Baby Jesus. *Point to the figures/pictures*

People who've had to leave their home
because someone's going to hurt them.

People who've had to run from their homes
are often called 'refugees'.
Can you say 'refugees'?
Refugees.

There are 'refugees' who've come to OUR country,
looking for a safe place to live.
What do you think it feels like
to have to pack and run away like that?
Can you show me with your face?

If your group is creating person templates afterwards, place a representative number of these in the centre of the circle, or you may like to use 'small world' people or recent pictures of refugees from newspapers.
I'm going to place these people here now
with Baby Jesus, Mary and Joseph
in the middle of our circle
to remind us of the refugees in OUR country.

They've come a long way and they're still scared.
Let's open our hands out to them to show they're welcome.
Lead the children in opening hands out to Mary, Joseph, Jesus and the other refugees.
Let's help them to feel safe.

Either, if your group is familiar with Welcome Song: Option 1:
Let's sing 'Welcome friends to St Mary's*' to them!
Welcome friends to St Mary's*,
Wave to the centre of the circle.
Welcome friends to St Mary's*,
Wave to the centre of the circle.
you are welcome in the name of the Lord!

* *Insert the name of your church or children's group, or sing 'our worship', 'England' or another country.*

Or, if your group is familiar with Welcome Song: Option 2:
Let's sing our Welcome Song to them.

Let's wave with one hand. *Lead waving*
Then with our other hand. *Lead waving*
Then let's show God's 'glory' all over the refugees.
Move arms up and down in front of you with fingers wiggling, palms facing out, towards the centre of the circle.
Then let's wave with both hands to give them a big welcome.
Lead waving.

You are welcome in the name of the Lord!
Wave with right hand to the centre of the circle.
You are welcome in the name of the Lord!
Wave with left hand to the centre of the circle.
I can see all over you, the glory of the Lord!
Move arms up and down in front of you with fingers wiggling, palms facing out, towards the centre of the circle.
You are welcome in the name of the Lord!
Wave with both hands to the centre of the circle.

Or, if your group is familiar with the Gathering Song for this unit:
Let's sing 'You are welcome! You are welcome!' to them!

Lead the group in singing the following words to the tune of 'We are marching in the light of God', waving throughout to the figures/pictures of the refugees:

You are welcome! You are we-elcome!
You are welcome! You are we-elcome!
You are welcome! You are we-elcome!
You are welcome! You are we-elcome!
You are welcome! You are welcome! Oh! Jazz hands
You are welcome! You are we-elcome!
You are welcome! You are welcome! Oh! Jazz hands
You are welcome! You are we-elcome!

Or sing another Welcome Song to the figures/pictures of refugees.

If possible, include one of the following activities as part of your worship, or another response to support refugees that's appropriate for your group and resources.

We've been telling stories about Jesus, the Light of the World.
Jesus asks us to be little lights in the world, too.

Either:
Today we're going to be part of
shining God's light in the dark.
We're going to make some pictures of refugees
and give them to our family
and friends/people in our church.
We're going to ask them/our church to remember
people who've had to run and need a safe place to live.
We're going to ask them to pray that we will welcome them.

And if you're wondering what 'refugees' look like,
they might look just like you or just like me!

Anna the Prophet's Story

→ Luke 2.36–38; Isaiah 40; 60
→ Song: Words: © Sharon Moughtin.
→ Tune: 'Swing low, sweet chariot' (traditional).

Look up, Je - ru - sa - lem! Your God is com - ing strong to save! Stand tall, Je - ru - sa - lem! Your God is com-ing strong to save!

Appropriate for mixed groups of babies, toddlers and children up to the age of 9. Groups that only include children up to the age of 7 may prefer to focus on the story of Zechariah in the Temple: 'Jesus, Light of the World!' (p. 12).

Today we're telling Anna, the prophet's, story.
In the Bible, a prophet is someone
who learns to see with God's eyes.
Let's imagine for a moment we can see through God's eyes!
Let's close our eyes . . . .
Lead the group in closing eyes

And open them.
Imagine we're seeing with God's eyes!
The world looks different!
Everything looks different!

To tell Anna's story, first we need to tell Jerusalem's story.
It's time to learn a song.

'My turn' *Point to self*, 'your turn' *Leader's hands out to group.*
Singing:
Look up, Jerusalem! *Point to horizon with chin raised*

79

See Story Starter Ideas on p. 148 for details.

Or:

Today we're going to be part of shining God's light in the dark.
We're going to make _____ and sell them.
We're going to give the money to _____
name of a local, national or international charity
who are helping refugees
who've had to run and need a safe place to live.
See Story Starter Ideas on p. 148 for ideas.

You may like to lead your congregation in a suitable prayer for refugees, for instance *Common Worship*'s Prayer for Refugees, below.[1] The children could then give their creations after the service to family, friends or members of the congregation.

Heavenly Father,
you are the source of all goodness, generosity and love.
We thank you for opening the hearts of many
to those who are fleeing for their lives.
Help us now to open our arms in welcome,
and reach out our hands in support.
That the desperate may find new hope,
and lives torn apart be restored.
We ask this in the name of Jesus Christ Your Son, Our Lord,
who fled persecution at His birth
and at His last triumphed over death. Amen.

Your God is coming strong to save! *Strong arms then crossed arms*
Can you sing that?
Look up, Jerusalem! *Point to horizon with chin raised*
Your God is coming strong to save! *Strong arms then crossed arms*

Then we need to get up for this bit!
Lead the group in standing.
Stand on tiptoes and sing:
Stand tall, Jerusalem! *Tiptoes and chin up*
Your God is coming strong to save! *Strong arms then crossed arms*

We're ready to tell Jerusalem's story.
Let's sit down.
When the group is ready:
In the Bible, Jerusalem is a city, a capital city like *London*.
Change as appropriate.
The Bible tells Jerusalem's story.
It's a hard and sad story.
Let's show tears on our face for Jerusalem.
Lead the group in showing tears running down face.
The Bible has songs crying for Jerusalem. *Show tears if appropriate.*
  Like the book of 'Lamentations' – which means lots of crying.
But it also has songs to free Jerusalem from her sadness:
to comfort her.

One of those songs is the song we just sang.
Let's sing our song to 'comfort' Jerusalem together.
Let's free her from her sadness. *Show tears*

Look up, Jerusalem! *Point to horizon with chin raised*
Your God is coming strong to save! *Strong arms then crossed arms*

Stand tall, Jerusalem! *Tiptoes and chin up*
Your God is coming strong to save! *Strong arms then crossed arms*

Jerusalem, the city, needed freeing from her sadness,
Because soldiers had come.
Let's march on the spot and be the soldiers.
1, 2, 3, 4, 1, 2, 3, 4! *Marching on the spot*
The soldiers had ruined and broken Jerusalem.
Mime breaking (like breaking bread).
Lots of people were hurt, and died, and had been stolen away.
The whole city of Jerusalem was weeping!
Let's bend our whole body down low
to show how sad Jerusalem is.
Lead the group in bending low.

Then a prophet came, singing a song of comfort to Jerusalem.
That's our song.
Let's comfort Jerusalem.

Look up, Jerusalem! *Point to horizon with chin raised*
Your God is coming strong to save! *Strong arms then crossed arms*
Stand tall, Jerusalem! *Tiptoes and chin up*
Your God is coming strong to save! *Strong arms then crossed arms*

Then, one day, Jerusalem was set free!
She was set free from the soldiers!
God had come, strong to save! *Strong arms then crossed arms*

And many people sang for joy!
Let's dance together and sing our song.
This time sing loud and joyful and double fast!

Look up, Jerusalem! *Point to horizon with chin raised*
Your God is coming strong to save! *Strong arms then crossed arms*

Stand tall, Jerusalem! *Tiptoes and chin up*
Your God is coming strong to save! *Strong arms then crossed arms*
Lead the group in clapping.

But then soldiers came again.
Lots of people died and were hurt again!
Jerusalem was filled with tears again!
Let's kneel down and bend down low to show Jerusalem's sadness.
Lead the group in kneeling and bending low.

People tried to keep singing the song to comfort her.
But it felt so hard. Where was God?
The song became just a whisper and a question.
Let's sing our song as a whisper and a question.
And this time, we're not going to get up: we're too sad.

As a whisper:
Look up, Jerusalem? *Point sadly to horizon with chin raised*
Your God is coming strong to save? *Strong arms then crossed arms*
Stand tall, Jerusalem? *Point upwards with chin raised*
Your God is coming strong to save? *Strong arms then crossed arms*

That's Jerusalem's story so far.
Jerusalem's still waiting for her God.
So what about Anna's story?

Let's stand up and be Anna.
When the group are ready.
Anna was an old woman.
Let's bend over a bit and show how old we are.
Lead the group in bending low like a very old woman.
Her story was sad too, like Jerusalem's story.
Anna's husband had died.
Let's show tears for Anna.

Lead the group in showing tears.

Anna lived in Jerusalem
when Jerusalem was filled with soldiers.
There was no one to keep her safe.
So Anna stayed in the Temple, God's House, and prayed.

In the Temple, the songs and prayers for Jerusalem
became her songs and prayers.
One of them was the song we've been singing.
Anna learned not to sing it as a question.
And not to sing it in a whisper.
And even though Anna was old and bent low,
she could stand on her tiptoes for Jerusalem!
Let's sing like Anna!
Lead the group in singing loudly and expectantly.

Look up, Jerusalem! *Point to horizon with chin raised*
Your God is coming strong to save! *Strong arms then crossed arms*
Stand tall, Jerusalem! *Tiptoes and chin up*
Your God is coming strong to save! *Strong arms then crossed arms*

And Anna learned to see with God's eyes.
She became a prophet.

Then one day, Baby Jesus came into the Temple.
Let's be Mary holding Baby Jesus in our arms.
Lead the group in miming holding a baby
And Anna the prophet looked at Baby Jesus with God's eyes.

And Anna the prophet knew in here *Tap heart* that this tiny baby
was the one coming 'strong' to save! *Strong arms then crossed arms*

'Strong'? Can a tiny baby be 'strong'? *Strong arms*
'Save'? Can a tiny baby 'save'? *Crossed arms*

Anna the prophet was seeing differently!
She was seeing with God's eyes!
Anna could see that something is stronger than 'everything'?
If the group are familiar with the 'Love is stronger' song from Good Friday and the Paul the Letter Writer Unit:
What's stronger than everything?

Love!
Love *Cross arms* is stronger *Strong arms*
than everything. *Fling arms outwards*
And Anna the prophet could see that this baby,
the God of love *Cross arms*
was coming strong to save. *Strong arms then crossed arms*
And the best thing about this story?
Anna couldn't keep it in! She told everyone!
She told everyone that God is coming
strong to save. *Strong arms then crossed arms*

Let's be like the prophet Anna!
Let's make her song our song!
Let's make it a prayer for our place!
Let's sing 'Look up, London town!' *Change to the name of your place*
first as a quiet prayer. . . .

Lead the group in singing quietly:
Look up, London town! *Point to horizon with chin raised*
Your God is coming strong to save! *Strong arms then crossed arms*
Stand tall, London town! *Tiptoes and chin up*
Your God is coming strong to save! *Strong arms then crossed arms*

And now let's sing so that everyone can hear
Like the prophet Anna!

Lead the group in singing loudly and joyfully:
Look up, London town! *Point to horizon with chin raised*
Your God is coming strong to save! *Strong arms then crossed arms*
Stand tall, London town! *Tiptoes and chin up*
Your God is coming strong to save! *Strong arms then crossed arms*

Jesus, Light of the World!

→ **The Presentation of Jesus**
→ Luke 2.22–33
→ Song: 'Jesus, Light of the World (Epiphany)' Words: © Sharon Moughtin.
→ Tune: 'What shall we do with the drunken sailor?' (traditional).

[Musical score with lyrics: Walk-ing, walk-ing, walk-ing, walk-ing, walk-ing to the Temp-le, walk-ing, walk-ing, walk-ing to the Temp-le! The Light of the World is SHIN-ING! Je - sus, Light of the World! Je - sus, Light of the World, is SHIN-ING in the dark - ness!]

Appropriate for mixed groups of babies, toddlers and children up to the age of 9.

Some leaders/children might notice that this week's song shares its tune with Zechariah's song from Week 1 and the Gathering Song of Advent. In Luke's Gospel, the stories of Zechariah and Simeon are strongly connected with all sorts of similarities:

| Zechariah is an old man, who encounters God (via an angel) in the Temple, and sings a song about Jesus, Light of the World. Luke 1.5–23, 59–79 | Simeon is an old man, who encounters God (in the Spirit) and is sent to the Temple, where he sings a song about Jesus, Light of the World. Luke 2.25–32 |

In Luke, these stories are like 'bookends', showing the beginning and end of the stories about Jesus' birth. We've also used these stories as bookends in Sowing Seeds: Zechariah's song started off our stories about Baby Jesus in Advent and now Simeon's song (sung to the same tune) will bring them to an end. Both celebrate Jesus, Light of the World!

Tip

If your group is meeting during a Sunday service and you're a church that is celebrating the Presentation of Jesus at the Temple, you might also like to invite the children, if they want, to present what they've made to the congregation at the end of the service. You could use this as an opportunity to challenge your congregation to wonder how we can be part of shining God's light in the darkness for all those who are looking for safety.

Optional: What's in the Box? (see p. 7):
Invite one of the children to open the box.
Inside are two pictures or figures: one is Baby Jesus and the other is an old man (Simeon). For Simeon, you could use a biblical painting, a picture from a children's Bible or a modern photo of an old man.

What's in the box? *Invite the child to respond*

Today we're going to tell the story
about when this old man met Baby Jesus.

Or, if your church calls this Sunday 'Candlemas', you may wish to use a candle:

Today we're going to tell the story of 'Candlemas'.
Candlemas is the day when we celebrate
Jesus, the Light of the World, with candles.
If appropriate: Look out for the candles today in church.

Introduction to the song: Option 1

For groups that are familiar with the 'Jesus, Light of the World!' song from the 'Getting Ready for Baby Jesus (Advent and Christmas)' unit:

Today's our last story about Baby Jesus,
the Light of the World.
We sang a song when we were getting ready
for Baby Jesus before Christmas.
It's our 'busy, busy, busy' song about
Jesus, Light of the World . . . DAWNING in the darkness.

Say these words in a way that invites the children to join in:
Jesus, Light of the World . . . DAWNING in the darkness.

But this time Jesus isn't DAWNING in the darkness! *Action for the rising sun.*
Jesus is SHINING in the darkness! *Jazz hands*
Can you show me your jazz hands for 'shining'? *Jazz hands*

Let's try singing our song
with Jesus SHINING in the darkness at the end.
Lead the children in singing:

Jesus, Light of the World, *Action for the rising sun*
Jesus, Light of the World, *Action for the rising sun*
Jesus, Light of the World . . . *Action for the rising sun*

Interrupt the singing Remember Jesus is SHINING!
is SHINING in the darkness! *Jazz hands*

Continue with the material for all groups, below.

Introduction to the song: Option 2

For groups that are not familiar with the 'Jesus, Light of the World!' song from the 'Getting Ready for Baby Jesus (Advent)' unit:

We're going to learn a song today.
It's about Jesus being the Light of the World, like the sun.

Let's crouch down and show the sun hiding
before it comes up in the morning.
Lead the children in crouching down.
Now let's show the sun rising with our bodies . . .
Up, up, up and out!
Raise hands upwards and outwards as you stand up.

We're going to use that action for our song.
And then because Jesus is SHINING bright, *Jazz hands*
we're going to finish with jazz hands! *Jazz hands*

Let's try that.
Lead the children in singing with the actions of the rising sun:

Jesus, Light of the World, *Action for the rising sun*
Jesus, Light of the World, *Action for the rising sun*
Jesus, Light of the World . . . *Action for the rising sun*
is SHINING in the darkness! *Jazz hands*
Repeat if necessary until the children are basically familiar with the tune.

All groups

We're ready to tell our story.
Our story today is about two people. *Show two fingers*

Number 1: *Show one finger*
a tiny baby. He's only six weeks old! *Mime holding a baby*
It's Baby Jesus!

So number 1: *Show one finger a VERY young baby. Mime holding a baby*
And number 2: *Show two fingers a VERY old man.*
Let's look old and hunched over.
Lead the children in bending over.
Let's hold our stick to help us to walk.
Lead the children in leaning on an imaginary walking stick.

So 1: a VERY young baby. *Lead the children in holding the baby*
And 2: a VERY old man. *Lead the children in hunching over*

They're going to meet in the biggest house!
The Temple, God's House!
Can you show me big?
Lead the children in stretching upwards and outwards as high as you can.
Bigger and bigger! Reach up high!
That's God's House, the Temple,
where people go to meet with God, a bit like our church.

First, Baby Jesus is on the way to God's House.
Lead the children in holding an imaginary baby in your arms.
Mary and Joseph want to say thank you to God
for Baby Jesus, so they're taking him to the Temple.

Let's stand up and be Mary or Joseph.
Lead the children in standing.
Let's carry Baby Jesus in our arms.
Let's walk on the spot and sing: 'Walking, walking to the Temple'.

Walk on the spot, cradling Jesus as you sing:
Walking, walking to the Temple,
walking, walking to the Temple,
walking, walking to the Temple!
The Light of the World is SHINING! *Jazz hands*

Sing louder and take the speed up a bit.
Jesus, Light of the World! *Action for the rising sun*
Jesus, Light of the World! *Action for the rising sun*
Jesus, Light of the World, *Action for the rising sun*
is SHINING in the darkness! *Jazz hands*

Someone else is on the way to the Temple, too:

If appropriate: hunch over an imaginary stick and ask the children:
Who else is in our story today?

The old man!
Let's hunch over and hold our stick and be the old man together.
Lead the children in being the old man.

We've been looking out for God's helper our whole life!
Let's hold our hand over our eyes and look . . . .
Lead the children in looking around.

Let's sing together, 'Looking, looking, looking, looking for God!'
Lead the children in continuing to look around as you sing:
Looking, looking, looking for God!
Looking, looking, looking for God!
Interrupt the song.

Sssssh! Can you hear that? *Hand behind ear*

Is that God? . . . .
That's GOD whispering! *Look shocked*
What's God saying?

Whisper loudly with hands around your mouth:
'Go to the Temple!' *Point*

85

Baby Jesus!
Can you make the tiniest shape you can with your body?
Lead the children in crouching down into a tiny shape.

Baby Jesus was tiny.
But the old man saw that Jesus' light FILLED God's House!
Let's make the biggest shape we can with our body!
Lead the children in making a big shape with their body.

Jesus' light FILLED God's House!
The tiny baby's light . . . *Lead the children in making a tiny shape*
FILLED the massive Temple! *Lead the children in making their big shape*

Not only that! The baby's light filled the whole WORLD!
Let's make our shape even bigger! BIGGER!
Lead the children in stretching out as far as they can.
Freeze!

The old man saw the baby:
and he knew that's who he'd been looking for:
Jesus, the Light of the World!

How do you think he felt?
Can you show me?

The old man took the tiny baby in his arms. *Hold baby*
And he sang the song we've been singing, about
Jesus, the Light of the World.
That's the old man's song!

> *If appropriate:* Some churches all through the world
> still sing the old man's song every day.

Let's be the old man singing to Baby Jesus.
Let's start by showing the tiny Baby Jesus with our bodies.

After 3, let's all be God and whisper, 'Go to the Temple'.
Lead the children in whispering loudly with hands around your mouth:
'1, 2, 3 . . . go to the Temple!' *Point*

And what do you think the old man did?
Invite responses from the children.

He went to the Temple as fast as he could!
Let's be the old man again and sing our song quickly
to show how quickly we want to get to the Temple.

But, remember, we're very old so we can't run.
We can only hobble with our stick.

At speed, hobbling on the spot, lead the children in singing:
**Hurry, hurry, hurry, hurry to the Temple,
hurry, hurry, hurry, hurry to the Temple,
hurry, hurry, hurry, hurry to the Temple!
The Light of the World is SHINING!** *Jazz hands*

Jesus, Light of the World, *Action for the rising sun*
Jesus, Light of the World, *Action for the rising sun*
Jesus, Light of the World *Action for the rising sun*
is SHINING in the darkness! *Jazz hands*

We're here! We're in God's House, the Temple.
Look around: it's huge!
Let's show with our bodies how big the Temple is!
Lead the children in each making the biggest shape they can with their bodies.

But wait a minute, *Point* who's that?
Who do you think the old man saw?
Accept the children's responses if there are any.

The old man saw a tiny baby!

86

Lead the children in making a tiny shape, e.g. crouching.
Let's sing 'Shine, shine, shine' and show our tiny shape.

Then let's sing 'in all the world!' *Big shape*
and show our biggest shape for the world.
'Shine, shine, shine' *Tiny shape*
'in all the world.' *Biggest shape*

Let's sing!
Lead the children in singing:

Shine, shine, shine in all the world! *Tiny shape followed by big shape*
Shine, shine, shine in all the world! *Tiny shape followed by big shape*
Shine, shine, shine in all the world! *Tiny shape followed by big shape*
The Light of the World is SHINING! *Jazz hands*

Jesus, Light of the World, *Action for the rising sun*
Jesus, Light of the World, *Action for the rising sun*
Jesus, Light of the World *Action for the rising sun*
is SHINING in the darkness! *Jazz hands*

Let's sit down for a moment.
When the children are ready:
Let me tell you something.
The Light of the World isn't just shining in Baby Jesus.

Jesus said that you *Point to a child*
and you . . . and you . . . and you . . . *Point to three more children*
All of us . . . *Point in a circle to everyone in the room*
All of us are the light of the world!
Jesus' light shines inside all of us!
Trace your finger in a circle around your heart.

To finish our stories about Jesus, Light of the World,
let's make our song into a prayer.
Let's sing 'Shine, shine, shine in me, in me!'

Let's start off singing quietly
Trace small circle on your heart.

Then as we sing let's get louder and louder
and show our light shine brighter and brighter inside us.
Show the circle that you are tracing on your heart getting bigger and bigger.

Let's imagine Jesus' light filling us,
then filling our church/school/name of place,
then bursting out to fill the whole world! *Jazz hands*

Let's close our eyes and pray our song.
Show the circle that you are tracing on your heart getting bigger and bigger as you lead the children in singing:

Shine, shine, shine, in me, in me-e!
Shine, shine, shine, in me, in me-e!
Shine, shine, shine, in me, in me-e!
The Light of the World is shining! *Jazz hands*

Lead the children in standing for the final verse.

Jesus, Light of the World, *Action for the rising sun*
Jesus, Light of the World, *Action for the rising sun*
Jesus, Light of the World *Action for the rising sun*
is shining in the darkness! *Jazz hands*

John the Baptist unit (the weeks before Lent)

This unit introduces groups to John the Baptist and baptism and includes an optional baptism workshop. Other opportunities to explore baptism can be found in the 'God's Best Friend, Moses' unit.

For groups that follow the church seasons, the 'John the Baptist' unit works well in the weeks running up to the beginning of Lent, introducing the wilderness. For years where there are very few Sundays between Epiphany and Lent, there is an option to combine the first two stories (Meet John and John Baptizes Jesus) into a single story. This is outlined within the storytelling material. The story of Jesus' baptism is traditionally told in Epiphany season, but was moved here as the switch from Jesus as baby to adult then back again can be confusing for children.

John the Baptist storybox

Choose from the stories according to your own context.

Meet John (Matthew 3.1–6) 88
Appropriate for mixed groups of 0–9 years

John Baptizes Jesus (Matthew 3.13–17) 92
Appropriate for mixed groups of 0–9 years

Extra: Our Baptism: a baptism roleplaying workshop 97
Appropriate for mixed groups of 0–9 years or whole school or all-age services

Jesus Is Thrown into the Wilderness (Mark 1.9–12) 107
Appropriate for mixed groups of 0–9 years

> **Tip**
> Even if you don't use the other Building Blocks, you may find it helpful to use the Gathering Song 'Get ready for our God' just before the storytelling in every session of this unit as it gathers together the themes of the unit as a whole. See p. 177.

Meet John

→ Matthew 3.1-6

Appropriate for mixed groups of babies, toddlers and children up to the age of 9.

If you are using 'Introducing the Unit' as one of your Building Blocks, some of the introduction is repeated here in the first paragraph. Adapt the material accordingly.

Optional: One or more bowls of water for the optional Saying Sorry material towards the end of the storytelling. You can simply use normal tap water, or you may like to use water from your baptism font.

to get the world ready for Jesus!
Let's stand up and be John the Baptist together.
Lead the children in standing.

John wore clothes made from camel hair!
Let's put our camel-hair coat on!
Lead the children in putting on a coat and scratching.
It's very itchy!

John's job was to get the world ready for God!
John called out,
'Get ready for God!' *Cup hands around mouth*

After 3, let's shout, 'Get ready for God!'
1, 2, 3 . . . Get ready for God! *Cup hands around mouth*

Look around I'm not sure anyone heard that.
Let's try that again even louder.
1, 2, 3 . . . Get ready for God! *Cup hands around mouth*

Look! *Point* The people are coming!
And do you know what John did?
He washed the people in the river!
Let's be the people coming to John.
The people wanted to get ready for God.
But they'd done wrong things that made them feel sad.
Can you show me sad?
Lead the children in looking sad.

They didn't really feel ready for God.
Lead the children in shaking head.
Let's shake our heads and look sad.
The people felt like they needed a new start!
We're going to learn a new song!
It's the people's song when they met John the Baptist.

The 'I'm Sorry' and 'New Start' signs are among the very few Sowing Seeds signs and actions that are fixed. In this story, the I'm Sorry' sign is used to show the washing away of the wrong things people have done in the river. The 'New Start' sign shows our desire to 'start over' but also has resonances of the rolling away of the stone on Easter Day when Jesus wins a 'new start' for all of us. See p. 8 or the website (www.sowingseeds-online.org) for a description and explanation.

If your group would like to tell the stories of 'Meet John' and 'John Baptizes Jesus' as a single story, follow the instructions set out in boxes like this during the storytelling.

Optional: What's in the Box? (see p. 7)

Invite one of the children to open the box. Inside is a picture of John the Baptist.
What's in the box? *Invite the child to respond*
It's John the Baptist!
If appropriate:
Look what he's wearing! It's made of camel hair!

It's time to get ready *If appropriate:* again!
This time, it's time to get ready for Jesus the grown-up.
To help us get ready,
we need to meet a man called John the Baptist.

Even when John was still in his mummy's tummy,
God knew that John would have a special job:

89

Let's say the words 'my turn', *Point to self*, 'your turn' *Leader's hands out to group.*

Wash me in the river, *'I'm Sorry' sign*
wash me in the river. *'I'm Sorry' sign*
Wash me in the river, *'I'm Sorry' sign*
wash me in the river. *'I'm Sorry' sign*

O wash me, O wash me, *'I'm Sorry' sign twice*
I need a new start! *'New Start' sign*
O wash me, O wash me, *'I'm Sorry' sign twice*
I need a new start! *'New Start' sign*

Now let's try and add the tune.
Repeat the 'my turn', 'your turn' introduction above, this time with the tune (p. 131).

Wash me in the river, *'I'm Sorry' sign*
wash me in the river, *'I'm Sorry' sign*
Wash me in the river, *'I'm Sorry' sign*
wash me in the river. *'I'm Sorry' sign*

O wash me, O wash me, *'I'm Sorry' sign twice*
I need a new start! *'New Start' sign*
O wash me, O wash me, *'I'm Sorry' sign twice*
I need a new start! *'New Start' sign*
Repeat as appropriate.

When the group is ready, continue with the following material.

It's time to get into the river with John!
Let's dip our toe in.
Lead the children in dipping a toe in imaginary water.

Is the water warm or cold today?
Let one of the children decide. According to their response:
   Either: Oh no! It's freezing!
   Or: Oooh! It's lovely and warm!

Let's walk on the spot into the river . . .
Lead the children in walking in slowly on the spot into warm/cold water.
Deeper . . . *Show the water level on your ankle*
and deeper . . . *Show the water level at your knee*
and deeper . . . *Show the water level at your thighs*
and deeper . . . *Show the water level at your waist*
until the river's up to our waist!

We're in the river!
Now we're going to let John baptize us.
After 3, we're going to take a deep breath,
then we're going to go down *Point down* right under the water . . .
and up again. *Point up*
Down . . . *Point down*
then up . . . *Point up*

Are you ready to take a deep breath?
Don't forget to hold your nose!

1, 2, 3, breathe! *Lead the children in taking a deep breath then hold nose and down . . . Lead the children in crouching down to go under the water* and up! *Lead the children in standing up again*

This was called BAPTISM.
Can you say 'baptism'?
Baptism.

Let's go down again and this time we're going to stay underwater.
1, 2, 3 . . . *Deep breath, hold nose*
Down into the water . . . and FREEZE!
Stay crouched down with the children.

In the water, God made the people clean.
Not just clean OUTside *Rub arms*
but clean INside too. *Trace a circle on your heart*
God gave them a new start!

After 3, let's go up out of the water and shout,

90

'God gives me a new start!'
1, 2, 3 . . . *Lead the children in jumping up*
God gives me a new start!

So John called to the people.
Let's stand up and after 3,
let's be John calling, 'Get ready for God' again.
1, 2, 3 . . . Get ready for God! *Hands around mouth*

And more and more and more people came!
Let's show John's baptism one more time.
After 3, let's go down and stay down. *Point down*
1, 2, 3 . . . *Deep breath, hold nose*
Lead the children in crouching down.
and FREEZE!

Now we're going to jump back up *Point up*
and shout *Hands cupped around mouth*
'God gives me a new start!'
1, 2, 3 . . . Jump up God gives me a new start!

> If you're telling 'Meet John' and 'John Baptizes Jesus' as a single story, move straight to 'John Baptizes Jesus' on p. 94 at this point. If you'd like to continue with a time of saying sorry, use the following material.

Let's sit down for a moment.
When the group is ready:
I wonder how the people felt when God gave them a new start?
Can you show me with your face?
Accept the children's responses.

Sometimes we do things we wish we hadn't done.
Sometimes it can feel like we've done it all wrong.
We wish we could have a new start!

Let's put our hands on our head.
I wonder if there's anything we've thought this week
that we wish we hadn't thought?

Wash me in the river, *'I'm Sorry' sign*
Wash me in the river, *'I'm Sorry' sign*
O wash me, O wash me, *'I'm Sorry' sign twice*
I need a new start! *'New Start' sign*

I wonder if there's anything we've said this week
that we wish we hadn't said?

Wash me in the river, *'I'm Sorry' sign*
Wash me in the river, *'I'm Sorry' sign*
O wash me, O wash me, *'I'm Sorry' sign twice*
I need a new start! *'New Start' sign*

Let's cross our hands on our chest.
I wonder if there's anything we've done this week
that we wish we hadn't done?

Wash me in the river, *'I'm Sorry' sign*
Wash me in the river, *'I'm Sorry' sign*
O wash me, O wash me, *'I'm Sorry' sign twice*
I need a new start! *'New Start' sign*

Let's open our eyes again.
The Good News is that God LOVES giving new starts!
God can wash us, not just OUTside,
but INside too! *Trace a circle on your heart* *Rub arms*

One very special way God does this is through baptism,
like John's baptisms.

Put your hand up if you've seen a baptism or been baptized?
If appropriate: We'll be talking more about baptism next time.

But God loves giving new starts all the time!
Not just in baptism.
We don't have to go to a river!
We don't even have to use water, but we're going to today!

If there is an older child present who is unlikely to spill the water you could invite her or him to take the water around the circle. You may wish to ask more than one child to take bowls around the circle, going opposite ways or starting at different points in the circle. Alternatively take a bowl around yourself and/or ask adults to help.
Here I have a bowl of water

If appropriate taken from our baptism font at church.

Name is going to bring this bowl of water around.

If you'd like a new start from God,
You could dip your finger in the water in the bowl and
Either: draw a cross on your forehead.
Or: draw a smile on your forehead
to show that God is happy with you.

Let's ask God to wash us INside as well as OUTside!
Let's ask God to give us a brand new start!
Let's sing as we wait for the water.

Lead the group in singing:
Wash me in the river, *'I'm Sorry' sign*
Wash me in the river, *'I'm Sorry' sign*
O wash me, O wash me, *'I'm Sorry' sign*
I need a new start! *'New Start' sign*

When all the children and adults who wish to take water have done so:
Look at all those beautiful new starts! *Point around the room*
After 3, let's shout, 'God gives me a new start!'
1, 2, 3 . . . God gives me a new start!

I wonder how you'll use your new start today?

Optional: If you're meeting within a church school setting, you could send each class back with the water in a little dish to place on their RE table in the classroom:

I'm going to give *Name* this water
to take back to your classroom.
When you do something
you wish you hadn't done,
if you like, you can come and ask God
to give you a new start.
You can dip your finger in here
Mime dipping finger into the bowl.
and draw a cross/smile on your forehead.
Mime drawing a cross/smile on your own forehead.
God always loves to give new starts!

John Baptizes Jesus

→ Matthew 3.13–17

Appropriate for mixed groups of babies, toddlers and children up to the age of 9.

This storytelling starts with a recap of the previous story, 'Meet John'. If your group is telling 'Meet John' and 'John Baptizes Jesus' as a single story, start with the material immediately following the box like this below.

92

Optional: What's in the Box? (see p. 7)
Invite one of the children to open the box. Inside is a picture of John the Baptist.

What's in the box? *Invite the child to respond*
This is John the Baptist!
If appropriate:
Look what he's wearing! It's made of camel hair!

Let's stand up and be John the Baptist together.
Let's call out after 3, 'Get ready for God!'
1, 2, 3 . . . Get ready for God!

Look! *Point* The people are coming!
Can anyone tell me what John the Baptist's going to do?
Accept the children's responses.

John's going to wash them in the river!
It's time to get into the river with John!
Let's dip our toe in.
Lead the children in dipping a toe in imaginary water.

Is the water warm or cold today?
Let one of the children decide. According to their response:
   Either: Oh no! It's freezing!
   Or: Ooooh! It's lovely and warm!

Let's walk on the spot into the river . . .
Lead the children in walking in slowly on the spot into warm/cold water.
Deeper . . . *Show the water level on your ankle*
and deeper . . . *Show the water level at your knee*
and deeper . . . *Show the water level at your thighs*
and deeper . . . *Show the water level at your waist*
until the river's up to our waist!

Now we're going to let John baptize us.
After 3, we're going to take a deep breath,
then we're going to go down *Point down*
and up again. *Point up*
Don't forget to hold your nose!

Lead the children in taking a deep breath.
1, 2, 3, breathe! *Hold nose*
and down . . . *Lead the children in crouching down to go under the water*
and up! *Lead the children in standing up again*

This was called baptism.
Can you say 'baptism'?
Baptism.

Let's go down again.
1, 2, 3 . . . **Deep breath, hold nose**
Down into the water . . .
and FREEZE!
This time stay crouched down with the children.

In the water, God made the people clean.
Not just clean OUTside *Rub arms*
but clean INside too. *Trace a circle on your heart*
God cleaned their hearts! *Trace a circle on your heart*
God gave them a new start!

After 3, let's go up out of the water and shout
'God gives me a new start!'
1, 2, 3 . . . Up out of the water
God gives me a new start!

93

If your group is telling 'Meet John' and 'John Baptizes Jesus' as a single story, move straight from the place indicated in 'Meet John' to pick up the story again from here.

So John was at the river baptizing people.
Then, one day, JESUS came to the river!
Let's stand up tall and be the grown-up Jesus. *Lead the children in standing up tall.*

Jesus said, 'Baptize me!'
After 3 let's say, 'Baptize me!' *Point to self like Jesus.*
1, 2, 3 . . . **Baptize me!** *Point to self*
John was shocked!
Can you show me your shocked face?
Lead the children in looking shocked.

John shook his head.
Let's shake our head. *Lead the children in shaking head*
I can't baptize YOU!' said John. *Point in front of you*
You don't need a new start!
You're clean ALREADY!
You should baptize ME! *Point to self*

Let's all shake our heads like John again and say, 'No!'
'No!' *Shaking head*
But Jesus said, 'Yes!' *Nod head*
After 3 let's say, 'Baptize me!' *Point to self like Jesus.*
1, 2, 3 . . . **Baptize me!** *Point to self*

Jesus stepped into the river.
Let's be Jesus and get into the river together.

Lead the children in miming walking on the spot and showing the water level rising with your hands up to your waist.
Deeper and deeper until the water is up to our waist.

So John baptized Jesus.
Jesus went down into the river and then back up again.
After 3, let's be Jesus.
Let's go down into the river . . . .
1, 2, 3 . . . *Deep breath, hold nose*
. . . and up again!

Then when Jesus came up out of the water, *Point back up*
Something amazing happened!
Look! *Point heavenwards*

The sky is opening up!
Move arms from both pointing upwards, down to your sides.
The Holy Spirit is flying down like a dove!
Show a dove flying down with your hands.

Let's make a dove shape with our hands.
Show the children how to make a dove shape by linking your thumbs.
Let's make the dove fly down from heaven.
Lead the children in making a dove fly down from the sky.

Let's sit down for a moment.
When the group is ready:
God flew down like a dove and landed on Jesus
and a voice said . . .
Can you say these very special words after me,
'my turn' *Point to self,* 'your turn' *Leader's hands out to group?*

'This is my child.' *Mime rocking a baby*
'This is my child.' *Mime rocking a baby*
'I love him!' *Hands crossed over chest*

'I love him!' *Hands crossed over chest*
'I am very happy with him!' *Trace smile on face*
'I am very happy with him!' *Trace smile on face*

Jesus' baptism made baptism special.
Now, if we want to follow Jesus, we get baptized too!
Can you put your hand up if you've been baptized?
Acknowledge those who've put their hands up.

When the group is ready:

God has said those special words to you!
God wants to say those special words to ALL of us!

Let's all close our eyes for a moment . . . .
Let's imagine getting baptized like Jesus:
going down . . . then up . . . .
Let's imagine the Holy Spirit
flying down on us like a dove.

Let's say God's special words again
but this time let's say them quietly.
Let's imagine God saying them to us too!

'You are my child.'
'You are my child.'
'I love you!'
'I love you!'
'I am very happy with you!'
'I am very happy with you!'

Let's open our eyes.
I wonder how those words make you feel?
Can you show me?
Accept all responses.

God is VERY happy with us!
There's nothing we can do to make God love us less.
Shake head and smile.
And there's nothing we can do to make God love us more.[2]
Shake head and smile.

If your group is telling 'Meet John' and 'John Baptizes Jesus' as a single story, you could end here.

If you would like to continue with a time of saying sorry, use the following material. Your group will need to know the 'Wash me in the river' song from the previous story or you could teach it here (see p. 131). Alternatively you could replace it with the Sorry Song (p. 180).

The 'I'm Sorry' and 'New Start' signs are among the very few Sowing Seeds signs and actions that are fixed. In this story, the I'm Sorry' sign is used to show the washing away of the wrong things people have done in the river. The 'New Start' sign shows our desire to 'start over' but also has resonances of the rolling away of the stone on Easter Day when Jesus wins a 'new start' for all of us. See p. 8 or the website (www.sowingseeds-online.org) for a description and explanation.

But sometimes we don't feel READY to be with God.
Like the people who came to John didn't feel ready. *Shake head*

The people asked John to wash them in the river first. *'I'm Sorry' sign*
Sometimes WE can feel not ready for God. *Shake head*

I need a new start! *'New Start' sign*

Let's open our eyes again.
The Good News is that God LOVES giving new starts!
God can wash us, not just OUTside, *Rub arms*
but INside too! *Trace a circle on your heart*

One very special way God does this is through baptism,
But God loves giving new starts all the time!
We don't have to go to a river!
We don't even have to use water, but we're going to today!

If there is an older child present who is unlikely to spill the water you could invite him or her to take the water around the circle. You may wish to ask more than one child to take bowls around the circle, going opposite ways or starting at different points in the circle. Alternatively take a bowl around yourself and/or ask adults to help.

Here I have a bowl of water

If appropriate: taken from our baptism font at church.
Name is going to bring this bowl of water around.

If you'd like a new start from God,
You could dip your finger in the water in the bowl and
 Either: draw a cross on your forehead.
 Or: draw a smile on your forehead to show that God is happy with you.

Let's ask God to wash us INside as well as OUTside!
Let's ask God to give us a brand new start!
Let's sing as we wait for the water.

Lead the children in singing the following, or the 'I'm sorry' refrain from your usual Sorry Song.

Wash me in the river, *'I'm Sorry' sign*
Wash me in the river, *'I'm Sorry' sign*

Sometimes we feel like we need a new start.

The Good News is:
God LOVES to give us a new start.

Let's have a time of saying sorry to God now.

Sometimes we do things we wish we hadn't done.
Sometimes it can feel like we've done it all wrong.
We wish we could have a new start!

Let's put our hands on our head.
I wonder if there's anything we've thought this week that we wish we hadn't thought?

Wash me in the river, *'I'm Sorry' sign*
wash me in the river, *'I'm Sorry' sign*
O wash me, O wash me, *'I'm Sorry' sign twice*
I need a new start! *'New Start' sign*

Let's put our hands by our mouths.
I wonder if there's anything we've said this week that we wish we hadn't said?

Wash me in the river, *'I'm Sorry' sign*
Wash me in the river, *'I'm Sorry' sign*
O wash me, O wash me, *'I'm Sorry' sign twice*
I need a new start! *'New Start' sign*

Let's cross our hands on our chest.
I wonder if there's anything we've done this week that we wish we hadn't done?

Wash me in the river, *'I'm Sorry' sign*
Wash me in the river, *'I'm Sorry' sign*
O wash me, O wash me, *'I'm Sorry' sign twice*

**O wash me, O wash me, *'I'm Sorry' sign*
I need a new start! *'New Start' sign***

When all the children and adults who wish to take water have done so:
Look at all those beautiful new starts! *Point around the room*
After 3, let's shout, 'God gives me a new start!'
1, 2, 3 . . . God gives me a new start!

I wonder how you'll use your new start today?

Extra: Our Baptism: a baptism roleplaying workshop

Appropriate for mixed groups of babies, toddlers and children up to the age of 9.

Optional: a baptism roleplaying workshop based on themes from the 'John the Baptist' unit.

Introductory notes

Baptism roleplaying workshops using dolls are becoming increasingly common. Witnessing or taking part in roleplay can accelerate and deepen learning experiences among children (and adults!). The following material is offered as an option for churches, groups or schools who would like to offer a baptism roleplaying workshop to give children opportunities to make connections between the Bible stories about baptism that you've been telling together and the Christian baptisms they see in their place of worship.

Baptism looks different in every church and setting. The following material is based on infant baptism material in *Common Worship* (both *Christian Initiation* 2006 and *Additional Baptism Texts in Accessible Language* 2015) and BCP 2004 (Church of Ireland). However, please adapt the Sowing Seeds resources freely so your workshop reflects baptism in your church as closely as possible. It may also be appropriate for your group to omit some sections because of time limitations.

The words and symbols of baptism are full of meaning! This workshop concentrates solely on the meanings brought to baptism by the stories about John the Baptist and the baptism of Jesus, building on the songs and actions that the children have learned over the unit. For an opportunity to explore more meanings of these rich symbols, see the similar baptism roleplaying workshop in the 'God's Best Friend, Moses' unit (Book 3). Other Sowing Seeds workshops for baptism (for instance, exploring baptism in the context of the Easter stories and the death and resurrection of Jesus) will become available on the website over time.

> The 'I'm Sorry' and 'New Start' signs are among the very few Sowing Seeds signs and actions that are fixed. In this story, the I'm Sorry' sign is used to show the washing away of the wrong things people have done in the river. The 'New Start' sign shows our desire to 'start over' but also has resonances of the rolling away of the stone on Easter Day when Jesus wins a 'new start' for all of us. See p. 8 or the website (www.sowingseeds-online.org) for a description and explanation.

97

> **Tip**
>
> The titles used for the different sections in this workshop match the ones used in *Common Worship* and BCP 2004 so, if you like, you can compare the material easily. Some of the order of the service has been changed for practical reasons (e.g. the Signing with the Cross is before the Prayer over the Water): to bring together the parts of the workshop that will take place at the tables. If you prefer, you can adapt the material to follow *Common Worship*'s order of service.

For today's session, you will need:

- a range of baby dolls or figures set out in a line in front of the group: one for each child. To represent 'babies' we provide a baby doll. To represent 'adults' we provide a 'small world' figure. It can be so good to see the range of farmers, police officers, shopkeepers, soldiers, elderly people, etc., who are brought to 'baptism'. If your church does not have infant baptism, you could use adult figures only.

For the baptism demonstration (leader) in the first part of the session:

- a baby doll (or adult figure if your church does not have infant baptism);
- a large, transparent bowl of water;
- a white robe or dress, or a piece of white cloth to act as a robe (if your church dresses baptism candidates in white after baptism);
- a pot of oil (if your church uses oil for the Signing with the Cross).

For the baptism workshop (whole group) in the second part of the session, you will need to set up tables beforehand with:

- a bowl of water for each child filled with water beforehand, just deep enough for the children to be able to scoop water out easily;
- a piece of white cloth to act as a robe for each child (if your church dresses baptism candidates in white after baptism);
- access to towels to dry hands and for inevitable spillages;
- two or more pots of oil on each table that the children can easily access (if your church uses oil for the Signing with the Cross and/or anointing).

> **Tip**
>
> You may like (or need) to invite children to bring their own dolls or figures to the baptism workshop. If you do invite children to bring a favourite toy, it's important to then honour this invitation (even if the favourite toy turns out to be a teddy or a rabbit, for instance). Psychology suggests that favourite toys can represent much more than the toy itself for many children. The danger of rejecting such a toy as 'not quite right' is that children may then feel rejected themselves. If your group might find this challenging, then it may be best not to make an invitation like this.

Tip

We would recommend not giving the children access to the dolls/figures until later in the session, as we've found that they can prove really distracting to the children if given out early on. If children have brought toys with them, you could ask them to place them in a special place so you can make sure they're reunited for the workshop.

Introduction

As the baptism workshop is longer than most stories, it may make sense to skip the Gathering Song this week even if you usually use it.

If appropriate, encourage the children to join in at the dots.
We've been telling stories about John the . . . **Baptist.**
Let's stand up, put our itchy camel-hair coat on . . .
Lead the children in standing up, putting coat on and scratching.
and be John the Baptist together.

John's job was to get the world ready for God!
Cup hands around mouth
After 3, let's shout, 'Get ready for God!'

1, 2, 3 . . . Get ready for God! *Cup hands around mouth*
Look around I'm not sure anyone heard that.
Let's try that again even louder.
1, 2, 3 . . . Get ready for God! *Cup hands around mouth*

People heard John! And they came!

If appropriate: Can anyone tell us what John did?
Accept responses.

John washed the people in the river!

Let's show John's baptisms.
After 3, we're going to take a deep breath, then we're going to go down under the water and stay down. *Point down.*

Don't forget to hold your nose!
Lead the children in taking a deep breath.
1, 2, 3, breathe! *Hold nose*
and FREEZE!

Go down and stay crouched down with the children.
In the water, God made the people clean.
Not just clean OUTside *Rub arms*
but clean INside too. *Trace a circle on your heart*
God gave them a new start!
After 3, let's go up out of the water and shout 'God gives me a new start!'
**1, 2, 3 . . . *up out of the water*
God gives me a new start!**

We get baptized in our church.

If appropriate:
Put your hand up if you've been baptized.

All groups:
Put your hand up if you've seen a baptism in our church.
Baptism in our church LOOKS different from John's baptisms but it's doing the same thing.

Today we're going to 'baptize' one of these friends.
Indicate dolls/teddies/figures to be 'baptized'.

99

Presentation of the Candidates

→ Song: 'I am going to follow Jesus'. Words: © Sharon Moughtin.
→ Tune: 'Bobby Shaftoe' (traditional).

'I am going to follow Jesus' will become the Gathering Song for the 'Journey to the Cross' unit. As the words are so repetitive, don't worry about teaching the song, just start singing and the children will naturally begin to join in.

When our friends are baptized,
they promise to 'follow Jesus'.
Let's show our friends how to follow Jesus.
Let's stand up and march on the spot.
Lead the children in marching on the spot, counting in beat with the song you'll sing.
1, 2, 3, 4! 1, 2, 3, 4!

Continue marching as you sing.
**I am going to follow Jesus,
I am going to follow Jesus,
I am going to follow Jesus,
follow, follow Jesus!**

Let's practise following Jesus!
Invite one of the children to stand in the centre of the circle or at the front.
Name is going to be Jesus!
To the child: 'Jesus!' Can you show us an action?
Let's all copy what 'Jesus' does.

Let's 'follow Jesus'.

Continue 'following' the child's action as you sing:
**I am going to follow Jesus,
I am going to follow Jesus,
I am going to follow Jesus,
follow, follow Jesus!**
Invite another child to be 'Jesus' and repeat.

When the group is ready to finish:
Let's sit down for a moment.

When the group is ready:
We've shown our friends how to follow Jesus. *Indicate dolls/figures*
Now I'm going to ask three questions. *Hold three fingers up*

If our friends are going to be baptized,
we need to answer, 'We will!' for our friends. *Thumbs up*
Let's practise saying, 'We will!' *Thumbs up*
We will! *Thumbs up*

Question number 1: *Show one finger*
Will you welcome these friends into God's family?
We will! *Thumbs up*

Question number 2: *Show two fingers*
We've been practising how to do this in our song!
Will you show these friends how to follow Jesus?
We will! *Thumbs up*

Question number 3: *Show three fingers*
Will you help these friends be part of the Church?
We will! *Thumbs up*

The Decision

Either:

➤ **Song: 'Wash me in the river'** (the Gathering Song for the John the Baptist unit).
   Words: © Sharon Moughtin.
➤ **Tune:** 'Alive, alive-o' from 'Molly Malone' (traditional). For the music see p. 131.

Or:

➤ **Song: 'The Sowing Seeds sorry song'. Words:** © Sharon Moughtin
➤ **Tune:** © Sharon Moughtin. For the music see p. 180.

Or:

You may prefer to use the words from *The Decision* (Common Worship or BCP 2004) that you use for baptism in your church.

If your church lights the Easter Candle visibly during baptisms, you could light a real candle in a safe place at this point.

Now we light a candle to remind us
of God's bright light, shining in the darkness.

When we're baptized, Jesus gives us a new start.
Before we get baptized,
we say a really big sorry to God.

If you've lit a candle:
We promise to walk in God's light! *Point to the lit candle*

Let's teach our friends *Point to dolls/figures* how we say sorry.
Let's put our hands on our head
I wonder if there's anything we've thought this week
That we wish we hadn't thought?

Lead the children in singing the following. Or change the words to the Sorry Song here and below. If your group isn't familiar with either song, you could use simply the refrain from the Sorry Song: "I'm sorry, I'm sorry. I need a new start'. Or another sorry song that your group is familiar with.

**Wash me in the river, *'I'm Sorry' sign*
wash me in the river, *'I'm Sorry' sign*
O wash me, O wash me, *'I'm Sorry' sign twice*
I need a new start! *'New Start' sign***

Let's put our hands by our mouth.
I wonder if there is anything we've said this week that we wish we hadn't said?

Lead the children in singing.

**Wash me in the river, *'I'm Sorry' sign*
wash me in the river, *'I'm Sorry' sign*
O wash me, O wash me, *'I'm Sorry' sign*
I need a new start! *'New Start' sign***

Let's cross our hands on our chest
I wonder if there is anything we've done this week that we wish we hadn't done?

Lead the children in singing.

**Wash me in the river, *'I'm Sorry' sign*
wash me in the river, *'I'm Sorry' sign*
O wash me, O wash me, *'I'm Sorry' sign*
I need a new start! *'New Start' sign***

The Good News is that God
always wants to give us a new start!
Let's tell our friends about our amazing new start.

After 3, let's shout, 'God gives us a new start!'
1, 2, 3: God gives us a new start!

If you're in a church building and are going to show the children the font:
It's time to go to the 'font'.
Let's sing 'I am going to follow Jesus' while we go there.

101

Let's tiptoe! *We've found that this helps the children not to run from excitement!*
Lead the children in singing as you move to the font.

I am going to follow Jesus,
I am going to follow Jesus,
I am going to follow Jesus,
follow, follow Jesus!

Invite the children to sit around the font.
This is a 'font'. It's like a big bowl filled with water.

....
Tip

If you're moving to the font, you could take this opportunity to ask a helper to move the dolls/figures to the baptism tables ready for their 'baptism'. We place the dolls/teddies/figures on the floor around the tables: one for each bowl. You can place figures on top of the tables: one next to each bowl. If any children have brought their own toys, keep these to one side and make sure the children are reunited with them for the workshop.
....

All groups:
Now we need some water.
Show the children water in a transparent bowl so they can see it.
This is just ordinary water.
But we say a prayer over the water to make it special.

If appropriate: Let's hold our hands up
over the water to show our prayer.
Lead the children in holding hands up over the water.

The prayer remembers
how important water is in our Bible stories.

One of the prayers remembers
John baptizing Jesus in the river.

Let's tell the story together.
Let's stand up and be Jesus.

When the group is ready:
After 3, let's go down into the river . . . .
1, 2, 3 . . . *Deep breath, hold nose*
. . . *and up again!*

Jesus made baptism special!
When we follow Jesus we get baptized too!
But we don't have a river in our church!

If appropriate: and WE don't go right under the water,
Point down.
though some churches do!

Let's show how we baptize in our church.

Signing with the Cross
....
If your church does not make the sign of the cross here, skip this section and continue at 'Baptism', below.

Pick up the doll that you will use to demonstrate baptism.
First, when we baptize someone,
we draw a cross on their forehead.

If your church uses oil for the Signing with the Cross.
I'm going to dip my finger/thumb in this oil.
Dip finger in oil and show the oily finger/thumb.

If it's the oil of catechumens:
This oil is the oil of getting ready and learning.
It shows that we're getting ready to be baptized.

102

All groups:
I'm going to draw a cross on this baby's forehead.
Can you say the words after me,
'my turn' *Point to self*, 'your turn' *Leader's hands out to group*.

You belong to Jesus. *Look baby in the eyes*
You belong to Jesus.
I sign you with the cross. *Sign cross on forehead*
I sign you with the cross. *Sign cross on forehead*

Baptism

Continue from here if your church doesn't make the sign of the cross before the baptism.

[Now] I'm going to 'baptize' this baby.
Let's see if you can count on your fingers
how many times I pour water.

Hold the doll like a baby in one arm and look into its eyes.

Alex, *Or another unisex name*
I baptize you in the name of . . . *Pause*
the Father, *Pour*
and of the Son, *Pour*
and of the Holy Spirit. *Pour* Amen.
Can you show me on your fingers
how many times I poured water?
Accept the children's responses.

Three times! *Show three fingers*
The three are:
Father, *Bend first finger up and down*
Son *Bend second finger up and down*
and Holy Spirit. *Bend third finger up and down*

When we're baptized, we show that's what we believe.
Can you show me one finger?
Lead the children in holding up index finger.

When the group is ready:
Watch this!
Demonstrate to the children:

I believe in the Father. Nod, nod, nod. *Nod first finger three times*
Let's try that together.
I believe in the Father. **Nod, nod, nod.** *Nod first finger three times*

Now two fingers: *Lead the children in holding up two fingers*
I believe in the Son. **Nod, nod, nod.** *Nod second finger*

Three fingers: *Lead the children in holding up three fingers.*
I believe in the Holy Spirit. **Nod, nod, nod.** *Nod third finger*

So we pour water THREE times.
Father, Son and Holy Spirit!

If your church places a white robe on the newly baptized, you could do this at this point.
Then we put a white robe on our friend
to show they've been 'baptized'.

If your church makes the sign of the cross at this point,
Now I'm going to make the sign of the cross
on the baby's forehead
Demonstrate to the group.

If your church anoints with oil of Chrism:
Now we're going to 'anoint' the baby's head with oil.
This oil is the same oil
used to sign the King with the cross
when he was made King!

We could say it's 'Royal Oil'.
Can you say 'Royal Oil'?
Royal Oil!

The oil reminds us that our baby or adult
is going to be part of a ROYAL family: God's family!

I'm going to dip my finger/thumb in this oil.
Dip finger in oil and show the oily finger/thumb.

Either: Now I'm going to rub oil on the baby's head.
Or: Now I'm going to draw a cross
on the baby's head with oil.
Demonstrate to the group.

Baptism Workshop

So you've watched how we baptize in our church.
I think you're ready for our baptism roleplay.
At the tables, there's a bowl of water

If you've moved the toys to the tables:
and a friend who's asked to be 'baptized'.

If the toys are still gathered elsewhere.
On the way, we'll give you a friend to 'baptize'.
Get ready to distribute the toys to the children. If any of the children have brought toys, make sure they're reunited with the right toy!

Let's go to our table(s) and find a place.
But wait!
Don't touch the water until we're all ready!
Let's sing as we go . . . .
Let's tiptoe!
Lead the children in singing 'I am going to follow Jesus' as they find a place next to a bowl of water.

Roleplay: Signing with the Cross

As in the demonstration above, if your church does not make the sign of the cross here, skip this section and continue from 'Roleplay: Baptism', below.

When the group is ready:
Can anyone remember what we did just before we poured water on our friend?
Encourage the children to join in after the dots:
We signed our friend with the . . . **cross!**

Let's make the sign of the cross on our friend's forehead.

If you're using oil:
Let's dip our finger/thumb in the oil
and hold it up in the air to show we're ready.
Show the children your oily finger/thumb and wait as all the children dip their finger/thumb in oil and hold it up.

When the group is ready:
Let's say the words
'my turn' *Point to self,* 'your turn' *Leader's hands out to group.*
You belong to Jesus.
You belong to Jesus.
I sign you with the cross. *Draw a cross on the doll's forehead*
I sign you with the cross. *Draw a cross on the doll's forehead*

Roleplay: Baptism

Now let me tell you something important!
You can't be baptized without a name!
So let's call our babies and adults 'Alex', *Or another unisex name*

Now say these words after me,
and copy my actions,
'my turn' *Point to self,* 'your turn' *Leader's hands out to group.*

104

Alex! *Look into the doll/figure's eyes*
Alex!
I baptize you
I baptize you
in the name of . . .
in the name of . . . .

Aside to the children quietly: Now let's put our hand in the water ready . . .
Scoop one: the Father,
Scoop one: **the Father,**
Scoop two: and of the Son,
Scoop two: **and of the Son,**
Scoop three: and of the Holy Spirit.
Scoop three: **and of the Holy Spirit.**
Amen!
Amen!

If your church places a white robe on the newly baptized,
Then we put a white robe on our friends
to show they've been 'baptized'.

Lead the children in placing white robes on their friends.
If your church makes the sign of the cross at this point:
Now we're going to make the sign of the cross
on the baby's forehead.
Demonstrate to the group.

If your church anoints with oil of Chrism:
Now we're going to 'anoint' the baby's head with oil.

Let's dip our finger/thumb in the oil
and hold it up in the air to show we're ready.
Lead the group in rubbing oil on the toy's head or drawing the sign of the cross.

The Welcome

Then we welcome our friends into the church family.
Welcoming our new brothers and sisters
into God's family is really important!

Either:
Let's sing our Welcome Song to them!
If your group uses one of the Welcome Songs, sing your Welcome Song here. If you're using Welcome Song: Option 1, you could sing 'Welcome frie-ends to God's family!' throughout.

Or:
Let's give them all a big clap!
Lead the children in clapping.

Opportunity for 'overlearning'

Now, we only ever need to get baptized once
in our whole lives.
But as this is role play, shall we do that again?
Use the same pattern as you used earlier.

If appropriate:
Can anyone remember what we did first?
Encourage the children to join in after the dots:
We signed our friends with the . . . **cross!**

If you're using oil:
Let's dip our finger/thumb in the oil
and hold it up in the air to show we're ready.

When the group is ready:
Let's say the words 'my turn' *Point to self,* 'your turn' *Leader's hands out to group.*

105

Lead the children in signing cross and saying words.
You belong to Jesus.
You belong to Jesus.
I sign you with the cross.
I sign you with the cross.

Let's pretend to baptize our friends!
Alex! *Look into the doll/figure's eyes*
Alex!
I baptize you
I baptize you
in the name of . . .
in the name of . . .

Aside quietly: Now let's put our hand in the water ready . . .
Scoop one: the Father,
Scoop one: **the Father,**
Scoop two: and of the Son,
Scoop two: **and of the Son,**
Scoop three: and of the Holy Spirit.
Scoop three: **and of the Holy Spirit.**
Amen!
Amen!

If appropriate:
Then what do we do?
Accept children's responses.

If your church places white robes on the newly baptized,
Then we put white robes on our friends
to show they've been 'baptized'.
Lead the children in placing a white robe on their friends.

If your church makes the sign of the cross at this point:
Now I'm going to make the sign of the cross on the baby's forehead.
Demonstrate to the group.

If your church anoints with oil of Chrism:
We 'anoint' our friend's head with oil.

Let's dip our finger/thumb in the oil
And hold it up in the air to show we're ready.
Lead the group in rubbing oil on the head or drawing the sign of the cross.

And let's welcome our friends into the church family.
Use the same welcome as you did earlier.

Roleplay: Giving of a Lighted Candle

If your group includes children who are likely to want to continue exploring the water, you may find it helpful to say something like: 'Now let's take our friend and take one step back from our tables.'

When the group is ready:
If your church gives a candle at the end of the service, show one of the candles you use to the children.
The last thing we do in a baptism is give a candle
to remind our friends to shine like little lights
in the world for Jesus.

Let's hold our friends in one hand
and make our other finger into a candle now.
Lead the children in holding your finger up in front of you.

After 3, I'm going to light your friends' candles.
Are you ready?
1, 2, 3 . . . Tsssss!

Jesus Is Thrown into the Wilderness

→ Mark 1.9–12
→ Poem: 'Look at that rubbish! Throw it away!' © Sharon Moughtin.

Appropriate for mixed groups of babies, toddlers and children up to the age of 9.

For today's session, you may like to use the following:

- a wilderness tray to support the children in imagining the wilderness: for instance, a tray filled with sand (or brown sugar) with a few rocks and stones placed around so that it looks desolate;
- a Jesus figure: for instance, Joseph figures from nativity sets can work well. If you have no appropriate figures, you could print a picture of Jesus to lay on the sand.

Resources for the 'Sorry Action': see below.

To tell our story today, we need to learn a chant.
Let's see if you can say this after me:
'my turn' *Point to self,* 'your turn' *Leader's hands out to group.*

Look at that rubbish! *Point to self to show your turn*
Throw it away! *Continue pointing to self to show your turn continues*
Look at that rubbish! *Hands out to group*
Throw it away!

Within the leader's material, different words are emphasized each time to help bring variety. Don't worry about the children following you precisely: the group can emphasize different words.

Let's try that again, this time with the actions:

LOOK at that rubbish! *Point and make a disgusted face*
Throw it away! *Mime picking up rubbish and throwing it*
Look at that **RUBBISH!** *Point elsewhere and make a disgusted face*
Throw it away! *Mime picking up rubbish and throwing it*

Mime striking a match in the air and hold it out towards the children's finger candles to 'light' them.

End with a suitable song. For example:

Either:

Let's sing to our friends and help them remember to be little lights in the world for Jesus.

Lead the children in waving their candle finger in front of their friend.

This little light of mine, I'm gonna let it shine!
This little light of mine, I'm gonna let it shine!
This little light of mine, I'm gonna let it shine!
Let it shine, let it shine, let it shine!

Continue with the rest of the song, if appropriate.

Or:

We give this candle to remind our friends
that everything they do is in the light of God.
Let's celebrate that they've been 'baptized'!
Let's dance and sing:
'We are living in the light of God'!
Lead the children in waving their candle finger as they sing.

We are living in the light of God,
we are living in the light of God!
We are living in the light of God,
we are living in the light of God!
We are living, we are living, oh!
We are living in the light of God!
We are living, we are living, oh!
We are living in the light of God!

Or: close by singing another song with which the group is familiar, either about living in God's light or being welcomed into God's family.

Look at THAT rubbish! *Point elsewhere and make a disgusted face*
Throw it away! *Mime picking up rubbish and throwing it*

We're ready to tell our story.
Jesus was baptized by John the Baptist.
Jesus stepped into the river.
What's the water like today? Hot or cold? *Let one of the children decide.*
Let's be Jesus and get into the *cold/warm* river together.

Lead the children in walking on the spot into the river, as if it's cold/warm according to the child's choice. With your hands, show the water rising higher and higher, starting with your ankles until it reaches your waist.
Deeper and deeper until the water is up to our waist.

After 3, let's be Jesus.
Let's go down into the river . . . .
1, 2, 3 . . . *Deep breath, hold nose*
. . . and up again!

When Jesus came up out of the water,
he was ready!
Ready to give the world a BIG new start! *'New Start' sign (p. 8)*

Then something VERY surprising happened.
The Holy Spirit **THREW* JESUS OUT** into the wilderness!
*This is actually the word that Mark's Gospel uses: ekballo, to throw out.

Can you show me how you throw something?
Lead the children in pretending to throw.
The Spirit THREW Jesus out into the wilderness!
Let's be the Spirit
and throw Jesus out into the wilderness.
Encourage the children to 'throw' Jesus out into the wilderness.

Optional: wilderness tray:
This is like the 'wilderness'.

Place your wilderness tray in front of the children. If your group usually uses the What's in the Box? option (p. 7), this can become the object for this story. You may like to have a cloth over it, in which case invite a child to remove the cloth at this point.

What do you see? *Invite a child to respond*

Sand, rocks and sky and nothing else. *Shake head*
Place the Jesus figure in the wilderness.
The Spirit threw Jesus into the wilderness!

Let's stand up and be Jesus.
Jesus looked one way.

Let's look this way . . . *Point one way*
Lead the children in looking the way you've pointed.
And there was sand and rocks and sky.

And Jesus looked the other way . . .
Lead the children in looking the other way.
And there was sand and rocks and sky.

Jesus looked behind him . . .
Lead the children in looking behind.
What do you think he saw?
Encourage the children to join you:
Sand and rocks and sky!

When Jesus was alive,
the 'wilderness' was where people went
when no one wanted them any more. *Shake head*
When people were thrown out like rubbish.
Let's see if we can remember our chant
about throwing rubbish out.

LOOK at that rubbish! *Point and make a disgusted face*
Throw it away! *Mime picking up rubbish and throwing it*

108

Look at that RUBBISH! *Point elsewhere and make a disgusted face*
Throw it away! *Mime picking up rubbish and throwing it*
Look at THAT rubbish! *Point elsewhere and make a disgusted face*
Throw it away! *Mime picking up rubbish and throwing it*

The wilderness was where the world threw people out that they didn't want any more. *Shake head*
Let's pretend to pick people up and throw them out.

LOOK at that rubbish! *Point and make a disgusted face*
Throw it away! *Mime picking up rubbish and throwing it*
Look at that RUBBISH! *Point elsewhere and make a disgusted face*
Throw it away! *Mime picking up rubbish and throwing it*

Look sad The world can be mean to people sometimes.
But let me tell you a secret! *Whisper behind hand*
God loves rubbish!

Let's sit down for a moment.
After 3, can you whisper our secret together:
Lead the children in whispering behind hand:
1, 2, 3 . . . God loves rubbish!

Talk normally again.
God loves things that have been thrown out.
God knows AMAZING things can be made from things and people that have been thrown out.

God doesn't see rubbish like we do. *Shake head*
When we see rubbish *Both hands to self,* we say:
LOOK at that rubbish! *Point and make a disgusted face*
Throw it away! *Mime picking up rubbish and throwing it*

God doesn't see rubbish like that. *Shake head*
God says . . . listen! . . .

Look at that RUBBISH! *Point and make an excited face*
What can I make?! *Pick it up and look excited*

Let's be God together. Let's say:
LOOK at that rubbish! *Point and make an excited face*
What can I make?! *Pick it up and look excited*
Look at THAT rubbish! *Point elsewhere and make an excited face*
What can I make?! *Pick it up and look excited*
Look at that RUBBISH! *Point elsewhere and make an excited face*
What can I make?! *Pick it up and look excited*

God loves rubbish!
So when Jesus began the big new start,
he began in the wilderness,
with all the things and all the people no one wants:
ready to make something exciting!

Let's be God together again.
Let's say:
Look at that RUBBISH! *Point and make an excited face*
What can I make?! *Pick it up and look excited*

At this point, your group can:
sing the Sorry Song, move straight to the Saying Sorry Action below, or end the storytelling with the words: 'We'll find out what happens to Jesus in the wilderness next time . . .' or similar.

Saying Sorry to God

Invite the children to sit down for a moment of quiet.
Let's close our eyes.
Sometimes we can feel like rubbish.
Sometimes it can feel like we've done everything wrong.
It's time to say sorry.

This is a good opportunity to learn the Sorry Song, if your group is not already familiar with it (see p. 180). You could then continue with the Saying Sorry Action as outlined below. This Saying Sorry Action is also one of the options for 'The Journey to the Cross' (Lent) unit in Book 2. So, if your group is telling this story in the weeks before the 'Journey to the Cross' unit, you could continue with it through that unit.

Saying Sorry Action

This action can be used whether or not the group has sung the Sorry Song.

You will need:

- a 'bare tree'
- Either of the following:
  - a large tree branch held in a Christmas tree holder or in a bucket filled with stones and sticky tack;
  - one or more copies of the bare tree template (see Book 2, p. 194 or website) printed on to white or blue paper.
- a wastepaper basket/battered cardboard box or old container with white and/or pink crumpled tissue/crepe/coloured paper torn into pieces that will look like blossom when crumpled up into a ball (not too big). If you've printed your tree outline on white paper, pink tissue paper will help to create a contrast.

Show the group the box of rubbish.

This paper has been thrown out as rubbish.
In a moment, *Name* and *Name* are going to come around with this rubbish.
If you like you can take a piece and hold it in the air.
Let's remember what it feels like to feel rubbish!

While all the children and adults who wish to take a piece of rubbish do so, lead the group in humming the Sorry Song (p. 177), or another appropriate song.

When the group is ready:
When we do things that make God or other people sad, it can make us feel like rubbish!
Let's crumple our paper up to show how we can feel when we feel like rubbish.

When the group is ready:
Let's open our eyes again.
The Good News is, that when we feel like rubbish God LOVES rubbish!
Let's be God again.
Let's imagine we're God, looking at us when we're feeling rubbish.

Look at that RUBBISH! *Point and make an excited face*
What can I make?! *Pick it up and look excited*
Look at THAT rubbish! *Point elsewhere and make an excited face*
What can I make?! *Pick it up and look excited*

It's time to give our rubbish to God the Maker.
Show the group the bare tree you have chosen.

If your group is using a tree branch (small groups only):
Let's take our rubbish paper and some sticky tack and stick our paper on our tree.

If your group is using a printed tree (large groups):
Either: Let's take our rubbish paper and place it on our trees.

Or: Name and *Name are going to come around now with these 'bare trees' on trays.*
If you like, you can place your rubbish paper on the trees.

While all the children and adults who wish to give their rubbish to God do so, lead the group in humming or singing again. Expect some of the blossom to end up looking as if it's blown from the tree or fallen to the floor. This is what blossom does!

When the group is ready:

What looked like rubbish becomes beautiful blossom,
a sign of new life!
God can make amazing things with rubbish!
After 3, let's say, 'God gives us a new start!'
1, 2, 3 . . . God gives us a new start!

Part 2
Bible storytelling for baby and toddler groups

Part 2

Introduction

This material is designed for groups of babies and toddlers (and their parents/carers) which don't currently include any children above the age of 2½. Groups which include children over the age of 2½ may find the material in Part 1 more helpful.

For tips on how to involve babies actively alongside older children when telling stories from Part 1, see 'Including babies in mixed groups' (p. 7).

You may like to make simple song sheets for each unit to help the adults, but most of the songs provided here simply repeat the first line, making it easy to join in. And everyone can join in the actions even if they're not sure of the words!

Choose a simple structure for your time together like the one outlined here and keep this pattern the same for every session (see below). Alternatively, you may simply like to choose one song to sing from the units below each time you gather. Please use and adapt the material as best suits your group.

Welcome Song: this stays the same across every unit
Introduction to the Unit: this changes every unit and helps to introduce the theme
Choice of Songs from the Unit: these change every unit: choose them from the material below or beyond
Optional: Prayer Song: this can stay the same across every unit, or you might like to alternate every so often
Closing Song: this stays the same across every unit

If your session will be followed by a time for refreshments, suggestions for relevant toys and sensory equipment for the children to play with during this time that can support their understanding of the unit can be found in Part 3: Creative Response starter ideas. Make sure that all the choices you make are appropriate to the ages and development stages of your group.

> **Tip: Presentation folders**
>
> Presentation folders can really help when leading Sowing Seeds. They're much easier to manage than loose sheets, especially when doing actions! We've found that A5 folders are best, and the Bible storytelling has been formatted to slip easily into A5 folders.

Basic Structure

Welcome Song

→ **Song**: 'The Sowing Seeds welcome song'. Words © Sharon Moughtin.
→ **Tune**: 'Glory, glory, alleluia!' (traditional).

Wel - come Name__ to St Mar - y's! Wel - come Name__ to St Mar - y's! Wel - come Name__ to St Mar - y's!

Wel - come Name__ to St Mar - y's! You are wel-come in the name of the Lord.

Welcome your group, which is, if possible, seated in a circle.
Let's start by going round the circle
and saying our name out loud.
My name's _____.
Go round the circle so that every adult and child has the chance to say his or her name (and introduce any dolls, teddies or toys). If any of the children don't want to say their name or aren't able to, you (an adult) could say it for them and wave.

When you're ready, start the song. Go around the circle the same way as above. See if each of you can remember the others' names and insert them into the song.

Welcome Name 1 to St Mary's*
Welcome Name 1 to St Mary's*
Welcome Name 1 to St Mary's*
You are welcome in the name of the Lord!
* Insert the name of your church or children's group.

Introducing the Unit

A simple introduction to each unit and its theme can be found below.

Choice of Songs from the Unit

Choose the songs from the units below that you think might work in your setting. How many songs you sing each week will be dependent on your group. It may even be just one!

In practice we've found that it is best not to change too abruptly between units/seasons with this age group. This would mean having to learn more than one new song in a single week! Instead, we've found it makes sense to add one new song, when the group feels ready, and say goodbye to one old song (which may be from the same unit or the previous unit) every now and again, moving around the year that way.

Every group is different and so is every leader! Over time, you will find the number of songs and the rhythm that works for your group.

Prayer Song

Option 1: Thank You, God

→ **Song**: 'My hands were made for love'. Words © Sharon Moughtin.
→ **Tune**: 'Hickory, dickory, dock' (traditional).

My hands were made — for love. My hands were made — for love.

Thank you for the love they've shown! My hands were made — for love.

Alternative prayer songs include the Sorry Song (p. 180) and the 'Jesus, hear our prayer!' song (p. 190).

Invite the children to sit in a circle for a moment of quiet.
It's time to remember all the things we've done this week.
It's time to say 'thank you' to God

Prayer Song

Option 2: Prayers for Other People

→ Song: 'The Sowing Seeds little prayers song'. Words © Sharon Moughtin.
→ Tune: 'Frère Jacques' (traditional).

For our food, — For our food, — thank you, God. thank you, God. For — our teach-ers,

For — our teach-ers, thank you, God. thank you, God. For Rach-el's Nan - ny,

For Rach-el's Nan - ny, hear our prayer. hear our prayer. For peo-ple with no homes, — for

peo - ple with no homes, — hear our prayer. hear our prayer.

Either choose what you'd like the group to pray for before the session, or ask the toddlers and adults at this point if there is anything or anyone that they'd like to pray for. You will need two different 'thank you' suggestions and two different 'hear our prayer' suggestions.

Tip
Try to encourage at least one prayer for other people outside the group.

---

for when we've been part of showing God's love.
Let's wiggle our fingers!
I wonder when you've shown love
with your hands this week?

Wiggle fingers as you sing.

My hands were made for love!
My hands were made for love!
Thank you for the love they've shown.
My hands were made for love!

Let's wiggle our feet!
I wonder when you've shown love
with your feet this week?

Wiggle feet as you sing.

My feet were made for love!
My feet were made for love!
Thank you for the love they've shown.
My feet were made for love!

Let's put our hands gently on our neck.
Let's sing 'Ahhh!'
Ahhhhh!
Can you feel your throat vibrating and dancing?
I wonder when you've shown love
with your voice this week?

Hold neck and feel your voice 'dancing' as you sing.

My voice was made for love!
My voice was made for love!
Thank you for the love it's shown.
My voice was made for love!

Invite the adults and the children to sing after you, repeating your words and their actions. Sometimes it might be almost impossible to fit a toddler's own words in! It's really valuable to do this where possible, however, resisting the urge to try and 'neaten' their suggestions.

For our foo-ood,
For our foo-ood,
Thank you, God!
Thank you, God!
F-or our frie-ends,
F-or our frie-ends,
Thank you, God!
Thank you, God!

For Rachel's Nanny,
For Rachel's Nanny,
Hear our prayer!
Hear our prayer!
For people with no homes,
For people with no homes,
Hear our prayer!
Hear our prayer!

Having sung your prayers, you could insert a Prayer Action (see the choices on p. 192), repeat the process or move straight on to close with the following (or other words that remain the same each week).

For today,	*Point hands down for 'now'*
For today,	***Point hands down for 'now'***
Thank you, God!	*Open hands upwards to God or hands together in prayer*
Thank you, God!	***Open hands upwards to God or hands together in prayer***
Fo-r your love,	*Cross hands on chest*
Fo-r your love,	***Cross hands on chest***
Thank you, God!	*Open hands upwards to God or hands together in prayer*
Thank you, God!	***Open hands upwards to God or hands together in prayer***

Closing Song

→ Song: 'I've got peace like a river' (traditional).
→ Tune: Traditional.

For this song you may like to use a long piece of blue fabric.

Either: invite the children each to hold a small section of the fabric, helped by adults, and to raise and lower it so it 'flows' like a river as you sing.
Or: Invite the children to lie beneath the fabric as two adults wave it over their heads.
Or: If you don't have any blue fabric, invite the group to join in raising and lowering their hands like the waters of a flowing river as you sing.

I've got peace like a river,
I've got peace like a river,
I've got peace like a river in my soul.
I've got peace like a river,
I've got peace like a river,
I've got peace like a river in my soul.

The Light of the World Is Dawning unit (Advent): Getting Ready for Baby Jesus

The 'I'm Sorry' sign and 'New Start' sign which appear in this unit are among the very few Sowing Seeds signs and actions that are fixed. See p. 8 or the website (www.sowingseeds-online.org) for a description and explanation. It's worth introducing this even at this very young age so the children do not have to 'unlearn' actions for the songs later.

The songs in this unit focus on getting ready for baby Jesus and the build-up to Christmas. If you'd like to include songs set just after the birth of Jesus, for instance, 'Away in a manger' and songs about the Magi/Three Kings/Wise Men, they can be found in the next unit, 'Jesus, Light of the World', see p. 124.

Introducing the Unit

Christmas is coming!
Someone very special is coming at Christmas:
Baby Jesus!

Getting Ready for Baby Jesus songbox

Choose from this songbox or elsewhere the songs that you think might work in your setting to add to the simple structure of your session (see pp. 115–16). Don't try to learn them all in one day! In practice, we've found it works to add a new song and to say goodbye to an old song every now and again, when your group feels ready, moving around the year that way.

'Busy, busy, busy, getting ready for Christmas!'

→ Luke 1.78–79
→ Tune: 'What shall we do with the drunken sailor?' (traditional).
→ Words © Sharon Moughtin.

Before Christmas only:
Everyone's very busy getting ready!
Let's sing our 'Busy, busy, busy' song.
Let's start off by decorating our Christmas tree while we sing.

Act out decorating a Christmas tree, or provide a little Christmas tree with wooden decorations for the children to hang as you sing.

Busy, busy, busy, getting ready for Christmas!
Busy, busy, busy, getting ready for Christmas!
Busy, busy, busy, getting ready for Christmas!
[The] Light of the World is dawning!

Hands together in front of your chest then reaching up and out, like the sun dawning. Toddlers might want to crouch down with the same action, then stand up as they bring their arms up and out.

Je-sus, Light of the World, *Sun dawning action*
Je-sus, Light of the World, *Sun dawning action*
Je-sus, Light of the World, is *Sun dawning action*
dawning in the darkness! *Sun dawning action*

If you're using imaginative aids (see p. 207), you might like to distribute them for this song using them for the various actions in the verses.
Either invite the toddlers, parents or carers to make suggestions about what they've been doing that week at home, or choose from some of the following suggestions. For each activity sing 'Busy, busy, busy, getting ready for Christmas' with an appropriate action, followed by the 'Jesus, Light of the World' refrain:

- *opening Advent calendars*
- *making Christmas cards*
- *cleaning*
- *baking and cooking*
- *wrapping up presents*
- *dancing at parties*

To end:
Getting ready for Christmas can be very busy!
You might see adults running around
and getting very busy!
Let's look all busy and stressed like the adults!
Lead children in waving imaginative aids or arms around madly and running on the spot.
Let's sing 'Busy, busy, busy, getting ready for Christmas' again.

Continue 'very busy' action as you sing.

Busy, busy, busy, getting ready for Christmas!
Busy, busy, busy, getting ready for Christmas!
Busy, busy, busy, getting ready for Christmas!
[The] Light of the World is dawning!

Crouch down then arms up and out like sun dawning.

Je-sus, Light of the World, *Sun dawning action*
Je-sus, Light of the World, *Sun dawning action*
Je-sus, Light of the World is *Sun dawning action*
dawning in the darkness! *Sun dawning action*

My goodness, that was busy!
In all the busyness,
let's remember to also have time for some quiet.
Let's imagine holding Baby Jesus in our arms
and singing to him quietly and gently.

Lead the children rocking a baby and singing quietly.

Je-sus, Light of the World,
Je-sus, Light of the World,
Je-sus, Light of the World, is
dawning in the darkness!

Let's get ready for Baby Jesus today
by singing our songs about when Baby Jesus was born.

'"Yes!" said Mary'

→ Luke 1.26–38
→ Tune: '"Pop!" goes the weasel' (traditional). Words © Sharon Moughtin.

Show an angel.
Shall we sing the story together of when an angel went to Mary?

The actions of this song are designed to mirror a jack-in-the-box, with its lid closing and the puppet bursting out at the 'pop' moment. Encourage the children to stand with their hands stretched high, or hold your hands high over the babies. You could make angel wings (like butterfly wings) with your hands if you like.

An angel came to Ma-a-a-ry. *Hands come down from on high*
'You will have a baby! *Rock like a baby standing at normal height*
He will be the Son of God!' *Crouch down on the ground like tiny child*
'Yes!' sa-id Mary! *Jump up or raise the baby high in the air and shout 'Yes!'*

You may like to continue with the following, sung to the second verse of 'Pop goes the weasel': 'Up and down the City Road . . .'

Angels singing in the sky. *Hands come down from on high*
came down to shepherds . . . *Wave arms like wings standing at normal height*
'Come and meet the new-born king!' *Beckoning gesture and point to king*
Up jumped the shepherds! *Jump up or raise the baby high in the air*

'My God is a topsy turvy God!'

→ Luke 1.39–55
→ Tune: 'O, the grand old Duke of York' (traditional). Words © Sharon Moughtin.

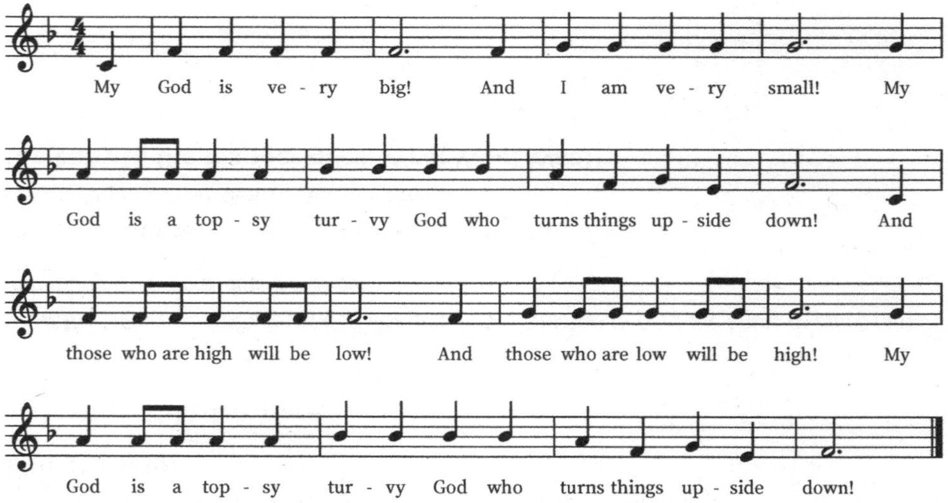

Mary was so excited about her special baby!
She sang a beautiful song to say 'thank you' to God.
Let's sing Mary's song together!

O my God is very BIG! *Make the biggest shape you can*
And I am very small! *Make the smallest shape you can*
My God is a topsy turvy God, *'New Start' sign (see p. 8)*
who turns things upside down!
And those who are low will be high!
Start low and end up high. Or lift babies from low to high.
And those who are high will be low!
Start high and end up low. Or lower babies from high to low.
My God is a topsy turvy God, *'New Start' sign*
who turns things upside down!

'Little donkey'

→ Luke 2.1–5
→ Tune and words: Eric Boswell © Warner Chappell Music, 1959.

Mary was going to have a baby.
But first she had to go on a journey to Bethlehem with Joseph. *Show a donkey*

Let's sing our story about Mary and Joseph travelling with a little donkey!

Sing Eric Boswell's 'Little donkey'. This song is under copyright but can be found in many hymn and carol books. If you're using imaginative aids (see p. 207), you might like to distribute them for this song and encourage the children to use them as donkey's tails, long donkey's ears, ringing bells, etc. for different verses through the course of the song.

'The cow by the manger'

→ Luke 2.6–7
→ Tune: 'The wheels on the bus' (traditional). Words © Sharon Moughtin.

When Mary and Joseph arrived at Bethlehem,
There was nowhere for them to stay. *Shake head*
Just a place full of animals!
Let's sing our song about the animals there.

For each verse, you might like to pull a toy animal or picture of an animal out of a bag and give it to a child, or place it in or next to a 'manger' (this could be as simple as a cardboard box). You could use the animals that follow, or go wherever your imagination takes you.

The cow by the manger goes 'Moo, moo, moo!
Moo, moo, moo! Moo, moo, moo!'
The cow by the manger goes 'Moo, moo, moo!'
all night long!

The sheep by the manger goes 'Baa, baa, baa!
Baa, baa, baa! Baa, baa, baa!'
The sheep by the manger goes 'Baa, baa, baa!'
all night long!

The fly by the manger goes 'Bzzz! Bzzz! Bzzz!
Bzzz! Bzzz! Bzzz! Bzzz! Bzzz! Bzzz!'
The fly by the manger goes 'Bzzz! Bzzz! Bzzz!'
all night long!

The goat by the manger goes 'Bleat! Bleat! Bleat!
Bleat! Bleat! Bleat! Bleat! Bleat! Bleat!'
The goat by the manger goes 'Bleat! Bleat! Bleat!'
all night long!

The mouse by the manger goes 'Squeak, squeak, squeak!
Squeak, squeak, squeak! Squeak, squeak, squeak!'
The mouse by the manger goes 'Squeak, squeak, squeak!'
all night long!

And in that dark, dark place,
Baby Jesus was born.

Show the children a Baby Jesus doll. Ask one of the children to hold the baby, or place him in something that represents a manger.

The baby in the manger goes 'Waa! Waa! Waa!
Waa! Waa! Waa! Waa! Waa! Waa!'
The baby in the manger goes 'Waa! Waa! Waa!'
all night long!

'Silent night'

→ Tune: Franz Xaver Gruber.
→ Words: Joseph Mohr, translated by John Freeman Young.

For groups that don't choose 'The cow by the manger':
And in a dark, dark place,
Baby Jesus was born.
Show the children a Baby Jesus doll.
Ask one of the children to hold Baby Jesus, or place him in something that represents a manger.

For groups that do choose 'The cow by the manger':
But sssh! Baby Jesus has fallen asleep!
In all of that noise, there was also silence.
Silence and peace! Sssh!
Let's sing 'Silent night' together!

For this song you might like to use a peace cloth (see p. 207). Depending on the age of the children present, you could encourage them to each hold a small section of the cloth and raise and lower it over Baby Jesus (as for the Peace Song), or you might like to encourage the children to lie underneath the peace cloth along with Baby Jesus instead.

Silent night, holy night,
all is calm, all is bright
round yon virgin mother and child!
Holy infant so tender and mild,
sleep in heavenly peace,
sleep in heavenly peace.

Jesus, Light of the World! unit (Christmas and Epiphany)

'Joy! Joy! Joy! It's Christmas!'

→ Luke 1.78-79
→ Tune: 'What shall we do with the drunken sailor?' (traditional).
→ Words © Sharon Moughtin.

Joy! Joy! Joy! It's Christ-mas, Christ-mas! Joy! Joy! Joy! It's Christ-mas, Christ-mas!
Joy! Joy! Joy! It's Christ-mas, Christ-mas! The Light of the World is shin - ing! Je - sus,
Light of the World! Je - sus, Light of the World!
Je - sus, Light of the World, is shin - ing in the dark - ness!

The songs in this unit focus on the celebrations of Christmas and the following visit of the Magi (Three Kings/Wise Men). If your group isn't one that follows the church year, you may find it makes more sense to move on to another unit at this point.

Choose from the songbox which songs you think will work best in your setting and add them into the structure of your session. An example structure can be found on pp. 115–16. In practice, we've found it's best to introduce new songs one at a time when you feel your group is ready (see tip on p. 116).

Introducing the Unit

Baby Jesus is here!
Baby Jesus is the Light of the World, shining bright. *Jazz hands*
Let's show jazz hands for Jesus' light. *Lead the group in jazz hands*
It's time to celebrate!

You may like to place a Baby Jesus doll in a manger/Moses basket/cardboard box in the centre of the circle. If the children like playing with Baby Jesus, you might like to have more than one doll ready!

Jesus, Light of the World! songbox

Choose from this songbox or beyond the songs that you think might work in your setting to add to the simple structure of your session (see pp. 115–16). Don't try to learn them all in one day! In practice, we've found it works to add a new song and to say goodbye to an old song every now and again, when your group feels ready, moving around the year that way.

This song is an easy update to the 'Busy, busy, busy getting ready for Christmas' song, making it applicable for after Christmas Day too!

Let's sing our 'Busy, busy, busy' song,
but with new Christmas words!
We're going to sing:
'Joy! Joy! Joy! It's Christmas! Christmas!'
And instead of 'the Light of the World is dawning',
let's sing 'the Light of the World is shining!' *Twinkle hands*

Joy! Joy! Joy! It's Christmas! Christmas!
Joy! Joy! Joy! It's Christmas! Christmas!
Joy! Joy! Joy! It's Christmas! Christmas!
The Light of the World is shining! *Twinkle hands*

Either invite the toddlers, parents or carers to make suggestions about what they've been doing over Christmas, or choose from the following suggestions. For each activity sing 'Joy!

124

'See in the darkness'

→ Tune: 'Incy, wincy, spider' (traditional).
→ Words © Sharon Moughtin.

See in the dark-ness a lit-tle light shines bright. Light of the World, shi-ning
love in dark-est night. Light of the World, shine for ev-'ry-one to
see! O, Light of the World, shine your light of love in me!

If appropriate (different parts of the world get dark at different times of the year!):
When people decided what day Christmas should be on,
they chose it because it was the darkest time of the year.

Jesus, the Light of the World, is born
in the deep, deep dark.
Let's close our eyes and feel the dark.
Lead the group in closing eyes or holding hands over babies' eyes.
And let's open our eyes!
Open eyes.

Show the children a child safe lantern or torch shining (make sure it is toddler friendly).
Jesus is like a light shining in the darkness.
Let's light our little light here.
Light the lantern or torch.
Let's sing our song about Jesus the light that shines bright!
Let's show our 'twinkle hands' as we sing!

Encourage the adults to open and close hands like 'twinkle stars' before the babies' or toddlers' eyes as you sing.
See in the darkness, a little light shines bright!
Light of the world, shining love in darkest night!
Light of the world, shine for everyone to see!

Joy! Joy! It's Christmas! Christmas!' with an appropriate action, followed by the *'Jesus, Light of the World'* refrain:

- *opening stockings*
- *dancing at parties*
- *unwrapping presents*
- *eating lots of food*

Je-sus, Light of the World, *Sun dawning action*
Je-sus, Light of the World, *Sun dawning action*
Je-sus, Light of the World, is *Sun dawning action*
shining in the darkness! *Twinkle hands*

My goodness, that was busy!
In all the busyness,
let's remember to also have time for some quiet.
Let's imagine holding Baby Jesus in our arms
and singing to him quietly and gently.

Lead the group in rocking the babies and singing quietly:
Je-sus, Light of the World, *Sun dawning action*
Je-sus, Light of the World, *Sun dawning action*
Je-sus, Light of the World, is *Sun dawning action*
shining in the darkness! *Twinkle hands*

Light of the world, shine your light of love in me!

Shall we try that again?
Turn lantern or torch off.
Let's close our eyes and feel the dark.
Lead the group in closing eyes or holding hands over babies' eyes.
And let's open our eyes!
Open eyes.

Let's light our little light here.
Light the lantern or torch.
Let's show our 'twinkle hands' as we sing!

Encourage the adults to open and close hands like 'twinkle stars' before the babies' or toddlers' eyes as you sing.

See in the darkness, a little light shines bright!
Light of the world, shining love in darkest night!
Light of the world, shine for everyone to see!
Light of the world, shine your light of love in me!

'Twinkle, twinkle, holy star'

→ Matthew 2.1–11, Luke 2.8–20
→ Tune: 'Twinkle, twinkle, little star' (traditional). Words © Sharon Moughtin.

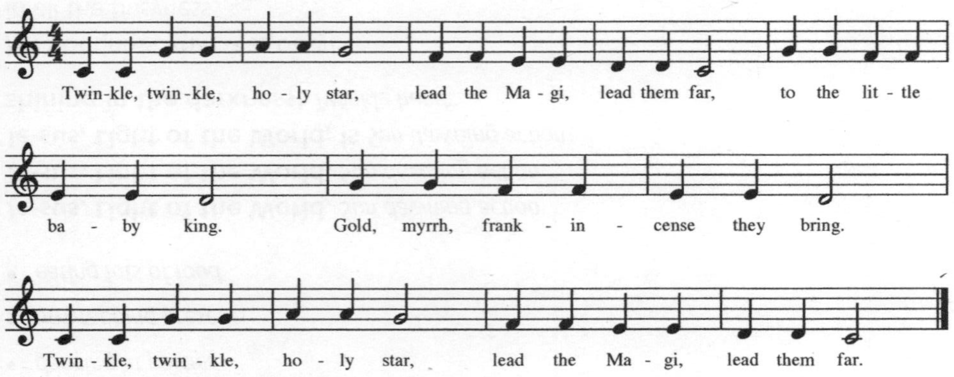

Twin-kle, twin-kle, ho-ly star, lead the Ma-gi, lead them far,
Gold, myrrh, frank-in-cense they bring.
Twin-kle, twin-kle, ho-ly star, lead the Ma-gi, lead them far.

Show the children a star on a stick with rounded edges (make sure it is toddler friendly).
That night, there was a special star shining in the dark sky.
The star was telling everyone that Baby Jesus, the new king, had been born!
Let's sing our song about the star together.

With such young children you may wish only to sing one verse, but I have included all three here. Adults will probably need song sheets or projected words for this song.

Twinkle, twinkle, holy star, *Twinkle sign*
lead the Magi, lead them far, *Twinkle sign*
to the little baby king. *Crown on head or point to Jesus*
Gold, myrrh, frankincense they bring. *Count on fingers*
Or: 1, 2, 3 presents they bring. Count on fingers
Twinkle, twinkle, holy star, *Twinkle sign*
lead the Magi, lead them far. *Twinkle sign*

Dazzle, dazzle, angels bright, *Wave arms like wings*
blaze God's love in darkest night! *Wave arms like wings*
'Glory in the highest!' sing! *Cupped hands round mouth*
Celebrate the baby king. *Crown on head or point to Jesus*
Dazzle, dazzle, angels bright, *Wave arms like wings*
Blaze God's love in darkest night. *Wave arms like wings*

Flicker, flicker, lanterns, show *Swing lantern in hand*
wondering shepherds where to go. *Point to Jesus*
Angels sang of peace on earth. *Wave arms like wings*
Shepherds speed to see Christ's birth. *Run on spot or cycle babies' legs*
Flicker, flicker, lanterns, show *Swing lantern in hand*
wondering shepherds where to go. *Point to Jesus*

'Follow, follow, follow the star'

→ Matthew 2.1–11
→ Tune: 'Here we go round the mulberry bush'. Words © Sharon Moughtin.

Let's fol-low, fol-low, fol-low the star, fol-low the star, fol-low the star! Let's fol-low, fol-low, fol-low the star, to meet the spe-cial king.

126

Tip

If the group includes babies only you can stay seated and move the babies' legs for them like 'cycling', or show two fingers walking around and following the actions. You may wish to cut the song to three verses: normal walking, rowing a boat, and tiptoeing quietly: 'Ssssh!'

Groups that haven't sung 'Twinkle, Twinkle':
That night, a special star shone in the dark sky, telling everyone a special baby was born!
Hold up a large yellow star on a stick with rounded ends (check it's toddler friendly).
Some clever people, (*If you like:* the Magi/Three Kings/Wise Men) saw a new king had been born.
They followed the star.

> *If toddlers are present:*
> Let's get up and follow the star together.

Lead the children in walking in a circle, following the star. You might like to take turns leading if appropriate.

[Let's] follow, follow, follow the star,
follow the star, follow the star!
[Let's] follow, follow, follow the star
to meet the special king.

Uh oh! It's the desert!
Let's climb on our camels
To help us through the sandy desert . . .

Show how a camel sways as you ride it, or give out toy camels or pictures of camels.

[Let's] follow, follow, follow the star,
follow the star, follow the star!
[Let's] follow, follow, follow the star
to meet the special king.

Uh oh! It's the sea!
Let's get in our boats to cross the sea.
Don't forget your camel!

Show the children how to sit down and row a boat as you sing.

[Let's] follow, follow, follow the star,
follow the star, follow the star!
[Let's] follow, follow, follow the star
to meet the special king.

Uh oh! A mountain!
Time for some climbing!

Lead the children in pretending to climb a very steep mountain.

[Let's] follow, follow, follow the star,
follow the star, follow the star!
[Let's] follow, follow, follow the star
to meet the special king.

Uh oh! A valley. It's a bit dark and a bit scary! Ssssh!
Let's sing really quietly!

Lead the children in tiptoeing around.

[Let's] follow, follow, follow the star,
follow the star, follow the star!
[Let's] follow, follow, follow the star
to meet the special king.

Look! The star's stopped!
Point to the manger.
What a long journey it's been!
Shall we look inside the manger . . .
Let's tiptoe there . . .
Tiptoe, tiptoe, tiptoe . . . .
Tiptoe back to your place around the manger.
It's Baby Jesus! The baby king!
> *If appropriate:*
> Let's kneel down around Baby Jesus.

'Giving a present to Jesus'

→ Matthew 2.11

The Magi (Wise Men/Three Kings) brought Jesus special presents.
We can give Baby Jesus a present too!

Show a basket of hearts. Use fabric hearts, or provide new paper hearts each week. If you'd prefer to emphasize the 'light' theme, you could use paper stars.

If you like, you can take one of these hearts/stars and give it to Baby Jesus to show your love.

As you sing, encourage the children to place their hearts/stars anywhere they like around Jesus.

Either: 'Away in a manger' by William James Kirkpatrick:

Away in a manger, no crib for a bed,
The little Lord Jesus laid down his sweet head.
The stars in the night sky
looked down where he lay,
the little Lord Jesus asleep on the hay.

Or: the refrain only from 'O come all ye faithful', attributed to John Francis Wade, trans. Frederick Oakeley and others:

O come, let us adore him!
O come, let us adore him!
O come, let us adore him!
Christ the Lord!

Or: to the tune of 'Here we go round the mulberry bush', like 'Follow the star to Bethlehem', words © Sharon Moughtin:

I'll show my love to Jesus,
Jesus, Jesus.
I'll show my love to Jesus,
The tiny baby king!

'We are marching in the light of God'

→ Tune and words: traditional.

Jesus the light of the world is here!
This song's all about Jesus' light shining.
It's about how everything we do is in 'the light of God'.

We are waking *Stretching action* **in the light of God,**
we are waking *Stretching action* **in the light of God!**
We are waking *Stretching action* **in the light of God,**
we are waking *Stretching action* **in the light of God!**
Interrupt the song: Breakfast time!
We are eating. *Eating action* **we are eating, oh!** *Jazz hands*
We are eating *Eating action* **in the light of God!**
We are eating. *Eating action* **we are eating, oh!** *Jazz hands*
We are eating *Eating action* **in the light of God!**

Repeat with different actions, changing actions halfway through the song. You may like to ask children or parents/carers what they will be doing that day to help make connections between this time of worship and the rest of each baby/toddler's day. For examples, see p. 8.

You may like to end with this final verse, sung quietly.
We are resting in the light of God, *Resting action*

128

we are resting in the light of God! *Resting action*
We are resting in the light of God, *Resting action*
we are resting in the light of God! *Resting action*

Interrupt: Sssh! Ssssh!
Lead the babies and toddlers in settling down to sleep.

We are sleeping, we are sleeping, ssssh!
We are sleeping in the light of God!
We are sleeping, we are sleeping, ssssh!
We are sleeping in the light of God!

John the Baptist and Baptism unit (the weeks before Lent)

This unit is particularly appropriate for groups who would like to explore baptism. It can be held in the weeks between Christmas and Lent or at any time of the year. Lent is a time when the Church turns its attention to baptism so if some of these songs end up being used in the Lent season as well, this is entirely appropriate.

The songs in this unit could also be used as a standalone baptism workshop with babies and toddlers. An alternative baptism workshop for mixed groups of babies, toddlers and children up to the age of around 9 is also available on p. 97.

Introducing the Unit

Our time today will include songs about baptism!
Has anyone here been to a baptism?
Accept responses.
Has anyone here been baptized?
Accept responses.
Today we get a chance to explore baptism together.

John the Baptist and Baptism songbox

Choose from this songbox or elsewhere the songs that you think might work in your setting to add to the simple structure of your session (see pp. 115–16). Don't try to learn them all in one day! In practice, we've found it works to add a new song and to say goodbye to an old song every now and again, when your group feels ready, moving around the year that way. With this unit, there is a connection between the songs so you could end the group by encouraging them to come back next time to find out what happens next.

> The 'I'm Sorry' sign and 'New Start' sign which appear in this unit are among the very few Sowing Seeds signs and actions that are fixed. See p. 8 or the website (www.sowingseeds-online.org) for a description and explanation. It's worth introducing this even at this very young age so the children do not have to 'unlearn' actions for the songs later.

'Get ready for our God!'

→ Words: © Sharon Moughtin.
→ Tune: 'She'll be coming round the mountain' (traditional).

Get rea-dy, get rea-dy for our God! ___ Get rea-dy, get rea-dy for our God! ___ It's ___ time for a ___ new start, ___ time for a new start! Get rea-dy, get rea-dy for our God! ___

If your group has imaginative aids (see p. 207), you may like to use them for this song. Either choose some actions yourself, leave the group to wave their imaginative aids as they wish, or invite the toddlers/parents/carers to invent actions for the song.

In the Bible, one of the people that talked most about baptism was John the Baptist!
John's job was to get the world ready for God!
John called out, 'Get ready!' *Cup hands around mouth*
After 3, let's shout, 'Get ready!'

'Down, down, down into the water'

→ **Words:** © Sharon Moughtin.
→ **Tune:** 'Glory, glory, alleluia!' (traditional).

1, 2, 3 . . . **Get ready!** *Cup hands around mouth*
Let's sing our song about getting ready for God.
Get ready, get ready for our God! *Get ready action*
Get ready, get ready for our God! *Get ready action*
It's time for a new start, time for a new start! *'New Start' sign (p. 8)*
Get ready, get ready for our God! *Get ready action*
Repeat.

'Wash me in the river'

→ **Words:** © Sharon Moughtin.
→ **Music:** 'Alive, alive-o': the chorus to the traditional Irish song 'Molly Malone'.

People heard John the Baptist shouting 'Get ready!'
and they came!
But they didn't feel ready to meet with God. *Shake head*
They asked John to wash them in the river.
Let's sing the people's song together.

Wash me in the river, *'I'm Sorry' sign*
wash me in the river. *'I'm Sorry' sign*
O wash me, o wash me, *'I'm Sorry' sign twice*
I need a new start! *'New Start' sign*
Repeat as appropriate.

For this song you may like to use a long piece of blue fabric for the river that stretches around the group on the adults' knees. Alternatively, if your context allows (for instance, outside, or on a carpet which will prevent any slips), you could give each child a small tray of water and a 'small world' figure.

John the Baptist shouted, 'Get ready!' *Cup hands round mouth*
and the people came.
John helped the people get ready for God.
He washed them in the river!

Let's show the people going down into the water!

Either: Let's wiggle our fingers to show the water!
Lead the group in wiggling fingers.
Or: Let's make our river go up and down.
Lead the group in waving the blue fabric up and down.
Or: Give out the small trays of water and 'small world' figures at this point.

Let's show the people going down into the water!

If you're showing a river with your fingers, lead the toddlers in crouching down under the water as you sing each line, or invite adults with babies to raise and lower their baby accordingly as you sing.
If you're using a blue cloth stretched around the group to show a river, encourage the group to raise and lower it gently as you sing each line.
If you're using a water tray, lead the toddlers in making the 'small world' people go down under the water as you sing each line.

131

**Down, down, down into the water,
down, down, down into the water,
down, down, down into the water,
God gives you a new start!**

Repeat as above, this time emphasizing the 'up' motion out of the water with each line.

**Up, up, up out of the water,
up, up, up out of the water,
up, up, up out of the water,
God gives you a new start!**
Repeat as appropriate.

Then one day, Jesus came to the river!
Let's show John baptizing Jesus.

As before, lead the children in showing Jesus going down into the water with your bodies or with 'small world' people.

**Down, down, down into the water,
down, down, down into the water,
down, down, down into the water . . .**

Freeze!
But Jesus didn't need a new start! *Shake head*
A voice came from heaven:
Sing to the last line of the song.
'I love you! You're my child!'
Let's sing the story of Jesus' baptism again!

**Down, down, down into the water,
down, down, down into the water,
down, down, down into the water . . .
'I love you! You're my child!'**

**Up, up, up out of the water,
up, up, up out of the water,
up, up, up out of the water,
'I love you! You're my child!'**

Continue until the group are familiar with the change of words for Jesus' baptism.

Either continue with the following to sing about baptism in your place or move on to the next song.

Jesus was baptized.
When we follow Jesus, we get baptized too.
Let's show someone being baptized in our church.

If you've been showing a river with your fingers, this time either mime holding a baby in one arm and pouring water over its head, or mime pouring water over an adult's head.
If you've been using a piece of blue fabric around the group, lead the group in miming scooping water up from the river with one hand and 'pouring' it over the head of the children.
If you're using a water tray, lead the toddlers in using your hand to pour water over the head of one of the figures.
If your church has baptism by full immersion, repeat the 'Down, down, down' and 'Up, up, up' verses, ending with your choice of final line.

**Pour, pour, pour with the water,
pour, pour, pour with the water,
pour, pour, pour with the water,**

Choose from the following last lines, according to what is most relevant to your setting.

. . . **'I love you! You're my child!'** *Cross on forehead or dove flying down*
. . . **to follow Jesus Christ!** *Walk on spot*
. . . **God gives you a new start!** *Cross on forehead or another suitable action*
. . . **now you belong to God!** *Cross on forehead or another suitable action*
Repeat as appropriate.

'The welcome'

- → 'The Sowing Seeds welcome song': words: © Sharon Moughtin.
- → Tune: 'Glory, glory, alleluia!' (traditional).
- → 'You are welcome in the name of the Lord': words and music traditional.

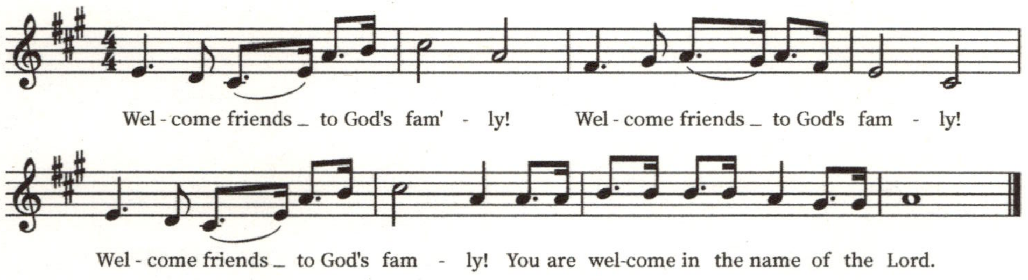

Wel - come friends _ to God's fam' - ly! Wel - come friends _ to God's fam - ly!

Wel - come friends _ to God's fam - ly! You are wel-come in the name of the Lord.

When we baptize people,
we welcome them into God's family *or:* the church family.

Either:
Let's sing a welcome song to them!
Let's wave as we sing.
Lead the toddlers and parents/carers in waving and singing:
Welcome frie-ends to God's fam'ly!
Welcome frie-ends to God's fam'ly!
Welcome frie-ends to God's fam'ly!
You are welcome in the name of the Lord!

Or:
Let's sing a welcome song to them!
Let's wave with one hand. *Lead waving*
Then with our other hand. *Lead waving*
Then let's show God's 'glory' in them!
Move arms up and down in front of you with fingers wiggling, palms facing out, towards one person then another.
Then let's wave with both hands.
Lead waving.
We're ready to sing!

You are welcome in the name of the Lord!
Wave with right hand.
You are welcome in the name of the Lord!
Wave with left hand.
I can see all over you, the glory of the Lord!
Move arms up and down in front of you with fingers wiggling, palms facing out, towards one person and then another.
You are welcome in the name of the Lord!
Wave with both hands all around the circle.

'Shine like a light in the world!'

- → 'This little light of mine': words and tune traditional.
- → 'We are marching in the light of God': words and tune traditional.

Singing a song about light when exploring baptism is particularly relevant for groups from churches which give out candles at the end of their baptism service.
When we baptize someone, we give them a candle.
If appropriate, show one of the candles you use to the group.
Like this!

We tell our friends to shine like little lights in the world for Jesus.
Let's make our finger into a candle now.
Lead the children in holding your finger up in front of you.
After 3, I'm going to light your candles.
Are you ready?
1, 2, 3 . . . Tsssssss!
Mime striking a match in the air and hold it out towards the children's finger candles to 'light' them.

Either:
Let's sing about shining our light in the world!
Lead the group in waving their candle fingers
This little light of mine, I'm gonna let it shine!
This little light of mine, I'm gonna let it shine!
This little light of mine, I'm gonna let it shine!
Let it shine, let it shine, let it shine!
Repeat or continue with the following verses.

Blow on your finger as if blowing out a candle on 'puff'. Then hold it up high.

**Won't let no one puff it out! I'm gonna let it shine!
Won't let no one puff it out! I'm gonna let it shine!
Won't let no one puff it out! I'm gonna let it shine!
Let it shine, let it shine, let it shine!**

*Hold your finger behind a cupped hand, then take your cupped hand away
to reveal the 'candle' and hold it high!*

**Hide it under a bushel? No! I'm gonna let it shine!
Hide it under a bushel? No! I'm gonna let it shine!
Hide it under a bushel? No! I'm gonna let it shine!
Let it shine, let it shine, let it shine!**

Or:

Let's march on the spot and sing about God's light!

**We are marching in the light of God,
we are marching in the light of God!
We are marching in the light of God,
we are marching in the light of God!
We are marching, we are marching, oh!
We are marching in the light of God!
We are marching, we are marching, oh!
We are marching in the light of God!**

*Or: the extended version of 'We are marching in the light of God' from the material
for the weeks after Christmas (see p. 172).*

Let's sing about how everything we do 'is in the light of God!'

Part 3
Creative Response starter ideas

Introduction

Sowing Seeds aims to create a space for children to encounter God for themselves. An important part of this is giving children the opportunity to respond creatively to what they've heard and experienced. This chapter provides starter ideas for each unit to encourage this.

These starter ideas deliberately offer very simple templates (all designed by children), or other open-ended activities, as starting points for the children to explore for themselves. Our hope is that in their hands these resources and initial ideas will be transformed into wholly unique and individual responses, according to the children's gifts, interests and abilities.

When leading a time of Creative Response, we recommend providing children with choices rather than a single option. Choice-making encourages children to begin to take responsibility for their own responses and their own relationship with God. Some young children can be overwhelmed by too much choice so it may help to begin by offering just two or three starter ideas to choose from. This will help to build their confidence and give them experience in exercising their imagination.

As the children grow in confidence, try providing only open-ended resources (paints, clay, play dough, collage materials (p. 208) and glue, recycling materials, Lego, Kapla blocks, or other interesting media (p. 209) for at least one week per unit to encourage their creativity and sense of personal responsibility.

> **Tip**
>
> Imagination and creativity can be vital to our relationship with God. After all, we're made in the image of God the Maker.

The Light of the World Is Dawning unit (Advent and Christmas)

These starter ideas are designed to spark imaginations and open up opportunities for the children to respond creatively in their different ways to the worship and storytelling you've taken part in together.

Story Starter Ideas relate directly to the Bible Storytelling of each session, including a print-and-go option.
Sensory Starter Ideas are designed for sensory explorers, including babies and toddlers. These can remain the same through the whole unit.
Unit Starter Ideas are designed to remain relevant throughout the whole unit. Keeping these resources available each time gives children the opportunity to deepen and develop their responses, while making preparation more manageable for leaders.

> **Tip: Free response area**
>
> In addition to any other resources you provide, keeping a free response area available every time will give the children the opportunity to create anything they wish in response to the story they've told, building their sense of confidence and personal responsibility. In this area you could simply provide blank paper and crayons, pencils, paints or pastels. If you have them, other interesting media (p. 209) will provide even more scope for the children to nurture and strengthen their imaginative skills.

Story Starter Ideas

The four nativity stories told in this unit share a number of strong themes and memorable characters. For this reason, there are more unit starter ideas than story starter ideas for this unit, so do take look at pp. 144–5 as well.

Baby John's Story

- Invite the children to explore light shining in the darkness by creating their own 'light' patterns with oil pastels, paint, or chalk on dark paper. *Provide dark paper plus oil pastels/paint/chalk.*

- Invite the children to make a representation of the angel Gabriel, providing angel templates for those who'd like a starting point but also encouraging free exploration of what an angel might look like. *Provide paper, pencils/crayons, scissors, glue, angel templates (p. 213 or website). Optional: collage materials (p. 208), ribbon/string/wool, in case the children would like to convert the angel into a Christmas tree decoration.*

- Invite the children to make little bags that smell like incense from squares of fabric, filled with pleasant-smelling spices that you have in the cupboard (e.g. cinnamon, allspice) and tied together with string/wool. Encourage the children to imagine the smell of the Temple as the prayers go up to God with the incense. *Provide fabric squares, string/wool, cupboard spices. Little socks can also make great incense bags when tied with string/wool. If you prefer, you could add popcorn and a few drops of essential oil to the bags.*

Mary's Story

- Invite the children to make a puppet of Mary. 'I wonder what Mary looked like?' *Provide body template (p. 218 or website), crayons/pencils/pastels, masking tape, lollipop sticks/straws/twigs.*

- The story of the angel Gabriel visiting Mary has been the subject of many stained-glass windows in churches. Give the children the opportunity to design their own stained-glass window to tell the story. *Provide paper, felt tips, pencils, or pastels and stained-glass window templates (p. 229 or website).*

- Invite the children to make a representation of the angel Gabriel, providing angel templates for those who'd like a starting point but also encouraging free exploration of what an angel might look like. *Provide paper, pencils/crayons, scissors, glue, angel templates (p. 213 or website). Optional: collage materials (p. 208), ribbon/string/wool, in case the children would like to convert the angel into a Christmas tree decoration.*

Mary's Song

- Invite the children to paint Mary's face with pastels or paints. 'I wonder what Mary looked like?' Encourage the children to think of a 'strong woman' they know who would be brave enough to say 'yes' to God like Mary (their mum, teacher, aunt, head teacher, granny, a friend) to use as a model. Or the children might like to let their imagination go wild. *Provide paper, crayons/pencils or paints/pastels, or other interesting media (p. 209). Optional: you may like to provide face templates (p. 222 or website) as a guide..*

- Give the children the opportunity to make Christmas cards, or to send a Christmas postcard to someone to share the Good News that Baby Jesus is coming! *Provide card-making materials. You might also provide scissors, glue, and last year's Christmas cards with characters from the Nativity story in case the children would like to cut them up to use on their own cards. Optional: you may like to provide postcard templates (p. 227 or website).*

- Give the children the opportunity to tape paper to the bottom of a chair, to lie down under the chair and draw a picture while upside down. The world looks different from down there! Everything is topsy turvy! *Provide paper, masking tape, and pencils/crayons/pastels.*

The Angels' Song

- Give the children the opportunity to make paper angels that multiply before their eyes. *Provide fold-out paper angel templates (p. 214 or website, instructions on p. 212), scissors, and pencils/crayons/pastels.*

- Invite the children to make their own sheep to retell the story at home. *Provide sheep template (p. 218 or website), pencils/crayons. Optional: glue and collage materials (p. 208), including cotton wool and black/brown crepe or tissue paper.*

- Give the children the opportunity to explore van Gogh's picture *The Starry Night* and then to paint or draw their own night sky filled with the light from stars and angels. *Provide copies of van Gogh's* The Starry Night *(search online) and paints/crayons/pencils/pastels.*

- Invite the children to turn pre-made (or bought) gingerbread people into shepherds or angels with icing and sprinkles. Try to leave as much space as possible for their own imagination and interpretation. If you have the facilities, you could even make the gingerbread shapes together using Nativity dough cutters. *Provide: pre-made (or bought) gingerbread people (or dough and cutters), bowls of different coloured icing with teaspoons, sprinkles.*

Meet Baby Jesus!

- This story is much shorter than other stories in the storybox, to open up the opportunity for a longer Creative Response time. You may wish to use this time for the children to make their own presents for Baby Jesus or you could offer a range of choices from any of the Creative Response starter ideas in this unit. You may like to offer Christmas wrapping paper and sticky tape so that the children can wrap the present that they will give to Baby Jesus.

The Shepherds' Story!

- Invite the children to make their own sheep to retell the story at home. *Provide sheep template (p. 228 or website), pencils/crayons. Optional: glue and collage materials (p. 208), including cotton wool and black/brown crepe or tissue paper.*

- Give the children an opportunity to create a picture of the sky filled with angels or light or both! *Provide black or dark paper, white, yellow, orange, gold and silver pastels, crayons or chalks. Optional: glue and light-coloured collage materials (p. 208).*

- Invite the children to create pictures of the shepherd children running fast! *Optional:* what is the fastest they have ever run? Can you draw a picture of yourself with the shepherd children running as fast as you can?! What about drawing as fast as you can too?! *Provide paper, crayons/pencils or paints/pastels, or other interesting media (p. 209).*

- *See also ideas from 'The Angels' Song' above*

Candle 1: The Patriarchs and Matriarchs (Abraham and Sarah)

- Give the children the opportunity to explore van Gogh's picture *The Starry Night* and then to paint or draw their own night sky filled with the light from stars and angels. *Provide copies of van Gogh's* The Starry Night *(search online) and paints/crayons/pencils/pastels.*

- Invite the children to create pictures of the sky filled with stars! *Provide black or dark paper, white, yellow, orange, gold and silver pastels, crayons or chalks. Optional: glue and white/gold/silver-coloured tissue paper squares (3–5 cm) which could be rolled into balls to create the stars.*

- Give the children the opportunity to make a 'journey stick', which tells the story of Abraham and Sarah's journey (or their journey to church, or another journey that's important to them). Journey sticks have been used for a long time in many cultures around the world. They can help retell the story of a journey through the use of colour, or by means of things collected along the journey (leaves, feathers, seed pods, etc.). Encourage the children to remember moments in the journey from start to finish and add different-coloured wool – or tie a symbol to their stick – for each part of that journey. They can use their stick to tell the story of the journey. *Provide real sticks, wool, string, collage materials and age-appropriate things to tie on such as leaves and feathers.*

- Invite the children to create a collage of people from all over the world cut out from magazines or newspapers. Abraham and Sarah had so many children's children! Look how different they all are! *Provide appropriate newspaper and magazine pages, glue, scissors and paper.*

- Challenge the children to draw as many people on a piece of paper as possible. How many can fit on? When they've finished ask them to see if they can count them! *Provide paper, crayons/pencils or paints/pastels, or other interesting media (p. 209).*

Candle 2: Prophets of Old (Isaiah)

- Invite the children to explore light dawning in the darkness by creating their own 'light' patterns with oil pastels, paint, or chalk on dark paper. Optional: draw silhouettes of people walking in the dark with black oil pastels. *Provide dark paper plus oil pastels/paint/chalk.*

- Today's story is all about the names of Jesus. Our names are important! Give the children a choice of name to write themselves and decorate or provide paper with a name already written on it. They could write the name 'Jesus', one or more of the names that Isaiah gives 'Wonderful Guide/Almighty God/Father for ever/Prince of Peace', or they could write their own name. When we're baptized into God's family our name is always said over us. You can't be baptized without a name! Our names matter and God knows each of us by name! *Provide paper, crayons/pencils or paints/pastels, or other interesting media (p. 209).*

Candle 3: John the Baptist

- Invite the children to make their own wilderness scene. All we can see in the wilderness is sand and rocks and sky! The children may like to draw John the Baptist in the wilderness, or leave it empty. *Provide paper, glue, sand (or brown sugar) and small pebbles.*

- Invite the children to make their own wilderness tray (see p. 47). *Provide sand, pebbles and a box or tub from recycling. Tubs with lids (e.g. margarine tubs, takeaway containers) are ideal for transportation home.*

- Invite the children to make their own figure of John the Baptist wearing sackcloth. Give them the chance to explore what they think the prophet may have looked like. Would they like to model John on a strong person they know themselves? They might like to attach a stick to their figure with masking tape. *Provide body template (p. 218 or website), pencils/pastels/ crayons/paints. Optional: glue and camel/sand/brown-coloured collage materials, twigs and masking tape.*

- Give the children the opportunity to make their own John the Baptist figure from a dolly peg or takeaway wooden spoon or fork. *Provide dolly pegs/wooden spoon/fork, sackcloth/brown fabric/felt, felt tips/pencils/crayons, glue.*

- Invite children aged 6+ to create an image of the way through the wilderness that John is preparing! Give them an A4 landscape piece of paper folded in two on the short edge. Ask them to draw a really challenging path in the top half over high mountains and low valleys, on rough ground and very winding paths. Then on the bottom half a complete straight path that everyone can walk on easily. *Provide A4 paper folded in half plus crayons/pencils or paints/pastels, or other interesting media (p. 209).*

Candle 4: Mary, Jesus' Mummy

- Choose from the Creative Response starter ideas for 'Mary's Story' (p. 138) and 'Mary's Song' (p. 138) above.

Candle 5: Jesus, Light of the World!

- Invite the children to make a darkness/light collage by decorating one half of a piece of paper with dark colours and the other half with light colours. *Provide white/dark paper folded in half, glue, dark collage materials and gold, white, yellow, orange and silver collage materials (p. 208; e.g. tinfoil).*

- Invite the children to explore light shining in the darkness by creating their own 'light' patterns with oil pastels, paint, or chalk on dark paper. *Provide dark paper plus oil pastels/paint/chalk.*

- Invite the children to create a collage of the sun rising behind a silhouetted building. *Provide: white card, glue, orange/pink/ yellow/red tissue or crepe paper squares to create a sunrise collage, the shape of a silhouetted building on black paper, as well as blank sheets of black paper for children who prefer to create their own silhouette. For the silhouetted building, you may like to use the church template (see website), or you may prefer to ask an artistic adult or child to make a simple outline of your own church or a local building. Note: the silhouette only needs to be drawn once (on black or white paper) and placed on the top of a pile of black paper: the sheets of paper can then all be cut at the same time.*

- You may like to put a candle out of reach in a safe place and invite the children to make an observational drawing of it. Talk with them about which colours they can see in the light. *Provide pastels/chalks on dark paper, or crayons/felt tips/pencils on white paper.*

- Invite the children to explore light shining in the darkness by creating their own 'light' patterns with neon paints, or even glow-in-the-dark paints, on dark paper. *Provide dark paper plus neon or luminous paint.*

The Christingle's Story

> **Tip**
>
> There are more examples of creative starter ideas for the Christingle's Story within the Sowing Seeds resources on the Children's Society website (www.childrenssociety.org.uk).

- Give the children the opportunity to make their own Christingle. Try to provide only the support that they absolutely need. It's far more important that the child feels that this is THEIR Christingle, than that it looks perfect to an adult's eyes. To learn how to make a Christingle and for tips on how to do this most easily with small children (for instance, making mini versions from satsumas and birthday candles and using thin red sticky tape, which is easier for young children to manipulate than ribbon), go to the Sowing Seeds resources on the Children's Society website (www.childrenssociety.org.uk). Remember if you're using satsumas, it's easier for little hands to insert the candle if you turn it upside down. Encourage the child to sing the Christingle song quietly with you as you construct the Christingle to support their understanding of the different parts.

- Ask the children to draw pictures of your local area or church/school or provide them with a map, pictures or photographs of your local area to work with. Invite them to show Jesus' light shining bright in your place with white/yellow/gold/orange/red collage, or paint. *Provide drawing paper and pens/crayons/pastels/pencils or a map/pictures of your local area plus white/yellow/gold/orange/red/neon paint, or glue and tissue paper cut into small shapes.*

- Invite the children to draw themselves as a Christingle character! How will they make the Christingle look like them? Can they show their little light shining really bright and sharing light? *Provide Christingle character templates from the Children's Society website (www.childrenssociety.org.uk) or plain paper and crayons/pencils/pens/paints.*

- Challenge the children to make two or more Christingle characters that look like them and members of their friends or family. They could cut these Christingle characters out, attach them to a stick/lollipop stick/paper straw, and use them to tell stories of different ways that they could share Jesus' love and light in their place. *Provide Christingle character templates from the Children's Society website (www.childrenssociety.org.uk) or plain paper and crayons/pencils/pens. Optional: scissors, sticks/lollipop sticks/straws and tape.*

- Give the children the opportunity to make their own edible Christingles. Invite the children to spread orange icing over a biscuit to make the 'world'. Leaving space in the centre of the biscuit for the 'candle', a red strawberry lace can be placed on the biscuit to show Jesus' love. Raisins or soft sweets can be placed directly onto the biscuit (without the use of cocktail sticks) to show the fruits of the world. To create a 'candle', children could build up a small column of three white chocolate buttons (with orange icing between each layer) in the centre of the biscuit. A tiny dollop of orange icing or an orange or yellow jelly tot (or similar) can then be placed on top of the 'candle' to show Jesus, Light of the World. Alternatively, a jelly baby could be placed in the centre of the biscuit to represent Baby Jesus. If the children make more than one Christingle biscuit each, and you're meeting as part of a church, nursery, school, or similar, you could SHARE them with others, or sell them afterwards to raise money for the Children's Society. *Provide rich tea biscuits (or similar), orange icing (premade by mixing icing sugar, orange food colouring and a little water), red strawberry laces, raisins or small soft sweets (such as dolly mixtures, jelly tots, Smarties™ or similar), plus white chocolate buttons or jelly babies to represent Jesus, the Light of the World.*

Interactive Nativity with Mini Carols

- Choose from any of the Creative Response starter ideas in this unit and the next unit, 'Jesus, Light of the World!'

Sensory Starter Ideas (including for babies and toddlers)

Note: Some of these Creative Responses can remain the same for the 'Jesus, Light of the World! (Epiphany) unit in the weeks immediately after Christmas.

You could provide:

- a Baby Jesus doll along with a Moses basket, manger or cardboard box. You could even provide real hay for the children to explore;

- Christmas cards of famous Nativity paintings or major characters from the stories. You could also provide a box with a slot cut into it for the children to post the cards, or make them into sewing cards by punching holes and providing shoelaces for threading;

- a durable Nativity set (for example, PlayMobil 123's Christmas manger);

- a range of animals (either plastic or soft) from the Nativity stories: sheep, a donkey, cows, hens;

- Nativity figures in a cloth bag, box or socks for the children to discover and explore;

- torches or sensory light toys like flashing stars or light sticks;

- board books with Nativity stories, or *That's Not My Angel* by Fiona Watt and Rachel Wells (London: Usborne, 2009; 2012);

- dressing up materials: tea towels, Nativity outfits, angel outfits (white fairy costumes with a halo), sheep or donkey masks;

- a light box. Put battery fairy lights (or similar) into a transparent plastic box and tape the lid firmly shut. Provide different coloured cellophane paper, tissue paper or other child-safe items that light can shine through. Include some items that no light shines through to create a contrast;

- a small durable Christmas tree to decorate with Nativity characters cut from old Christmas cards and attached to ribbon;

- building bricks (or other construction toys, e.g. Mega blocks, Duplo, Stickle Bricks, Kapla, Polydron) and 'small world' figures. Invite the children to build the Temple, Mary's house, a shepherd's hut, the manger – anything they like;

- wooden, plastic or jigsaw numbers. You could even use these to count down the weeks (or days, if from ten) to Christmas together;

- a range of different Christmas smells for the children to explore. Add drops of essential oils to scraps of material and place in little pots for the children to investigate. Or make baby-safe versions of the bags from 'Baby John's Story' (p. 138), using small socks and tightly tied string.

Unit Starter Ideas

You could use any of the story starter ideas from 'Candle 5: Jesus, Light of the World!' (p. 141).

Advent wreaths and candles

- If your church uses an Advent wreath, give the children an opportunity to design their own wreath or wreath hat. Traditionally, four purple or blue candles (or three purple and one pink: check your church's wreath) are placed around the wreath, standing for the four weeks of Advent, with one white central candle. However, the children might like to explore their own symbolism. *Provide candle templates (p. 219 or website) and glue, paints/pens/crayons/pencils. You could also provide green paper strips to make hatbands, circle templates (p. 220 or website), and/or paper plates.*

- Invite the children to decorate a candle to celebrate Jesus, Light of the World. What would they like to do with their candle? Leave it as it is? Attach it to string to make a necklace or to a band of paper to make a hat? *Provide candle templates (p. 219 or website), scissors, crayons/pencils/pastels/paints. If you have collage materials (p. 208), glue, string, hatbands (p. 212), masking tape, make these available too.*

- Invite the children to make a candle from a cardboard roll wrapped in white/coloured paper or from white card, rolled and taped. Invite them to decorate the candle in their own way. They may like to collage it with purple or blue collage, or draw pictures from today's story, or they may have their own ideas. If they're using pencils, they may find it easier to decorate card before rolling it up to form the candle. *Provide cardboard rolls (e.g. kitchen/tinfoil/cling film rolls) or card and sticky tape, blue/green collage materials (p. 208), glue and pencils/crayons/pastels/paints.*

Christmas tree and other decorations

- Invite the children to make foil decorations by cutting different shapes from foil and asking an adult to add a hole before threading string/wool through. *Provide foil, ribbon/wool/string, hole punch (either A4 or a single hole punch).*

- Give the children the opportunity to make tree decorations from last year's Christmas cards. Encourage them to explore the cards and cut out different shapes. Once an adult has made a hole, they could then thread a string through to hang the decorations. *Provide Christmas cards, scissors, hole punch, wool/string/ribbon.*

God's messenger angels

- Invite the children to make their own angel mobile from simple angel templates hung with ribbon. *Provide wire coat hangers (or two sticks covered in tinfoil and fastened in a cross), angel templates (p. 213 or website), pencils/paints/crayons, glue and collage materials, hole punch, ribbon/string.*

- Give the children the opportunity to explore an angel detail from a famous painting (or a photograph), or an angel in your church building, then invite them to create their own painting. Encourage them to use their imaginations freely. *Provide an angel detail from a painting, interesting media (p. 209).*

- Invite the children to collage their own angel: 'I wonder what angels might look like?' *Provide: angel templates (p. 213 or website), glue, scissors, collage materials (p. 208).*

- Give the children the opportunity to make gingerbread people into angels. Encourage them to use their imaginations freely. *Provide pre-made (or bought) gingerbread people, bowls with different coloured icing, a range of sprinkles.*

- See also the Creative Response starter ideas for 'The Angels' Song' (p. 139).

Nativity characters

- Invite the children to make their own Nativity puppet sets so they can tell the story themselves at home. Remember to encourage the children to develop the resources in their own ways and to make their own connections. *Provide finger-puppet templates (p. 223 or website, instructions on p. 212), scissors, crayons/pencils.*

- Give the children the opportunity to experiment and create with Nativity stencils. *Provide Nativity stencils, paper, paint or pencils.*

- Invite the children to create their own Nativity scene. *Provide modelling clay or salt dough (which is softer for little fingers, recipe p. 210). Optional extras: rolling pins, salt dough tools or even Nativity-themed animal and people dough cutters.*

Jesus, Light of the World! unit (Epiphany)

These starter ideas are designed to spark imaginations and open up opportunities for the children to respond creatively in their different ways to the worship and storytelling you've taken part in together.

Story Starter Ideas relate directly to the Bible Storytelling of each session, including a print-and-go option.
Sensory Starter Ideas are designed for sensory explorers, including babies and toddlers. These can remain the same through the whole unit.
Unit Starter Ideas are designed to remain relevant throughout the whole unit. Keeping these resources available each week gives children the opportunity to deepen and develop their responses, while making preparation more manageable for leaders.

Tip: Free response area

In addition to any other resources you provide, keeping a free response area available every week will give the children the opportunity to create anything they wish in response to the story they've told, building their sense of confidence and personal responsibility. In this area you could simply provide blank paper and crayons, pencils, paints or pastels. If you have them, other interesting media (see p. 209) will provide even more scope for the children to nurture and strengthen their imaginative skills.

Story Starter Ideas

The Magi's Journey

- Invite the children to decorate their own star. What would they like to do with it: leave it as it is, add it to a picture or attach it to a hatband or lollipop stick or straw? Some children may even like to design their own star shape on blank paper. *Provide star template (p. 230 or website) and blank paper, scissors, pencils/pens/crayons. If you have glue, tinfoil, any collage materials (p. 208), make these available too. You could even provide ribbon, ribbon, crepe/tissue paper strips to trail from the star.*

- Give the children the opportunity to make their own telescope or pair of binoculars. Invite them to decorate a sheet of paper/card with patterns (and/or stars), then show them how to roll the paper up and secure it with tape to create a telescope (one roll) or binoculars (two rolls). *Provide A4 card/paper, masking/sticky tape. You could even provide readymade cardboard tubes (for example, from kitchen roll or tinfoil rolls) for the children to decorate.*

- Invite the children to make a star from salt dough and to make it shine with bright paints. *Provide salt dough (recipe p. 210) and bright paints.*

- Invite the children to create star shapes from spaghetti: these could be triangular stars or asterisk stars, or the children may like to explore other shapes. Your group may like to explore transient art (in which case simply provide dyed uncooked spaghetti). Alternatively, to create longer-lasting shapes (and for a messier option), provide cooked spaghetti and PVA glue (coloured by paint if you like) in small bowls. Encourage the children to dip the spaghetti into the glue, then to make shapes on waxed/baking paper. Once the shapes have dried (overnight), they can be lifted off the waxed paper and hung up. *Provide uncooked/cold cooked spaghetti, plus (optional) PVA glue in small bowls, waxed paper.*

- It's an ancient Epiphany tradition for families to gather to ask for God's blessing on their home and all who visit or live there. Chalk is used to write **20 + C + M + B + 25** (or whichever year you are in) on the lintel, the doorstep or close to the door of the house, along with prayers asking Jesus to visit and be present in that home. Give the children the opportunity to lead their family in this Epiphany tradition by offering them a piece of chalk, instructions and the prayers to take home (see the Sowing Seeds website). Your church might like to bless the chalk at the end of a Sunday service, before sending the congregation out to pray for God's blessing on their homes. *Note*: C M B represents the traditional names of the Magi (Casper, Melchior and Balthazar) as well as the Latin words *Christus mansionem benedictat*, 'May Christ bless the house.'

The Magi's Gifts

- Invite the children to design a Magi crown for themselves or a crown for Baby Jesus, the King of Kings. What will their unique crown look like? *Provide crown template (p. 221 or website), scissors, pencils/crayons/pastels and masking or sticky tape. You could also provide collage materials (p. 208) and glue if you have them.*

- Give the children the opportunity to create their own treasure chest, filled with their gifts. They may like to write or draw what their gifts are inside, or they may prefer to use collage materials or pencils/crayons to fill the chest with 'treasure'. Remember to give them space to explore freely their own ideas. *Provide treasure chest template (p. 232 or website), pencils/crayons/pastels, scissors. If you have collage materials (p. 208, especially gold/silver collage) and glue, make these available too.*

- Invite the children to write or draw their gifts on a star or heart shape, or they may prefer to use their creative gifts to decorate one of these shapes with collage materials. You could even invite the children to wrap them up with Christmas wrapping paper as a present for Baby Jesus. *Provide star and/or large heart templates (p. 230 and p. 226, or website) and scissors plus pencils/crayons/paints/pastels. If you have collage materials (p. 208), glue, wrapping paper and sticky/masking tape, make these available too.*

- Give the children the opportunity to use their creative gifts as a gift for Jesus by creating new things from recycling. Encourage them to use their imagination and creativity freely. *Provide recycled items such as boxes, tubs, cartons, pots, paper, newspaper plus glue, string, sticky/masking tape.*

- Invite the children to draw round their hands on paper or make handprints with paint or salt dough. As the children create and decorate their open hands, encourage them to wonder what gifts they have to give Baby Jesus. The most important gift that all of us are given is love. In what ways do we like to show our love to God and other people? *Provide paper and pencils/crayons and scissors, or paper and paints, or salt dough (recipe p. 210) and dough cutters.*

- Give the children the opportunity to explore their gifts and wonder what they could give to God by decorating a body template to look like themselves. In pictures, saints are often depicted holding something to symbolize who they are and the gifts they gave to God. What would the children like to show themselves holding as a gift they have to give to God? A pencil, a ball, a favourite toy, a heart? Give them lots of space to hold whatever they choose, or present themselves with empty, open hands. *Provide body template (p. 218 and website), pencils/crayons/pastels/paints. If you have collage materials (p. 208), make these available too.*

Tip

At Epiphany, your church might like to invite the children – if they would like – to present their Creative Responses – or another symbol of their gifts such as an undecorated heart or star – to Baby Jesus in a manger during the Sunday service. These could be wrapped in Christmas paper or simply come as they are. It may help to reassure the children that they can still take their responses home with them even if they choose to offer them up during the service like this.

Baby Jesus, the Refugee

- Invite the children to make a body template into an image of a refugee, themselves, Joseph, Mary or someone else as a reminder of our shared humanity. If the children choose to make a refugee, they may also like to give them a name and age. *Provide body template (p. 218 or website), pencils/crayons/pastels, scissors. If you have glue and collage materials (p. 208, including fabrics) make these available too.*

- Some children may like to explore Jesus, the baby refugee, and remember other baby refugees across the world. *Provide the baby template (p. 215 or website), pencils/crayons/paints and scissors.*

- Give the children the opportunity to make a refugee 'icon' from a body template, glued to thick card wrapped in tinfoil. *Provide body template (p. 218 or website), pencils/crayons/pastels, scissors, glue, card rectangles, tinfoil to wrap around the card.*

- Imagine having to pack your case quickly and run! What would the children take with them? Invite them to draw these things in their suitcase. *Provide suitcase template (p. 231 or website).*

Tip

You could invite the children to give their creations to friends and family, asking them to remember refugees who've had to flee their homes like Mary, Joseph and Jesus. You may like to provide the children with a note to attach to the back, for example:

Please pray with us for refugees. Thank you.

**Jesus, Light of the World,
as a baby, you were a refugee.
Help us to be part of shining your light
on refugees.
Help us to welcome them
and make a safe place for them. Amen.**

- Invite the children to decorate bought or pre-made biscuits with coloured icing and sprinkles. Shapes of people (e.g. gingerbread people) or stars would be particularly appropriate. Sell the biscuits to raise money for an appropriate charity connected with refugees.

- Give the children the opportunity to make their own biscuits. Provide them with readymade biscuit mixture or scone dough and biscuit cutters and invite them to make their own shapes. Shapes of people (e.g. gingerbread people) or stars would be particularly appropriate. Bake the biscuits and then sell them to raise money for an appropriate charity connected with refugees.

- Choose another starter idea from the 'Jesus, Light of the World!' unit or beyond to sell to raise money for a charity connected with refugees, or to give to people, asking them to remember refugees who've had to flee their homes like Mary, Joseph and Jesus.

Anna the Prophet's Story

- Invite the children to paint Anna's face with pastels or paints. 'I wonder what Anna looked like?' Encourage the children to think of a 'strong older woman' they know to use as a model. Or the children might like to let their imagination go wild. *Provide paper, crayons/pencils or paints/pastels, or other interesting media (p. 209). Optional: you may like to provide face templates (p. 222 or website) as a guide.*

- Anna was a prophet. A prophet is someone who learns to see the world differently: through God's eyes. Give the children the opportunity to make their own telescope or pair of binoculars. Invite them to decorate a sheet of paper/card with patterns (and/or stars), then show them how to roll the paper up and secure it with tape to create a telescope (one roll) or binoculars (two rolls). Imagine this telescope/these binoculars can help us see with God's eyes! How would things look different? *Provide A4 card/paper, masking/sticky tape. You could even provide readymade cardboard tubes (for example, from kitchen roll or tinfoil rolls) for the children to decorate.*

- Anna's song encouraged God's People to 'Look up!' and around them to see God at work. Encourage the children to look up and around them to notice something small in the room that people might not always notice: perhaps a spider's web or an interesting pattern or something else that people don't usually take time to see. Give the children the opportunity to draw what they see. *Provide paper, crayons/pencils or paints/pastels, or other interesting media (p. 209).*

- Anna's song encouraged God's People to 'Stand tall!' Invite them to create a picture of someone standing tall and strong, even when things feel hard. Do they know someone who stands tall and strong like that? *Provide dark or black paper plus oil pastels or chalks.*

Jesus, Light of the World!

- Invite the children to decorate a candle to celebrate Jesus, Light of the World. What would they like to do with their candle? Leave it as it is? Attach it to string to make a necklace or to a band of paper to make a hat? *Provide candle templates (p. 219 or website), scissors, crayons/pencils/pastels/paints. If you have collage materials (p. 208), glue, string, hatbands (p. 212), masking tape, make these available too.*

- Invite older children to make paper lanterns to celebrate Jesus, Light of the World. Show the children how to fold the lantern template in half and cut down the lines. Then show them how to reopen the paper, make it into a circular lantern, and tape or glue it together and attach the handle. If your group has a longer time for Creative Response, you could invite the children to decorate their paper before cutting it. *Provide lantern template (p. 225 or website) on coloured paper if possible, scissors, glue or sticky/masking tape, pencils/crayons.*

- Invite the children to create an image of Jesus, Light of the World, shining in their hearts and filling them with light. The children may like to draw a picture of Jesus, or they may prefer to create something more impressionistic. Give them space to explore their own response. *Provide large heart templates (p. 226 or website), scissors, gold and silver collage materials (p. 208) and glue.*

- Jesus is the Light of the World! Give the children the opportunity to create their own 2D globe by taking a paper plate and painting it with blue and green paints, sticking green and blue tissue/crepe paper to it or attaching green dried pasta with blue glue. Expect these 'globes' to be very impressionistic! *Provide paper plates, green and blue collage materials (p. 208), paints, or green dried pasta (p. 210) and PVA glue coloured with blue paint. Once the children have created their globe you could also provide yellow/gold collage materials and invite the children to add them on or around the paper plate to show Jesus, the Light of the World.*

- Invite the children to make a globe light-catcher by gluing green and blue tissue paper to a circle of wax paper. Expect these globes to be impressionistic! *Provide circles of wax/baking paper (some pound shops sell ready-cut circles), glue, green and blue tissue paper cut into small (if possible, irregular) shapes.*

- Invite the children to imagine Jesus' light spreading through the world by gluing red, yellow and orange tissue paper on a map of the world. *Provide a black-and-white map of the world, glue, orange, yellow and red tissue paper cut into small shapes.*

Sensory Starter Ideas (including for babies and toddlers)

Some of these Creative Responses can remain the same as those for the previous The Light of the World is Dawning unit (Advent–Christmas), giving young children the opportunity to strengthen and deepen their engagement with the stories around Baby Jesus.

Resources that you might provide for the children (including babies and toddlers) to explore for themselves include:

- a Baby Jesus doll along with a Moses basket, manger or cardboard box. You could even provide real hay for the children to explore;

- Christmas cards of famous paintings showing the Magi and star from the stories. You could also provide a box with a slot cut into it for the children to post the cards or make them into sewing cards by punching holes and providing shoelaces for threading;

- different terrain that the Magi may have travelled over for the children to explore (either on trays or in transparent plastic bottles): rocks, pebbles, sand, water;

- a durable Nativity set that includes the Magi figures;

- building blocks to create an obstacle course for the Magi;

- torches, camping lanterns or sensory light toys like flashing stars or light sticks;

- survival blankets and unwanted CDs (these make amazing sparkly sensory objects for young babies to explore light);

- a toddler-friendly globe, map jigsaw or map for the children to explore;

- a light box. Put battery fairy lights (or similar) into a clear box and tape the lid firmly shut. Provide different coloured cellophane paper, tissue paper or other child-safe objects that light can shine through. Include some items that no light shines through to create a contrast;

- board books telling the story of the star and the Magi;

- dressing up clothes: robes, crowns, gifts, telescopes, binoculars, stars, camel masks;

- salt dough (recipe p. 210) plus star, Nativity, crown, camel cutters, etc.;

- Epiphany smells: add drops of essential oils of myrrh and frankincense to scraps of material and place in little pots for the children to explore;

- pictures of stars, star globes, telescopes, binoculars.

Unit Starter Ideas

Jesus, Light of the World!

- Invite the children to add stars to a night sky. *Provide dark paper, star stickers or star shapes and glue.*

- Give the children the opportunity to create a light painting. Invite them to draw a star, or any picture they like, using yellow/white wax crayons on white paper. Encourage the children to paint over this drawing with a thin blue/black watercolour or watered-down paint. Watch the light shining through the darkness! *Provide white paper, white/yellow wax crayons, blue/black watercolour or thinned paint, paintbrushes.*

- Invite the children to explore the contrast of light and dark with collage materials or chalks/pastels. *Provide black/dark paper and yellow/white/orange chalks or pastels, or gold/silver/white collage materials (p. 208).*

- Give the children the opportunity to create a stained glass 'window' that they can see the light shine through, just as Jesus, the Light of the World, can shine through us. Invite them to glue brightly coloured tissue/cellophane/crepe paper to squares or circles of wax/baking paper. Older children may like to precede this by folding up a black or coloured piece of paper three to four times, cutting shapes out of it, opening it out again, then gluing this to the wax/baking paper to act as a backdrop or frame. *Provide rectangles or arched window shapes of baking/wax paper, glue and brightly coloured tissue/crepe/cellophane paper (e.g. transparent sweet wrappers from Christmas). Optional: black/dark paper and scissors. If you do use black paper, the stained glass 'windows' may need to be trimmed after the paper has been added. You may even like to have one or more torches available on the table so the children can see the light shining through for themselves.*

- See also the options from story starter ideas for 'Jesus, Light of the World!' (p. 146).

The Magi

- Give the children the opportunity to create their own collages of the Magi from old Christmas cards that include pictures of the Magi, Nativity and star. *Provide paper, old Christmas cards, glue, pencils/crayons/pastels.*

- Invite the children to make their own Magi from finger-puppet templates. *Provide finger-puppet template (p. 223 or website), pencils/crayons, scissors, glue. Optional extras: collage materials (p. 208 including fabric and coloured paper).*

- Invite the children to make their own Magi puppets from figures cut from Christmas cards then stood upright with plasticine, or attached to lollipop sticks/ twigs. You could even invite the children to make a backdrop for the Magi from Christmas cards or their own imagination (or a bit of both). *Provide Christmas cards featuring the Magi, scissors, plasticine or lollipop sticks/wooden twigs, plus glue/masking tape and plain paper.*

John the Baptist and Baptism unit (the weeks before Lent)

These starter ideas are designed to spark imaginations and open up opportunities for the children to respond creatively in their different ways to the worship and storytelling you've taken part in together.

Story Starter Ideas relate directly to the Bible Storytelling of each session, including a print-and-go option.
Sensory Starter Ideas are designed for sensory explorers, including babies and toddlers. These can remain the same through the whole unit.
Unit Starter Ideas are designed to remain relevant throughout the whole unit. Keeping these resources available each time gives children the opportunity to deepen and develop their responses, while making preparation more manageable for leaders.

Story Starter Ideas

The stories told in this unit share a number of strong themes, for instance the River Jordan and baptism. For this reason, there are more unit starter ideas than story starter ideas for this unit.

Meet John

- Invite the children to make their own figure of John the Baptist wearing sackcloth. Give them the chance to explore what they think the prophet may have looked like. Would they like to model John on a strong person they know themselves? They might like to attach a stick to their figure with masking tape. *Provide body template (p. 218 or website), pencils/pastels/crayons/paints. Optional: glue and camel/sand/brown-coloured collage materials, twigs and masking tape (p. 208).*

- Invite the children to make a moving picture of someone being baptized in the River Jordan. First, give them the opportunity to create their own man, woman or child (freehand or by decorating a body template). This could be someone they know, someone from the story or themselves. Older children may then like to have a go at making their own 'river', by folding the short edge of a piece of A4 blue paper approximately in half, cutting a wavy slit into the fold, then opening the paper up again. You may like to add the wavy slits before the session for very young children. Show the children how to slide the figure into the slit and move them up and down. They may even like to attach a lollipop stick or twig to their baptism candidate. *Provide small body templates (p. 217 or website), plain paper, pencils/pastels/crayons/paints and blue paper, lollipop sticks or twigs and masking tape. Masking tape will also come in handy for when the slits inevitably break or are cut close to the edges of the paper!*

- Give the children the opportunity to make their own John the Baptist figure from a dolly peg. *Provide dolly pegs, sackcloth/brown fabric/felt, felt tips/pencils/crayons, glue.*

- See also the various 'River Jordan' and 'Our Baptism' unit starter ideas below (p. 154).

John Baptizes Jesus

- Invite the children to make their own dove. What would they like to do with it? Keep it as it is? Or add it to a bigger picture or collage, attach string to make a necklace or tape it to a hatband (p. 212). Would they like to add wings? If you have curling ribbon/crepe streamers, would they like to add these to the dove's tail or elsewhere? Or do they have their own ideas? *Provide bird template (p. 216), scissors and glue. Optional extras: twigs/lollipop sticks, masking tape, string, white collage materials/feathers (p. 208), curling ribbon/crepe streamers (give the children the choice between blue/green for water or red/gold/orange/yellow for fire; they may even like to choose a bit of both!). If they are making necklaces, make sure the string/wool can easily snap when pulled and is attached as two separate ends to prevent accidents.*

- Invite the children to make giant medals to show how God is very happy with them! What will they draw on their medal? A smiley face, their name, a picture of Jesus or the water? Or do they have other ideas? *Provide circle templates (p. 220 or website), string/ribbon/wool and masking tape. Make sure the string/wool can easily snap when pulled and is attached as two separate ends to prevent accidents.*

- Give the children the opportunity to use interesting media to draw Jesus' face as they imagine it. I wonder what Jesus looked like? You could use different paintings or people you know as inspiration. *Provide interesting media (p. 209).*

- Give the children the opportunity to create their own icons of the baptism of Jesus. *Provide pencils/crayons/pastels, scissors, glue, a card rectangle, tinfoil to wrap around the card (to create a silver icon background), paper for the children's picture (which can then be glued to the icon background).*

- Invite the children to make a moving picture of Jesus being baptized. See option from 'Meet John' above, but add Jesus to the suggestions of the people they might choose to make.

- See also the various 'River Jordan' and 'Our Baptism' unit starter ideas below (pp. 154 and 155).

Our Baptism

- Give the children the opportunity to make a baptism card for their friends. If you like, you could provide a choice of templates (see below) for the children to use as they wish. Or you could leave it entirely up to their imaginations! *Provide card plus pencils/paints/pastels/crayons. Optional: bird template (p. 216 or website), candle templates (p. 219 or website), body template (p. 218 or website), blue collage materials for water (p. 208) and glue.*

- See also the 'Our Baptism' unit starter ideas below (p. 155).

Jesus Is Thrown into the Wilderness

- Give the children a (lightly) screwed up piece of paper and ask them to open it out. God can make amazing things from rubbish! What can they make from this piece of rubbish? There's nothing on this paper, just as there's nothing in the wilderness! What can they do with it? *Provide lightly screwed up paper and pencils/crayons/pastels/paints.*

- Invite the children to make their own wilderness scene. All we can see in the wilderness is sand and rocks and sky! The children may like to draw Jesus in the wilderness, or leave it empty. *Provide paper, glue, sand (or brown sugar) and small pebbles.*

- Invite the children to make something amazing from rubbish! God loves rubbish! Give them space to use their imaginations freely. *Provide a range of recycling materials plus craft materials and masking tape.*

- Give the children the opportunity to witness new life growing from 'rubbish'. Invite the children to decorate a recyclable container that can act as a plant pot with collage materials. When they're ready, invite them to place a few pieces of folded paper towel and a discarded carrot top (top upwards) in the container. When they get home, they can put a little water on the paper towel and keep it damp (not soaked). Green leaves will grow up from the carrot top! *Provide recyclable containers, collage materials (p. 208), glue, paper towel (or cotton wool), discarded carrot tops.*

- Invite the children to make their own wilderness tray (see p. 47). *Provide sand, pebbles and a box or tub from recycling. Tubs with lids (e.g. margarine tubs, takeaway containers) are ideal for transportation home.*

Sensory Starter Ideas (including for babies and toddlers)

- Your group may like to hold a pancake party, with mini pancakes or traditional pancakes and toppings.
- You may like to hold an egg hunt to make sure you're taking all the eggs out of the room for Lent! *Provide eggs to find: paper eggs, plastic eggs or even mini foil-wrapped eggs.*

You could provide:

- sand (or brown sugar) in clear plastic bottles filled to different levels. Tape the lids shut tight!
- water in clear plastic bottles filled to different levels. You could even add food colouring. Tape the lids shut tight!
- a river cloth and sackcloth;
- different sizes of stones and rocks in a box/feely bag/socks. Where Jesus went into the wilderness there were only rocks and sand. Make sure these are a suitable size for under threes. If they present a choking hazard place these also in a clear bottle and tape the lid shut tight;
- a long roll of paper taped to the floor for children and parents to add wavy blue or green lines with chunky crayons; a sand and/or water tray if appropriate for your setting;
- pictures of rivers or water made into sewing cards by punching holes, with blue or white wool/shoelaces to thread through the picture to look like waves; a wilderness tray (see p. 47);
- shallow tubs of water/blue fabric and 'small world' figures (such as Happyland or Fisher Price plastic figures, or wooden or knitted figures) for the children to roleplay baptizing the people in the water, just as John baptized people in the River Jordan.

Unit Starter Ideas

The River Jordan

- Invite the children to make a wavy River Jordan from spaghetti dyed in different shades of blue and green. *Provide cooked, dyed spaghetti (p. 210).*
- Invite the children to create a wavy River Jordan from string or wool. *Provide string/wool of lots of different lengths, glue, paper. Choose between blue/green wool and white PVA glue, or white string/wool and PVA glue dyed with blue/green paint.*
- Give the children the opportunity to finger paint the River Jordan. *Provide lots of different pots of cornflour paint (p. 210) in different shades of green and blue (created by adding varying amounts of green/blue paint or food colouring).*
- Invite the children to make a River Jordan necklace by threading blue/green dried pasta onto wool or string. *Provide green/blue dried pasta (p. 210), wool/string. It can help to tape both ends of the wool/string and to knot one piece of threaded pasta with the string beforehand. If they are making necklaces, make sure the string/wool can easily snap when pulled.*
- Invite the children to collage the River Jordan. *Provide blue paper and green/blue/silver/white/grey collage resources (p. 208).*
- Give the children the opportunity to explore the different colours in water by looking at a photograph or painting, for instance Monet's *Water-Lily Pond*, then creating their own River Jordan. Remember to give the children space to develop their own responses, even if these differ from the example given. *Provide a photograph or famous picture of water, plus paper and watercolours/pastels.*
- Invite the children to create the scene of John the Baptist by the River Jordan. *Provide rocks, blue fabric and 'small world' people. If your facilities allow for it, you could even provide a water tray instead of blue fabric.*
- Invite the children to create the River Jordan on a paper plate. Will they show the banks of the river, or just the water? *Provide paper plates and either blue/green and yellow/brown paints, or glue and blue/green yellow/brown collage materials (p. 208). You may also like to provide sand/soil.*

Our Baptism

- Invite the children to design a baptism candle with pictures of Jesus' baptism. *Provide candle template (p. 219 or website), pencils/crayons/pastels/paints. Optional: glue and water-coloured collage materials (p. 208).*

- Give the children the opportunity to design their own baptism font. They may like to use the template as a starter, or to create their own shape. Remind them to show the water inside! They might like to decorate the font with patterns, with pictures of John the Baptist or Jesus, or with pictures from the same stories as your church's font. Younger children may like to use collage materials. Remember to give them the space to develop their own ideas. *Provide font template (p. 224 or website), pencils/crayons/pastels/paints. Optional: glue, scissors, collage materials (p. 208).*

- Give the children the opportunity to design their own font, using interesting media. *Provide interesting media (see ideas on p. 209).*

- Invite the children to draw an observational picture of your church's font, either in situ or from a photograph. *Provide paper, pencils/pastels/paints/crayons or interesting media (see ideas on p. 209).*

- Your group may like to create a giant picture of your church's font surrounded by the people of your church. *Provide a large piece of paper/card, body templates (p. 218 or website), pencils/crayons/pastels/paints, a simple outline of your church's font, scissors and glue. Optional: collage materials (p. 208) to dress the people and/or to collage the font.*

- Give the children the opportunity to roleplay 'baptizing' dolls or figures as in your church (particularly if you're not going to do the optional 'Our Baptism' session. Show them how to 'baptize' the dolls with three scoops of water ('In the name of the Father, and of the Son and of the Holy Spirit') or by full immersion and invite them to 'baptize' a range of 'baptism candidates'. *Provide shallow tubs of water and dolls or 'small world' figures.*

- Invite the children to make a baptism candle from a cardboard roll wrapped in white/coloured paper or from white card, rolled and taped. Invite them to decorate the candle in their own way. They may like to collage it with blue/green collage to show the waters of baptism, to draw pictures of John the Baptist or Jesus' baptism, or they may have their own ideas. If they're using pencils, they may find it easier to decorate the candle before rolling it up. *Provide cardboard rolls (e.g. kitchen/tinfoil/cling film rolls) or white card and sticky tape, blue/green collage materials (p. 208), glue and pencils/crayons/pastels/paints.*

- If your church uses a shell to scoop baptismal water, give the children the opportunity to design their own baptism shell. *Provide the children with light-coloured shells from the seaside and invite them to decorate them with felt tips/pastels/paints.*

Part 4
The Building Blocks

Introduction

Sowing Seeds isn't just Bible storytelling. The Building Blocks provide a wide range of prayer, worship and creative materials to resource and nurture your group's time with God. Different groups work in different ways and so the idea is that you choose Building Blocks and options that are appropriate for your group to build your own service.

There's no single way of holding a Sowing Seeds gathering. Groups will continually be faced with developing and flexing as they change in number, experience and age range, as well as with adapting to new children who have different gifts and ways of being

The idea is for your group to explore the material and decide which Building Blocks you'd like to use to build your own session. It can be helpful to think of the Building Blocks as falling into four categories:

- beginning;
- middle;
- middle plus;
- end.

Aim to build a session or service that has a beginning, a middle and an end, which best reflects the shape and feel of worship in your church. In other words, if your church tends to have informal worship, create a session with an informal feel. If your gathering is held during a communion service, then build a communion service for your children (up to 'The Peace', at which you can rejoin the wider congregation to share communion together). If your church uses liturgical colours, then use liturgical colours; if your church has an informal prayer time, then have an informal prayer time, etc.

Because Sowing Seeds has been written to be used across a whole range of traditions, it's likely that there will be material in this chapter that you would never use in your setting! Simply skip over that material and find the options that best fit your group.

Whatever choices you make, we advise that you stick to those choices for one whole so your group can find a rhythm. This will encourage participation and allow for deeper engagement among the children and adults.

> **Tip**
>
> The material includes Building Blocks for every part of a communion service or a Service of the Word. However, it was never envisaged that any group would attempt to use all these Building Blocks each Sunday. That would be far too much for children and leaders alike! For this reason, we would suggest choosing carefully and using only one Prayer Building Block each time.

The Sowing Seeds Website

When building your own session and service, the Sowing Seeds website can be an invaluable resource. All the Building Blocks are laid out there in a format that is easy to cut and paste into your own document. Using the website for the Building Blocks is generally far easier than trying to photocopy the material from this book. In contrast, the Bible Storytelling material has been designed for easy photocopying.

The website also provides a guide to each of the Building Blocks as well as examples of services you could build.

> **Tip**
>
> The members' code for this book on the website is: mustard251.

> **Tip: Presentation folders**
>
> Presentation folders can really help when leading Sowing Seeds. They're much easier to manage than loose sheets, especially when doing actions! And most of the session or service will stay the same for the whole unit, once your group has made your choices so will only need to be printed once: it's only the Bible storytelling material that will change. We've found A5 folders are best.

Teaching Your Group New Songs and Responses

Many of the songs and responses from the Sowing Seeds Building Blocks remain the same every week even when the units change. Still, there will always be a first time these songs and responses need to be learned. Tips on teaching new songs and said responses can be found on the website.

The Building Blocks

Welcome

Welcome your group.

Let's start by going around the circle
and saying our name out loud.
My name's _____.

Go around the circle so that every adult and child has the chance to say her or his name (and introduce any dolls, teddies or toys). If any of the children don't want to say their name, or aren't able to, you (or a parent or carer) could say it for them and wave.

It's time to sing our Welcome Song!

Welcome Song: Option 1

→ Song: 'The Sowing Seeds welcome song'. Words: © Sharon Moughtin.
→ Tune: 'Glory, glory, alleluia!' (traditional).

Wel - come Name _ to St Mar - y's!   Wel - come Name _ to St Mar - y's!

Wel - come Name _ to St Mar - y's! You are wel-come in the name of the Lord.

Go around the circle the same way as above. See if you can remember one another's names and insert them into the song.
Welcome *Name 1* to *St Mary's**
Welcome *Name 1* to *St Mary's**
Welcome *Name 1* to *St Mary's**
You are welcome in the name of the Lord!

* Insert the name of your church or children's group, or sing 'our worship'.

Welcome Song: Option 2

→ **Song:** 'You are welcome in the name of the Lord' (traditional).
→ **Tune:** traditional.

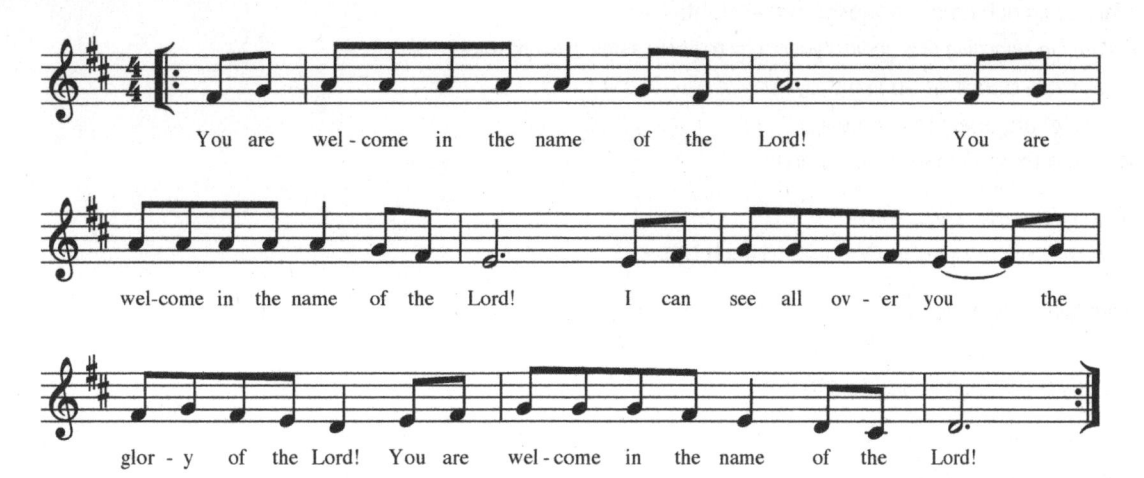

[Musical notation: You are wel-come in the name of the Lord! You are wel-come in the name of the Lord! I can see all ov-er you the glor-y of the Lord! You are wel-come in the name of the Lord!]

Welcome to St Mary's!
Let's wave with one hand. *Lead waving*
Then with our other hand. *Lead waving*
Then let's choose someone and show God's 'glory'!
Move arms up and down in front of you with fingers wiggling, palms facing out, towards one person.
And someone else! *Repeat*
Then let's wave with both hands all around the circle.
Lead waving.

We're ready to sing!
You are welcome in the name of the Lord!
Wave with right hand to one person.
You are welcome in the name of the Lord!
Wave with left hand to another person.
I can see all over you, the glory of the Lord!
Move arms up and down in front of you with fingers wiggling,
palms facing out, towards one person and then another.
You are welcome in the name of the Lord!
Wave with both hands all around the circle.

Getting Ready to Worship

This option is designed with churches or schools who regularly use the sign of the cross or 'The Lord be with you' in mind, to support the children in joining in. If other words of greeting are regularly used, you could use these here instead. If your church or school is more informal, then you could mirror that here.

Getting Ready to Worship: Option 1

→ **Action:** the sign of the cross.
→ **Words:** © Sharon Moughtin.

Invite the children to make the sign of the cross slowly with you. You could lead this 'my turn', 'your turn' or, as the children become more confident, invite a child to lead the action as the whole group says the words and makes the sign of the cross.

In my head,	*Touch head*
in my heart,	*Touch chest*
and all around me,	*Touch shoulders one by one*
Jesus is here.	*Open hands in front, facing upwards*

Getting Ready to Worship: Option 2

→ **Action: 'The Lord be with you' (open hands).**

Let's start by clenching our hands together tightly.
Lead children in clenching fists against your body to show a defensive posture.
When we close ourselves up like this,
it's hard to let anyone into our heart.
It's hard even to let God into our heart!

When we get ready to worship,
we show that we're open to God and to each other.

Open your hands out, facing up.
Can you show me your open hands?
We're ready to let God and each other in!

The Lord be with you.
Hold hands open to the children.

And also with you.
Invite the children to open their hands towards you.

Introducing the Unit

Introducing the Unit: Getting Ready for Baby Jesus: Option 1

It's time to get ready for Christmas!
Baby Jesus is coming!

Introducing the Unit: Getting Ready for Baby Jesus: Option 2

→ **Focus: the liturgical colour, purple.**

Who can tell us what colour season we're in now?
　　If appropriate: You may have seen it in church.

The colour purple
reminds us it's time to 'get ready'!
Baby Jesus is coming at Christmas!

　　If appropriate: Let's all look out for purple when we go back into church.
　　Or: Let's remember to look and see what colour we're in next time we go into church.

Introducing the Unit: Getting Ready for Baby Jesus: Option 3

→ **Optional focus: the liturgical colours white and gold.**
For Christmas Day or the week after Christmas before Epiphany starts on 6 January.

It's Christmas!
Baby Jesus is here!

　　If appropriate:
　　We have our Baby Jesus doll here to remind us.

　　If your church uses visible liturgical colours:
　　Who can tell us what colour Christmas is?
　　If appropriate: You may have seen it in church . . .

Invite a child to respond and accept his or her response.
Gold and white are the colours of joy!
Baby Jesus is here!

Introducing the Unit: Epiphany: Option 1

At the moment, we're celebrating Baby Jesus,
born at Christmas.

Let's close our eyes and feel the dark.
Let's imagine Jesus shining like a tiny star in the sky.
Now let's imagine that light growing brighter and brighter and brighter . . .
until it fills the whole world!
So bright we can't even look at it!
Let's open our eyes again.

Baby Jesus, the Light of the World, is shining bright. *Jazz hands*
Let's show jazz hands for Jesus' light. *Jazz hands*

> *If your group used the 'Busy, busy, busy' Gathering Song in the 'Getting Ready for Baby Jesus' unit (p. 165)*
> Before Christmas, we were 'busy, busy, busy'
> getting ready for Jesus, Light of the World,
> to DAWN in the darkness. *Show the sun rising up and out with your arms*

> Jesus' light was just beginning to come up,
> like the sun in the morning.
> Now Jesus' light is shining BRIGHT! *Jazz hands*
> It's time to celebrate!

Introducing the Unit: Epiphany: Option 2

→ **Focus: the liturgical colours white and gold.**

Who can tell us what colour season we're in now?
> *If appropriate:* You may have seen our colours in church.

White and gold are the colours of joy and celebration!
It's 'Epiphany'!
> *If appropriate:* Can you say 'Epiphany'?
> **Epiphany.**

In 'Epiphany' we celebrate Baby Jesus,
born at Christmas.

Let's close our eyes and feel the dark.
Let's imagine Jesus shining like a tiny star in the sky.
Now let's imagine that light growing brighter and brighter and brighter . . .
until it fills the whole world!
So bright we can't even look at it!
Let's open our eyes again.

Baby Jesus, the Light of the World, is
shining bright. *Jazz hands*
Let's show jazz hands for Jesus' light. *Jazz hands*

> *If your group used the 'Busy, busy, busy' Gathering Song in the 'Getting Ready for Baby Jesus' unit (p. 165)*
> Before Christmas, we were 'busy, busy, busy'
> getting ready for Jesus, Light of the World,
> to DAWN in the darkness. *Show the sun rising up and out with your arms*
> Jesus' light was just beginning to come up,

like the sun in the morning.
Now Jesus' light is shining BRIGHT! *Jazz hands*

That's the message of Epiphany:
Jesus is the Light of the World shining! *Jazz hands*
It's time to celebrate!

Introducing the Unit: John the Baptist unit

It's time to get ready [again]!
This time, it's time to get ready for Jesus the grown-up.

To help us get ready,

> *'Meet John' story:* . . . we need to meet a man called John the Baptist.
> *All other stories:* . . . can anyone remember who we met last week?

If necessary: John the . . . **Baptist**

Let's stand up and be John the Baptist together.
Lead the children in standing.

John wore clothes made from camel hair!
Let's put our camel-hair coat on!
Lead the children in putting on a coat and scratching.
It's very itchy!

John's job was to get the world ready for God!
John called out,
'Get ready for God!' *Cup hands around mouth*

After 3, let's shout, 'Get ready for God!'
1, 2, 3 . . . Get ready for God! *Cup hands around mouth*

Look around I'm not sure anyone heard that.
Let's try that again even louder.
1, 2, 3 . . . Get ready for God! *Cup hands around mouth*

Gathering Song

Choose a Gathering Song according to which unit you're in and the age range of your group. This Gathering Song can stay the same for the whole unit.

Gathering Song: Getting Ready for Baby Jesus: Option 1

→ 'Busy, busy, busy, getting ready for Christmas!' Words © Sharon Moughtin.
→ Tune: 'What shall we do with the drunken sailor?' (traditional).

Bu-sy, bu-sy, bu-sy, get-ting rea-dy for Christ-mas! Bu-sy, bu-sy, bu-sy, get-ting rea-dy for Christ-mas! Bu-sy, bu-sy, bu-sy, get-ting rea-dy for Christ-mas! The Light of the World is dawn-ing! Je-sus, Light of the World! Je-sus, Light of the World! Je-sus, Light of the World, is dawn-ing in the dark-ness!

In week 1, skip the Gathering Song, including the introduction, and move straight into the storytelling, which will introduce the Gathering Song for the rest of Advent.

Baby Jesus is the Light of the World!
Let's close our eyes and feel the dark . . .

We're waiting for Baby Jesus, the Light of the World,
to shine in the darkness!
Let's open our eyes again.

You might like to show the children a picture of the sun rising.
Like we wait for the sun to 'dawn',
to come up, in the morning.

If you're using imaginative aids, ask two or three children to give them out.
Let's show the sun 'dawning' with our bodies.
Let's crouch down low . . .
Let's show the sun coming up and up and out . . .
in the morning.
Lead the children in showing the sun rising with your hands as you stand up.

The sun is 'dawning' in the morning!
Now let's do that as we sing our song,
'Jesus, Light of the World'.

If you're singing this song for the first time with your group, you may find the following introduction helpful.
We have a new song about 'Jesus, Light of the World'.
Let's learn it 'my turn' *Both hands to self,* 'your turn' *Hands out to group*

Sing the words with the tune to the group.
Je-sus, Light of the World, *Both hands to self to show your turn*
Je-sus, Light of the World
Je-sus, Light of the World, *Both hands to group to show their turn*
Je-sus, Light of the World,
Je-sus, Light of the World is *Both hands to self to show your turn*
dawning in the darkness!
Je-sus, Light of the World, is *Both hands to group to show their turn*
dawning in the darkness!

Let's sing that all together and add our actions.

Je-sus, Light of the World, *Sun dawning action*
Je-sus, Light of the World, *Sun dawning action*
Je-sus, Light of the World, is *Sun dawning action*
dawning in the darkness! *Sun dawning action*

Getting ready for Christmas can be very busy!
What have we been doing to get ready for Christmas?

Either invite the children to make suggestions, or choose from the suggestions below. For each activity sing the 'Busy, busy, busy, getting ready for Christmas!' verse with an appropriate action designed by the children, followed by the 'Jesus, Light of the World' refrain:

- hanging lights on the Christmas tree . . . (we use lights at Christmas to remember that Jesus is the Light of the World!)
- opening our Advent calendars
- writing Christmas cards
- cleaning our home
- baking and cooking
- wrapping presents
- dancing at parties.

Don't worry about teaching the 'Busy, busy, busy' words. These are very repetitive, so that the children will pick them up as they go, and the tune is the same as the 'Jesus, Light of the World' refrain.

Busy, busy, busy, getting ready for Christmas!
Busy, busy, busy, getting ready for Christmas!
Busy, busy, busy, getting ready for Christmas!
The Light of the World is dawning! *Sun dawning action*

Je-sus, Light of the World, *Sun dawning action*
Je-sus, Light of the World, *Sun dawning action*
Je-sus, Light of the World, is *Sun dawning action*
dawning in the darkness! *Sun dawning action*

Getting ready for Christmas can be very busy!
You might see your parents or carers at home running around
and getting very busy!
> *If appropriate:* Or your teachers at school getting stressed
> about the Christmas/Nativity play!

Let's all look busy and stressed like the adults!
Lead children in waving imaginative aids or arms around madly and running on the spot.

Let's sing 'Busy, busy, busy, getting ready for Christmas' again.
Busy, busy, busy, getting ready for Christmas!
Busy, busy, busy, getting ready for Christmas!
Busy, busy, busy, getting ready for Christmas!
The Light of the World is dawning!

Je-sus, Light of the World, *Sun dawning action*
Je-sus, Light of the World, *Sun dawning action*
Je-sus, Light of the World, is *Sun dawning action*
dawning in the darkness! *Sun dawning action*

My goodness, that was busy!
Who's feeling tired?
When we're getting ready for Christmas
it can get really busy and really exciting!
Who's excited about Christmas?
In all the busyness,
let's remember to also have time for some quiet.
Let's remember to get ready for the very special baby
that's coming: Baby Jesus.

Let's sit quietly now and close our eyes . . .
Let's imagine holding Baby Jesus in our arms
and singing to him quietly and gently.
Baby Jesus will be born at Christmas!

Lead the children rocking a baby and singing quietly.
Je-sus, Light of the World,
Je-sus, Light of the World,
Je-sus, Light of the World, is
dawning in the darkness!

One of the ways we get ready inside *Trace a circle on your heart*
is to tell stories about Baby Jesus.
We're going to tell one of those stories today.

Gathering Song: Getting Ready for Baby Jesus: Option 2

→ 'Joy, joy, joy! It's Christmas, Christmas!' Words © Sharon Moughtin.
→ Tune: 'What shall we do with the drunken sailor?' (traditional). See Option 1 above for music.

Once it is Christmas, your group might like to use this version of the Gathering Song, which uses the same tune and structure but celebrates what happened at Christmas in our homes and communities, rather than preparing for it.

Baby Jesus is the Light of the World!
Let's close our eyes and feel the dark.

Lead the children in closing eyes.
Let's imagine Jesus shining like a tiny star in the sky.
Now let's imagine that light growing brighter and brighter and brighter –
until its light fills the whole world!
So bright we can't even look at it!
Let's open our eyes again.

Baby Jesus, the Light of the World, is
shining. *Jazz hands*
Let's show jazz hands for Jesus' light. *Jazz hands*

SOWING SEEDS • PART 4 — THE BUILDING BLOCKS — Gathering Song

Before Christmas, we were 'busy, busy, busy'
Move arms as if running.
getting ready for Jesus, Light of the World,
to DAWN in the darkness.
Show the sun rising up and out with your arms.

Jesus' light was just beginning to show,
like the sun dawning in the morning.
Now Jesus' light is SHINING, bright!
Lead the children in jazz hands.

Let's sing our Jesus, Light of the World, song again.
This time, at the end let's sing 'SHINING in the darkness'
Lead the children in jazz hands.
And show our jazz hands.

Lead the children in singing:
Je-sus, Light of the World, *Sun dawning action*
Je-sus, Light of the World, *Sun dawning action*
Je-sus, Light of the World, is *Sun dawning action*
SHINING in the darkness! *Jazz hands*

Let's sing our 'Busy, busy, busy' song,
But with new Christmas words!
Can you say after me?
'Joy! Joy! Joy! It's Christmas! Christmas!'
Joy! Joy! Joy! It's Christmas! Christmas!

And don't forget our *Jazz hands* for
'The Light of the World is shining!' at the end.

Joy! Joy! Joy! It's Christmas! Christmas!
Joy! Joy! Joy! It's Christmas! Christmas!
Joy! Joy! Joy! It's Christmas! Christmas!
The Light of the World is shining! *Jazz hands*

Je-sus, Light of the World, *Sun dawning action*
Je-sus, Light of the World, *Sun dawning action*
Je-sus, Light of the World, is *Sun dawning action*
shining in the darkness! *Jazz hands*

Let's think of some of the things we've done this Christmas.
Either invite the children to make suggestions, or choose from the suggestions below. For each activity sing 'Joy! Joy! Joy! It's Christmas, Christmas!' with an appropriate action designed by the children, followed by the 'Jesus, Light of the World' refrain:

- *opening stockings*
- *dancing at parties*
- *unwrapping presents*
- *eating lots of tasty food*
- *chocolate, chocolate everywhere!*

My goodness! That was exciting!
But in all that excitement,
let's remember to also have time for some quiet.
Let's remember to welcome Baby Jesus inside. *Trace circle on heart*
Let's sit quietly now and close our eyes . . .
Let's imagine holding Baby Jesus in our arms

Model rocking Baby Jesus.
and singing to him quietly and gently.
Ssssssssh!

Joy! Joy! Joy! It's Christmas! Christmas! *Rock Baby Jesus*
Joy! Joy! Joy! It's Christmas! Christmas! *Rock Baby Jesus*
Joy! Joy! Joy! It's Christmas! Christmas! *Rock Baby Jesus*
The Light of the World is shining! *Jazz hands*

Je-sus, Light of the World, *Sun dawning action*
Je-sus, Light of the World, *Sun dawning action*
Je-sus, Light of the World, is *Sun dawning action*
shining in the darkness! *Jazz hands*

'Advent Wreath' Song

→ **Song: The Sowing Seeds 'O Come' Antiphon. Words © Sharon Moughtin.**
→ **Tune:** *Veni Emmanuel* **(unknown).**

O come, O little baby, come! Come play with us and make our home your home! This world can feel as dark as night. Light of the world, come shine on us your light! Rejoice! Rejoice! Emmanuel shall come to thee, O Israel!

Groups from churches that sing 'O come, O come, Emmanuel' during Advent may like to use this verse of the song either in their church service, or instead of or alongside their Gathering Song.

O come, O little baby, come!
Rock Baby Jesus gently in your arms.
Come play with us
Hold hands out and move up and down as if dancing with the toddler Jesus.
and make our home your home.
Point to yourself, then to the toddler Jesus.
This world can feel as dark as night.
Hands over eyes.
Light of the world, come shine on us your light!
Sun rising action.

Rejoice! Rejoice!
Hands up in 'Alleluia' sign or waving.
Emmanuel shall come to thee, O Israel!
Rock Baby Jesus in your arms.

Gathering Song: Getting Ready for Baby Jesus: Option 3

→ 'In the first week of Advent. . .' Words © Sharon Moughtin.
→ Tune: 'On the first day of Christmas' (traditional).

(Musical notation with lyrics:)

In the first week of Advent, we light one candle! Abraham and Sarah! In the second week of Advent, we light two candles! Prophets of old and Abraham and Sarah! In the third week of Advent, we light three candles! John the Baptist, prophets of old, and Abraham and Sarah! In the fourth week of Advent, we light four candles! Mary, Jesus' mummy, John the Baptist, prophets of old, and Abraham and Sarah! On Christmas Day, we light five candles! Jesus, Light of the World! Mary, Jesus' mummy, John the Baptist, prophets of old, and Abraham and Sarah!

This option has been designed for groups who are using the 'Advent Wreath' storybox. It's appropriate for mixed groups of babies, toddlers and children up to the age of 9. Groups that only include children up to the age of 7 may prefer to use Option 1.

There are different traditions about the meaning of the five candles of the Advent wreath. If your church follows a different pattern, feel free to adapt the material accordingly.

Jesus is the light of the world
dawning in the darkness!
We have our Advent wreath here/in church
to show how the light is getting brighter and brighter
as we get nearer to Christmas!

  If appropriate:
  Can anyone tell us what 'Advent' means?
  Accept responses.

Advent means coming!
Our Advent wreath is reminding us
that Jesus – Light of the World – is coming!

Adapt material according to which week you are in:
Today is week number *one*.
How many candles do you think we'll light today? *Or 'did we light today'*
Accept responses.
One candle! *Show one finger*
One candle for week number one!

Can you show me your finger candle(s)?
Lead the children in showing the number of fingers for that week.
Let's light our candles together.
Lead the children in lighting their finger candle by striking an imaginary match in the air on three and pretending to light your finger.
1, 2, 3 . . . Tssss!

Lead the group in lighting the correct number of candles for that week. As the children light their finger candles, you could either do likewise or, if they haven't already been lit in the main church building, light the candles of the Advent wreath at the same time. As you light them, name the candles as follows, encouraging the children to join in where appropriate.

Candle number one is for. . . Abraham and Sarah!
Candle number two is for. . . prophets of old!
Candle number three is for. . . John the Baptist!
Candle number four is for. . . Mary!
And candle number five, the most important candle in the middle is for:
Baby Jesus!

When you've lit all the relevant candles for that week:
We're going to tell *Abraham and Sarah*'s story today! *Adapt as appropriate.*

> *First week:*
> We have a song to help us remember
> what all the candles are for.
> This week we're lighting just one candle.
> Can anyone remember
> whose story we're going to tell today?
> Abraham and Sarah!
> Candle number one is for Abraham and Sarah!
>
> Let's sing 'my turn' *Point to self*, 'your turn' *Leader's hands out to group*:
> In the first week of Advent,
> we light one candle!
> **In the first week of Advent,**
> **we light one candle!**
> Abraham and Sarah!
> **Abraham and Sarah!**
>
> Let's sing that all together:
> **In the first week of Advent,**
> **we light one candle!**
> **Abraham and Sarah!**
>
> *Following weeks:*
> Let's sing our song that helps us remember
> what all the candles are for.

Lead the children in singing the Advent Wreath Song up to the relevant verse for that week. If appropriate, you might find it helpful to ask the children if they can remember who the next candle is for before you start singing each verse.

In the first week of Advent,
we light one candle!
Abraham and Sarah!

In the second week of Advent,
we light two candles!
Prophets of old,
and Abraham and Sarah!

In the third week of Advent,
we light three candles!
John the Baptist,
prophets of old,
and Abraham and Sarah!

In the fourth week of Advent,
we light four candles!
Mary, Jesus' mummy,
John the Baptist,
prophets of old,
and Abraham and Sarah!

On Christmas Day,
we light five candles!
Jesus, Light of the World!
Mary, Jesus' mummy,
John the Baptist,
prophets of old,
and Abraham and Sarah!

Our Advent wreath is lit!
We're ready to tell today's story!

Gathering Song: Epiphany: Option 1

→ Song: 'We are waking in the light of God', based on 'We are marching in the light of God' (traditional).
→ Tune: traditional.

If your group has imaginative aids, you may like to think about whether you want to use them for this song, which also works well with whole body movements. If you do use the aids, they can add a great flourish on the word 'Oh!' and we've found the children can be wonderfully inventive in finding actions that use the aids. If you're using imaginative aids, ask two or three children to give them out at this point. Then invite the children to warm up their imaginations by exploring actions for different kinds of activities: writing, eating, painting, washing, cooking, eating, playing, hiding, brushing teeth, etc. 'Can you show me . . . writing!' etc.

Our song [for Epiphany] is all about Jesus' light shining.
It's about how everything we do is in 'the light of God'.

We started off our day in bed.
So let's start our song fast asleep in bed.

Who can show me fast asleep?
Lead the children in showing fast asleep.

Morning! It's time to wake up!
Let's stretch up high with our arms.
Lead the children in stretching and waking.
When we wake up, we wake up in the light of God!

Now let's eat our breakfast.
Maybe we had toast or cereal or something else . . .
Let's eat our breakfast together now.
Lead the children in miming eating their breakfast.

Let's sing 'We are waking in the light of God'. *Stretching action*
Then halfway through, let's change to
'We are eating'. *Eating breakfast action*

> *Either:*
> And when we sing 'oh!' *Jazz hands*
> let's show Jesus' light shining all around us with jazz hands.
> *Lead the children in jazz hands.*
>
> *Or (if you're using imaginative aids):*
> And when we sing 'oh!' *Fireworks action (aids moving very fast above head)*
> let's show Jesus' light SPARKLING like fireworks all around us. *Fireworks action*

This song is so repetitive it doesn't need to be taught line by line. Instead, start singing with the actions and the children and the rest of the group will gradually begin to join in. Some of the group may already know the traditional version of the song.

Let's start off asleep . . . Ssssssssh!
Lead the children in miming sleeping.
Time to wake up!

We are waking *Stretching action* **in the light of God,**
we are waking *Stretching action* **in the light of God!**
We are waking *Stretching action* **in the light of God,**
we are waking *Stretching action* **in the light of God!**
Interrupt the song: Breakfast time!
We are eating, *Eating action* **we are eating, oh!** *Jazz hands*
We are eating *Eating action* **in the light of God!**
We are eating, *Eating action* **we are eating, oh!** *Jazz hands*
We are eating *Eating action* **in the light of God!**

I wonder what else we'll do today?
Invite two different children to make two different suggestions together with an action. (We change actions halfway through the song.) If the group is part of a playschool/nursery/school you could also ask one of the teaching staff what the children will be doing that day to help make connections between this time of worship and the rest of each child's day.

> *Example: the children might suggest counting and playing.*
> Let's start by *painting* in the light of God.
> Can you show me painting?
> *Lead the group in following the suggested action for painting.*
>
> Then let's *play* in the light of God!
> Can you show me an action for playing?
> *Lead the group in following the suggested action for painting.*
> Let's go!
>
> *Lead the children in continuing painting as you sing.*
> **We are painting in the light of God,**

we are painting in the light of God!
We are painting in the light of God,
we are painting in the light of God!
Interrupt singing: Playtime!
Lead the children in their chosen playing action as they sing.
We are playing, we are playing, oh! *Jazz hands or fireworks action*
We are playing in the light of God!
We are playing, we are playing, oh! *Jazz hands or fireworks action*
We are playing in the light of God!
Depending on your group, you may like to repeat with two new actions.

Actions could include:
We are *learning* **in the light of God!** *Action for phonics sound of the week*
We are *singing* **in the light of God!** *Conducting action*
We are *jumping* **in the light of God!** *Jumping up and down*
We are *counting* **in the light of God!** *Counting on fingers*
We are *praying* **in the light of God!** *Hands together*
We are *brushing* **in the light of God!** *Mime brushing teeth*
We are *walking* **in the light of God!** *Walking on the spot*
We are *climbing* **in the light of God!** *Mime climbing a tree*
We are *reading* **in the light of God!** *Mime reading a book*
We are *cooking* **in the light of God!** *Mime stirring*
Encourage the children to make their own suggestions. Everything we do is in the light of God!

When it comes to the final time that you'll sing the song:
My goodness! We've done a lot today!
Who's feeling tired?
Let's rest.
Raise arms and wiggle fingers, slowly bringing arms downwards to show a resting action.

Can you show me resting? *Resting action*
And now sleeping . . . *Rest head to one side on joined hands*
It might be dark outside when we go to bed,
but let's remember Jesus' light is still shining in us.

So let's rest in the light of God. *Resting action*
Then let's sleep . . . *Sleeping action*

Sing quietly:
We are resting in the light of God, *Resting action*
we are resting in the light of God! *Resting action*
We are resting in the light of God, *Resting action*
we are resting in the light of God! *Resting action*
Interrupt: Sleepy time! Ssssh!
Lead the children in settling down to sleep.
We are sleeping, we are sleeping, ssssh!
We are sleeping in the light of God!
We are sleeping, we are sleeping, ssssh!
We are sleeping in the light of God!

Jesus is the Light of the World!
We'll be doing lots of things today.
Let's remember [the message of Epiphany].
Jesus' light is shining whatever we do.

Gathering Song: Epiphany: Option 2

→ Song: 'Epiphany: O let us see!'
→ Tune: 'The holly and the ivy' (traditional).

E - pi-pha-ny: O let us see! Let us see who Je-sus is! E - pi-pha-ny: O let us see! Let us see who Je-sus is.

This Gathering Song is designed for groups who wish to include children age 7+ alongside younger children, including babies and toddlers.

'Epiphany' means suddenly being able to see something!
To understand it!

> *Once the group are familiar with the song:*
> Can anyone tell us what 'Epiphany' means?
> *Accept responses.*
> *As a summary:* 'Epiphany' means suddenly being able to see something!
> To understand it!

Our song for Epiphany asks God to help us see!
Help us see who Jesus is.

> *To introduce the song for the first time or when there are many new people:*
> Let's sing it 'my turn' *Point to self*, 'your turn' *Leader's hands out to group.*

Epiphany: O let us see! *Hands over eyes then open*
Let us see who Jesus is!
Epiphany: O let us see! *Hands over eyes then open*
Let us see who Jesus is!

> *Speaking:* And then the same again, but we go down at the end.
> Let's sing 'my turn' *Point to self*, 'your turn' *Leader's hands out to group* again.

Epiphany: O let us see! *Hands over eyes then open*
Let us see who Jesus is!
Epiphany: O let us see! *Hands over eyes then open*
Let us see who Jesus is!

> Let's try that all together.
> **Epiphany: O let us see!** *Hands over eyes then open*
> **Let us see who Jesus is!**
> **Epiphany: O let us see!** *Hands over eyes then open*
> **Let us see who Jesus is!**

If you're using this Gathering Song before you've introduced the Magi's three gifts to the group, you could end here with a repetition of the song. Once the children are familiar with the Magi's three gifts, either from Sowing Seeds' storytelling in the Jesus, Light of the World unit or from elsewhere (e.g. school or church), it will help to recap what their meaning is.

If you're using imaginative aids (p. 207), give them out at this point.
When the group is ready:
First of all, we need an action
to show we're asking a big question.
Who can show me an action for 'big question'?
Choose one of the actions. This will become the 'question action'.

Epiphany: O let us see! *Hands/imaginative aids over eyes then open*
Let us see who Jesus is! *Question action*
Epiphany: O let us see! *Hands/imaginative aids over eyes then open*
Let us see who Jesus is! *Question action*

The clever Magi gave Jesus three gifts that show us who Jesus is.

> *If appropriate ask the group to remember the gifts one at a time:*
> Who can tell me what one of the gifts is?
> *Accept response.*
> And another one of the gifts?
> *Accept response.*
> And the third gift?
> *Accept response.*

The first gift was gold!
Gold is for a king!
Can you show me an action for 'king'?
Choose one of the actions. This will become 'the king' action.
Let's show that Jesus is king with our 'king action'.

Epiphany: O let us see! *Hands over eyes then open*
Let us see who Jesus is! *King action*
Epiphany: O let us see! *Hands over eyes then open*
Let us see who Jesus is! *King action*

The second gift was frankincense!
Frankincense shows that Jesus is holy!
Baby Jesus is GOD!
Can you show me an action for GOD!
Choose one of the actions. This will become the 'God action'.
Let's show that Jesus is GOD with our 'God action'.

Epiphany: O let us see! *Hands over eyes then open*
Let us see who Jesus is! *God action*
Epiphany: O let us see! *Hands over eyes then open*
Let us see who Jesus is! *God action*

So gold, frankincense, and. . . .
What's the third gift?
Encourage the group to join in: **Myrrh**
Myrrh shows that Jesus will die on the cross.
Can you stretch out wide to show me the cross?
Let's show the cross with our bodies as we sing.

Lead the group in singing:
Epiphany: O let us see! *Hands over eyes then open*
Let us see who Jesus is! *Cross*
Epiphany: O let us see! *Hands over eyes then open*
Let us see who Jesus is! *Cross*

The clever Magi's gifts show who Jesus is.
But that's just one story in Epiphany.
There are other stories as well.
I wonder what today's story will show about Jesus?

Let's sing our song one more time with our question action.
Epiphany: O let us see! *Hands over eyes then open*
Let us see who Jesus is! *Question action*

Epiphany: O let us see! *Hands over eyes then open*
Let us see who Jesus is! *Question action*
Gather imaginative aids and sing reflectively as they are gathered.

Gathering Song: John the Baptist unit

→ Song: 'Get ready for our God!' Words: © Sharon Moughtin.
→ Music: 'She'll be coming round the mountain' (traditional).

[Musical notation with lyrics:]
Get rea-dy, get rea-dy for our God! Get rea-dy, get rea-dy for our God!
It's time for a new start, time for a
new start! Get rea-dy, get rea-dy for our God!

The 'New Start' sign (the winding action from 'Wind the bobbin up'), used here to show how Baby John will 'get the world ready', is among the very few Sowing Seeds signs and actions that are fixed. See p. 8 or the website (www.sowingseeds-online.org) for a description and explanation.

The first time you sing this, you may find the following introduction helpful (before you distribute any imaginative aids that your group is using, p. 207):
We're going to learn a new song!
It's John the Baptist's song!
Let's say the words 'my turn' *Point to self*, 'your turn' *Leader's hands out to group*.

Say the words in the rhythm in which you will sing them.
Get ready, get ready for our God! *Both hands to self to show leader's turn*
Get ready, get ready for our God! *Hands out to group to show their turn*

It's time for a new start, time for a new start! *'New Start' sign*
It's time for a new start, time for a new start! *'New Start' sign*

Now let's try and add the tune:
Singing:
Get ready, get ready for our God! *Both hands to self to show leader's turn*
Get ready, get ready for our God! *Both hands to self to show leader's turn*
Get ready, get ready for our God! *Hands out to group to show their turn*
Get ready, get ready for our God! *Hands out to group to show their turn*

It's time for a new start, time for a new start! *'New Start' sign*
Get ready, get ready for our God! *Both hands to self to show leader's turn*
It's time for a new start, time for a new start! *'New Start' sign*
Get ready, get ready for our God! *Hands out to group to show their turn*

Let's try that all together . . .
Lead the group in singing the song as a whole. When the group is ready, continue with the material below.

If you're using imaginative aids (p. 207), ask two or three children to give them out at this point. Then invite the children to warm up their imaginations by exploring different shapes with their aids.

Let's sing John the Baptist's song about getting ready for God.
We need some actions!
We already have an action for 'new start'.
Lead the children in the 'New Start' sign
But we need an action for 'get ready'!
Who can show us a 'get ready' action?
Choose one of the actions and ask the group to copy it.

We're ready to sing!
Lead the group in singing:
Get ready, get ready for our God! *Get ready action*
Get ready, get ready for our God! *Get ready action*
It's time for a new start, time for a new start! *'New Start' sign*
Get ready, get ready for our God! *Get ready action*
Repeat. If you like, you could choose a different action for 'get ready' each time.

We're ready to tell our story.

Getting Ready for Bible Storytelling

Getting Ready for Bible Storytelling: Option 1

→ **Action: opening your group's box and naming this week's object.**

This Building Block is especially helpful for groups that include babies and toddlers who might need support with some of the vocabulary in the story. See the beginning of the weekly storytelling material for ideas of items to place in your box.

Invite one of the children to open the box.
What's in the box? *Ask the child to respond*

Getting Ready for Bible Storytelling: Option 2

→ Song: 'Jesus, open up my eyes'. Words: © Sharon Moughtin.
→ Tune: 'Michael, row the boat ashore' (traditional).

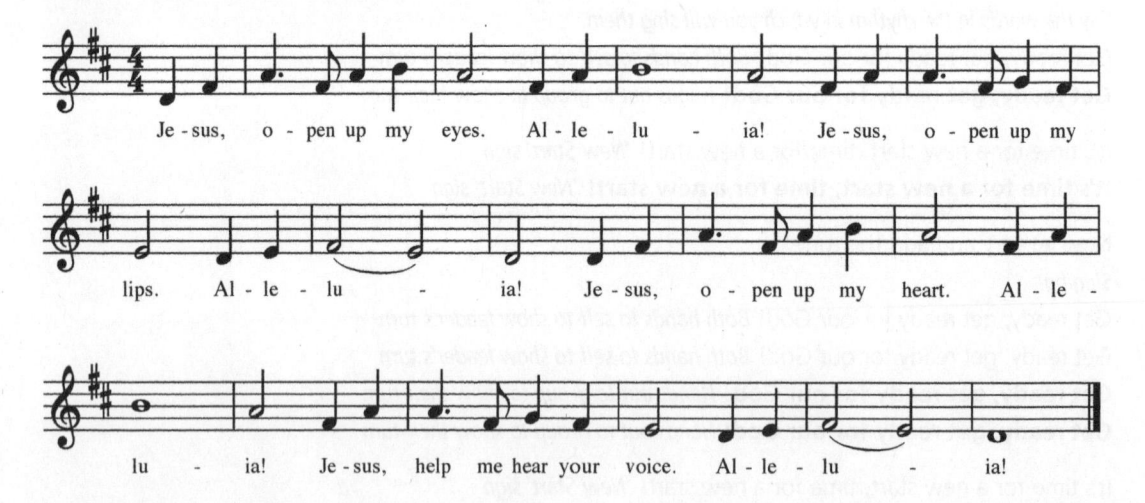

Je-sus, o-pen up my eyes. Al-le-lu - ia! Je-sus, o-pen up my lips. Al-le-lu - ia! Je-sus, o-pen up my heart. Al-le - lu - ia! Je-sus, help me hear your voice. Al-le-lu - ia!

This option has been created for churches who mark themselves with a cross three times before the reading of the Gospel in their church, to support children in understanding what is happening.

It's time to open the Bible.
Let's get ready!
Let's take our thumb *Lead children in showing thumb*
and draw our cross on our eyes, *Draw cross*
and our lips, *Draw cross*
and our heart. *Draw cross*

Let's ask Jesus to help us get ready to listen out for God!

Jesus, open up my eyes. Alleluia!
Trace a cross between your eyes.
Jesus, open up my lips. Alleluia!
Trace a cross on your lips.
Jesus, open up my heart. Alleluia!
Trace a cross on your heart.
Jesus, help me hear your voice. Alleluia!
Cup your hands behind your ears.

Interactive Bible Storytelling

See the Bible Storytelling material in Part 1 of this book.

Saying Sorry to God

Saying Sorry to God: Introduction: Getting Ready for Baby Jesus

Invite the children to sit in a circle for a moment of quiet.

In Advent we get ready to welcome Baby Jesus into the world.

One way we do this is by tidying up our home.
We can also get ready by asking God to help us tidy up our hearts.
It's time to sing our Sorry Song.

Saying Sorry to God: Introduction: Epiphany

Invite the children to sit in a circle for a moment of quiet.
Jesus is the Light of the World!

Jesus wants us to be like little lights, too.
It's time to say sorry for the times when we haven't
shone like little lights in the world.
For the times we've made the world
feel dark to other people instead.
Let's put our hands on our head.
I wonder if there's anything we've thought this week
that we wish we hadn't thought?

Saying Sorry to God: Introduction: John the Baptist unit

The 'Saying Sorry to God' Building Block, with its strong echoes of repentance and baptism, works particularly well with the John the Baptist unit. For this reason, saying sorry is an optional part of the storytelling itself for this unit.

Saying Sorry to God

→ Song: 'The Sowing Seeds sorry song'. Words: © Sharon Moughtin.
→ Tune: © Sharon Moughtin.

With my hands on my head, I re-mem-ber the things I've thought to-day, I re-mem-ber the things I wish I'd thought a diff'-rent way. I'm sor-ry, I'm sor-ry, I wish I could start a-gain. I'm sor-ry, I'm sor-ry, I wish I could start a-gain.

The 'I'm Sorry' and 'New Start' signs

The 'I'm Sorry' and 'New Start' signs are among the very few Sowing Seeds signs and actions that are fixed. Usually, the children are trusted with the responsibility for creating the actions for the songs and storytelling as the hope is that this will become *their* story and *their* song (p. 2). However, the 'I'm Sorry' and 'New Start' signs have been chosen for the resonances they create through the material. Videos of both signs can be found on the website next to the 'Sorry Song' Building Block in any of the units.

The 'I'm Sorry' sign

The 'I'm Sorry' sign not only conveys sadness. It calls to mind the waters of baptism being splashed over us. There echoes of an 'X' shape not only show that we know that we've got something wrong, but can also call to mind at the same time the cross of Jesus in the background. Start with your hands lightly crossed in front of your forehead, then move them in opposing arcs downwards towards your chest and round in opposing circles, and back just in front of your forehead. This opposing circular motion is the 'I'm Sorry' sign.

The 'New Start' sign

The 'New Start' sign can best be described as the 'winding' action from the nursery rhyme 'Wind the bobbin up'. Repeatedly rotate your arms around each other in front of your body. It shows that we want a chance to 'start again' but it has been chosen to point us also to the rolling away of the stone on Easter Day that brings about that great 'new start' for the whole world. The 'New Start' sign appears and reappears in so many of the stories. It's the sign for

- Mary's song about the 'topsy turvy God who turns things upside down' (which is sung in response to John's prophetic somersault)
- 'The first will be last and the last will be first' in God's revolutionary, 'topsy turvy' kingdom
- Jesus turning the tables 'topsy turvy' in the Temple – 'Look! Jesus is giving the Temple a new start!'
- Jesus washing the disciples' feet, as the longed for king turns everything upside down to become the servant
- The prayer 'Holy Spirit, come!' as Jesus' friends wait for the Spirit who will turn their lives (and the world) topsy turvy at Pentecost
- Paul falling 'topsy turvy' off his horse when he meets Jesus and is given his 'new start'

and more. Keep an eye out for the 'New Start' sign in the storytelling. It creates a golden thread of forgiveness and can appear in the most surprising of places!

Let's put our hands on our head.
I wonder if there's anything we've thought this week
that we wish we hadn't thought?

Lead the children in placing your hands on head, singing:
With my hands on my head,
I remember the things I've thought today,
I remember the things I wish I'd thought a different way.

I'm sorry, I'm sorry, *'I'm Sorry' sign twice*
I wish I could start again. *'New Start' sign*
I'm sorry, I'm sorry, *'I'm Sorry' sign twice*
I wish I could start again. *'New Start' sign*

Let's put our hands by our mouths.
I wonder if there's anything we've said this week
that we wish we hadn't said?

With hands by mouth, singing:
With my hands on my mouth,
I remember the things I've said today,
I remember the things I wish I'd said a different way.

I'm sorry, I'm sorry, *'I'm Sorry' sign twice*
I wish I could start again. *'New Start' sign*
I'm sorry, I'm sorry, *'I'm Sorry' sign twice*
I wish I could start again. *'New Start' sign*

Let's cross our hands on our chest.
I wonder if there's anything we've done this week
that we wish we hadn't done?

With hands crossed on chest, singing:
With my hands on my chest,
I remember the things I've done today,
I remember the things I wish I'd done a different way.

I'm sorry, I'm sorry, *'I'm Sorry' sign twice*
I wish I could start again. *'New Start' sign*
I'm sorry, I'm sorry, *'I'm Sorry' sign twice*
I wish I could start again. *'New Start' sign*

Continue with a Saying Sorry Action or move straight to 'God Gives Us a New Start', below.

Saying Sorry Action

You don't need to use a Saying Sorry Action. For some groups the song will be enough. However, if you would like to, choose from the following options according to which unit you're in.

Saying Sorry Action: any unit: Option 1

→ **Psalm 103.12**
→ **Action: crumpling a piece of paper to show how you feel when you're cross or sad and placing it in a basket.**

Invite two children to give out a piece of paper to everyone who would like one.
Name and *Name* are going to bring round some paper.
If you like, you can take a piece of paper
and hold it in the air
to show that there are things that you wish you hadn't done.

As the paper is given out, lead the group in singing the 'I'm Sorry' refrain.

Once all the children and adults who wish to take a piece of paper have done so:
When we do things that make God or other people sad,
it can make us feel sad and cross inside.
Let's crumple our paper up to show how we can feel
when we know we've made someone feel sad.
Let's put our feelings into the paper.

Lead the children in crumpling your paper to show your feelings: crossly, with frustration, sadly, etc. For example:
I'm feeling cross with myself for making my friend feel sad.
I'm going to put my crossness into this paper.

Crumple the paper crossly.
Whatever we're feeling, we can give our feelings to God.
Name is going to bring this basket around.
If you like, you can put your paper in the basket
and give it to God.

While all the children and adults who wish to place their paper in the basket do so, lead the group in singing the 'I'm Sorry' refrain,

Place the basket in the centre of the circle or on the focal table (see p. 208).
Continue with one of the New Start Actions on p. 188.

Saying Sorry Action: any unit: Option 2

→ **Action: crumpling a piece of paper representing *other* people's feelings and placing it in a basket.**

Invite two children to give out a piece of paper to everyone who would like one.
Name and Name are going to bring round some paper.
If you like, you can take a piece of paper
and hold it in the air
to show that there are things that you wish you hadn't done.

As the paper is given out, lead the group in singing the 'I'm Sorry' refrain.

Once all the children and adults who wish to take a piece of paper have done so . . .
Sometimes we can do things that make OTHER people sad.
Let's crumple our paper up to show
how we can make other people feel when we hurt them.
Let's put their feelings into the paper.

Lead the children in crumpling your paper with feelings: e.g. crossly with frustration, or gently with sadness, etc.
We can do things that hurt other people.
The Good News is:
we can give the hurtful things we've done to God
and God will give us a new start.
Name is going to bring this basket around.
If you like, you can put your paper in the basket
and give it to God.
Let's ask God for a new start.

While all the children and adults who wish to place their paper in the basket do so, lead the group in singing the 'I'm Sorry' refrain.

Place the basket in the centre of the circle or on the focal table (p. 208).
We've said sorry to God.
I wonder if there's anyone else you need to say sorry to this week?

Continue with one of the New Start Actions on p. 188.

Saying Sorry Action: any unit: Option 3

→ **Micah 7.19; Psalm 38.4; Hebrews 12.1; Matthew 11.28**
→ **Action: placing a pebble on a piece of fabric or in a bowl of water.**

Make sure the pebbles are large enough not to present a choking hazard and that this action is appropriate for your current group. For instance, assess whether they are likely to be thrown.

Invite two children to take around two baskets of pebbles to everyone who would like one.
Name *and* Name *are going to bring round some pebbles.*
If you like, you can take a pebble
and hold it in the air
to show there are things you wish you hadn't done.

As the pebbles are given out, lead the group in singing the 'I'm Sorry' refrain.

Once all the children and adults who wish to take a pebble have done so:
Let's hold our pebble in our hand.
Lead the children in weighing the pebble in their hand.

When we do things that make God or other people sad,
it can make us feel heavy and weighed down inside
like this pebble weighs our hand down.
When we're feeling sad and heavy,
we can give our feelings to God.

Place a basket, a piece of fabric, or a bowl of water in the centre of the circle and invite the children to place their pebble within it. Or ask two children to take baskets around the circle to collect the pebbles.

> *If your group is using water, make sure it's in a container that is deep and transparent, so the children can see their pebbles sinking.*
> The Bible says:
> God will sink all our wrong things
> to the bottom of the sea!
> Let's put our pebbles in gently
> and watch them sink to the bottom.
> Let's imagine God sinking the wrong things we've done
> to the bottom of the sea.

Let's give our sad and heavy feelings
to God now as we sing.

While all the children and adults who wish to place their pebbles do so, lead the group in singing the 'I'm Sorry' refrain.

The Good News is:
God always wants to give us a new start!
God doesn't want us to carry round
things that make us feel sad and heavy!
God takes them from us!
After three, let's jump up high
and shout 'God gives me a new start!'

1, 2, 3 . . . God gives me a new start!
Let's use our new start to share God's love this week!

Saying Sorry to God Action: Getting Ready for Baby Jesus: Option 1

→ **Action: placing a paper star on a piece of dark fabric.**

When we do things that make God or other people feel sad
everything can feel dark and lonely.

The Good News is that Jesus is the Light of the World.
Jesus can shine in any dark place.

In a moment, *Name* and *Name* are going to bring around these stars.
If you like, you could take one
and hold it gently in your hands like this.

Model to the children holding a star.
Imagine Jesus' love shining on you.
We're going to sing as we wait for Jesus,
Light of the World, to come to us.

While all the children and adults who wish to take a star do so, lead the group in singing the 'I'm Sorry' refrain.

God gives us a new start!
Let's hold our star high! *Joyfully, hold star high*
But there are other people
feeling like they're in a dark place.
Let's ask God to help us give other people a new start, too.

Lay a dark piece of fabric in the centre of the circle.
If you like, you can put your star in the centre of the circle
and promise to give other people a new start this week, too,
especially when they've made us feel cross or sad.

Lead the group in singing again as the stars are placed. When all the children and adults who wish to place their star have done so:
After three, let's say 'God gives us a new start!'
1, 2, 3 . . . God gives us a new start!
Let's use our new start to share God's love this week!

Saying Sorry to God Action: Getting Ready for Baby Jesus: Option 2

→ **Action: scribbling on a whiteboard/chalkboard then wiping it out.**

Place a single collective whiteboard/chalkboard in the centre of the circle, or ask one or more children to distribute individual smaller whiteboards/blackboards. Ask two more children to take around chalk/pens and a piece of kitchen roll to give to each child as you sing.
We all make bad choices sometimes.
When we make bad choices,
it can feel like we've made a big mess.
Let's scribble on our board
to show the mess we can make of things.

While the children and adults scribble, lead the group in singing the 'I'm Sorry' refrain.

Once all the children and adults have had the chance to scribble:

Look at that mess!
Bad choices can make everything feel messy
and all tangled up.
They can make us feel not ready for Baby Jesus!
The Good News is:
God always wants to give us a new start!
Let's be God, and wipe our scribble away!

Lead the children in wiping away their scribble. If you're using a collective board, invite one or more children to wipe out the scribble on behalf of the group; then invite another child to draw a smile.
Now let's draw a big smile . . .
and after three say 'God gives me/us a new start!'
1, 2, 3 . . . God gives me/us a new start!

Let's use our new start to share God's love this week!

Saying Sorry to God Action: Getting Ready for Baby Jesus: Option 3

→ **Action: sprinkling water or tracing a smile/cross with water.**

> **Tip**
>
> This option is particularly appropriate for churches that use the sprinkling of water (asperges) in Advent. When inviting children to lead by taking the water around, you may find it helps to make it clear to them that they can keep both hands on the bowl while the other children dip their finger in. Standing with the children, with your hands placed over theirs on the bowl, as they offer the water to the first participant may help very young children understand the pattern.

When we make bad choices,
it can feel like we've made a big mess of things.
The Good News is:
God always wants to give us a new start!
Sometimes we use water to show
that God's making us clean again:
not just on the OUTside, *Rub arms*
but on the INside too. *Trace a circle on your heart*

> *Either:*
> In a moment, I'm going to sprinkle us with water.
> When the water splashes us
> let's remember God is making us clean inside and out.

> *Or: Invite two children to take round bowls of water, going opposite ways around the circle.*
>
> *Name* and *Name* are going to bring round some water.
> If you like, you can dip your finger in the water
> and draw a smile/cross on your forehead
> to show that God gives you a new start!
>
> *Model to the children drawing a smile/cross on your own forehead. While the water is taken around, lead the children in singing the 'I'm sorry' refrain.*

Once all the children and adults who wish to have taken some water, or everyone who wishes to has been sprinkled with water:
That's better! Our hearts are lovely and clean again!
After three, let's jump up and say 'God gives me a new start!'
1, 2, 3 . . . God gives me a new start!
Let's use our new start to share God's love this week!

Saying Sorry Action: Epiphany: Option 1

→ **Action: placing hands over eyes then removing them.**

Let's put our hands on our eyes.
Lead the children in placing hands over eyes.

When we do something that makes God sad
or other people sad,
it can make us feel sad and dark inside.

When we say sorry, we ask God
to shine like a light in the dark.
Let's imagine Jesus, Light of the World,
shining bright inside us!

Let's take our hands off our eyes.
Now we can see what we've done wrong.
We can see that God gives us a new start too!

> *Either:*
> After 3, let's shout, 'God gives us a new start!'
> **1, 2, 3 . . . God gives us a new start!**
>
> *Or: choose one of the 'God Gives Us a New Start' options from p. 188.*

Saying Sorry Action: Epiphany: Option 2

→ **Action: shining a torch on the group or lighting a real candle (out of reach).**

Ask an adult to turn off the lights in the room.
When we do something that makes God sad
or other people sad,
it can make us feel sad and dark inside.

When we say sorry,
we ask God to shine like a light in the dark.

Turn on a torch or light a candle in a safe place.
We can see what we've done wrong,
but we can see that we have a new start too!

> *Either go around the circle and shine the torch on each child and adult. As you do so, either invite the children to go around the circle and say together:*
> **Name, God gives you a new start!**
>
> *Or, if you're using a real candle or are in a large group, ask the children, after 3, to say, 'God gives us a new start!'*
> **1, 2, 3 . . . God gives us a new start!**

Saying Sorry Action: Epiphany: Option 3

→ **Action: placing a star on a [white/gold] cloth in the centre of the circle.**

The Good News is:
God always wants to give us a new start!

Show the children the stars.

When we do something that makes God sad
or other people sad,
it can make us feel sad and dark inside.

When we say sorry,
we ask God to shine like a light in the dark in us.

I'm going to ask *Name* and *Name*
to bring around these stars now.
If you like, you can take one
and let God's light shine on you.

While the stars are taken around, lead the group in singing the 'I'm Sorry' refrain.

When the group is ready:
The Good News is:
God is always ready to give us a new start!
God's light is shining on and in us!

Let's hold our lights high!
After 3, let's say: 'God gives us a new start!'
1, 2, 3: God gives us a new start!

Let's promise to use our new start
to shine like lights in the world this week.
Let's give our stars to God
and promise to share God's love with each other.

Invite the children to place their star on a [gold/white] cloth in the centre of the circle as the group sings one of the following songs, or another that the children are familiar with.

Either:
→ **Song: 'We are loving in the light of God', based on 'We are marching in the light of God' (traditional).**
→ **Tune: 'We are marching in the light of God' (traditional).**

**We are loving in the light of God,
we are loving in the light of God!
We are loving in the light of God,
we are loving in the light of God!
We are loving, we are loving, oh!** *Jazz hands*
**We are loving in the light of God
We are loving, we are loving, oh!** *Jazz hands*
We are loving in the light of God!

Or:
→ **Song: 'This little light of mine' (traditional).**
→ **Tune: traditional.**

**This little light of mine, I'm gonna let it shine!
This little light of mine, I'm gonna let it shine!
This little light of mine, I'm gonna let it shine!
Let it shine, let it shine, let it shine.**

Or:
→ **Song: 'God loves to give me a new start!' Words: © Sharon Moughtin.**
→ **Tune: 'Give me oil in my lamp' (traditional). For the music see p. 189.**

[Yes, my] God loves to give me a new start! *Trace a smile/cross on own forehead*
How amazing God's love for me! *Cross hands on chest*
[Yes, my] God loves to give me a new start! *Trace a smile/cross on own forehead*
How amazing is God's love for me! *Cross hands on chest*

Sing hosanna! Sing hosanna! *Wave hands in the air*
Sing hosanna to the King of Kings! *Wave hands in the air followed by crown on head*
Sing hosanna! Sing hosanna! *Wave hands in the air*
Sing hosanna to the king! *Wave hands in the air followed by crown on head*

Saying Sorry Action: Epiphany: Option 4

→ **Action: placing a paper star on a piece of dark fabric, with a focus on giving other people a new start too.**

Show the children one or more baskets/trays with stars.

When we do things that make God or other people feel sad
everything can feel dark and lonely.

The Good News is that Jesus is the Light of the World.
Jesus can shine in any dark place.

In a moment, *Name* and *Name* are going to bring around these stars.
If you like, you could take one
and hold it gently in your hands like this.

Model to the children holding their star.
Imagine Jesus' love shining on you.

> We're going to sing as we wait
> for Jesus, Light of the World, to come to us.

While the stars are taken around, lead the group in singing the 'I'm Sorry' refrain.

When the group is ready:
God gives us a new start!
Let's hold our star high!
Joyfully, lead the children in holding your star high.

But there are other people
feeling like they're in a dark place.
Let's ask God to help us give other people a new start, too.

Lay a dark piece of fabric in the centre of the circle.
If you like, you can put your star here
and promise to give other people a new start this week,
especially when they've made us feel cross or sad.
When we give other people new starts
It can fill dark places like this with light!

Lead the children in singing/humming again as the stars are placed. Some groups may like to ask two children to take two trays covered with dark fabric opposite ways around the circle to collect the stars. The trays can then be placed in the centre of the circle.
When the group is ready:
After 3, let's say, 'God gives us a new start!'
1, 2, 3 . . . God gives us a new start!
Let's use our new start to share God's love this week!

Saying Sorry Action: John the Baptist unit

The 'Saying Sorry to God' Building Block, with its strong echoes of repentance and baptism, works particularly well with the 'John the Baptist' unit. For this reason, saying sorry is an optional part of the storytelling itself for this unit.

God Gives Us a New Start

> **Tip**
>
> Every time of Saying Sorry should end by assuring the children that God gives them a new start. Most Sowing Seeds Sorry Actions already include this promise of a new start. If they don't – or if you've created your own Sorry Action – you should choose one from the following New Start options, or create your own assurance of forgiveness. You could also choose to move straight from the Sorry Song to God's promise of a new start, without any Sorry Action.

New Start Action: Option 1

→ **Action: tracing a cross or smile on each other's forehead.**

The Good News is:
God always wants to give us a new start!
Let's turn to the person next to us
and show that God gives them a new start.
Let's take our thumb/finger *Show thumb/finger*
and draw a cross/smile on their forehead *Draw a cross/smile in the air*

If your group is drawing a smile, add:
to show that God is very happy with them!

Let's say 'God gives you a new start!'
Then let them give you a new start, too!

When the group has finished drawing a cross/smile to show each other God's new starts:
Let's use our new start to share God's love this week!

New Start Action: Option 2

→ **Action: standing up and hugging each other.**

The Good News is: God always wants to give us a new start!
Let's help someone next to us stand up from the floor.
Then let them help you stand up too!
Lead the children in helping each other stand up.

Then let's give each other a hug and say:
'God gives you a new start!'

When the group has finished helping one another up to show one another God's new starts:
Let's use our new start to share God's love this week!

New Start Action: Option 3

→ **Song: 'God loves to give me a new start!' Words © Sharon Moughtin.**
→ **Tune: 'Give me oil in my lamp' (traditional).**

[Musical notation with lyrics:]
God loves to give me a new start! How amazing God's love for me!
God loves to give me a new start! How amazing is God's love for me! Sing hosanna!
Sing hosanna! Sing hosanna to the King of Kings!
Sing hosanna! Sing hosanna! Sing hosanna to the king!

The Good News is: God always wants to give us a new start!
Let's sing our New Start song together.

God loves to give me a new start! *Trace a smile/cross on your own forehead*
How amazing God's love for me! *Cross hands on your chest*
God loves to give me a new start! *Trace a smile/cross on your own forehead*
How amazing is God's love for me!

Sing hosanna! Sing hosanna! *Wave hands in the air*
Sing hosanna to the King of Kings!
Wave hands in the air followed by placing crown on head.
Sing hosanna! Sing hosanna! *Wave hands in the air*
Sing hosanna to the king!
Wave hands in the air followed by placing crown on head.

Prayers for Other People

Introduction to Prayers: Getting Ready for Baby Jesus

Before Christmas:
It's time to bring our prayers to Jesus, Light of the World.

Christmas Day and Christmas 1:
It's Christmas! All our waiting is over.
It's time to bring our prayers to the tiny Baby Jesus.

Introduction to Prayers: Epiphany

It's time to bring our prayers to Jesus, Light of the World.

Prayers for Other People: Option 1

→ Song: 'Jesus, hear our prayer!' Words: © Sharon Moughtin.
→ Tune: 'Brown girl in the ring' (traditional).

For the world: Jesus, hear our prayer. For the Church: Jesus, hear our prayer. For our place London: Jesus, hear our prayer. Lord Jesus, hear our prayer. A - men. For the sick and lonely: Jesus, hear our prayer. For our friends and family: Jesus, hear our prayer. For ourselves: Jesus, hear our prayer. Lord Jesus, hear our prayer. A - men. Take our prayers: Jesus, hear our prayer. Make them holy: Jesus, hear our prayer. Make them beautiful: Jesus, hear our prayer. Lord Jesus, hear our prayer. A - men.

* Insert local area/school/church/community/parish.

For the sick and lonely:	**Jesus, hear our prayer!**
Fingers showing tears falling down cheeks.	*Open hands upwards to God.*
For our friends and family:	**Jesus, hear our prayer!**
Arms around yourself.	*Open hands upwards to God.*
For ourselves:	**Jesus, hear our prayer!**
Both hands on heart.	*Open hands upwards to God.*
Lord Jesus, hear our prayer. Amen.	
Open hands upwards to God.	

Let's close our eyes for a moment.
I wonder if there's someone special
you'd like to pray for?
Let's imagine that person now.

Now, let's imagine Jesus coming to them.
Does Jesus say anything?
Does Jesus do anything?

Let's open our eyes.

Continue with one of the Prayer Action options outlined below. Once the Prayer Action has been completed, you may like to use the following verse to close this time of prayer.

Take our prayers:	**Jesus, hear our prayer!**
Hands together gently.	*Open hands upwards to God.*
Make them holy:	**Jesus, hear our prayer!**
Hands together gently.	*Open hands upwards to God.*
Make them beautiful:	**Jesus, hear our prayer!**
Hands together gently.	*Open hands upwards to God.*
Lord Jesus, hear our prayer! Amen.	
Hands together gently, then open hands upwards to God.	

Prayers for Other People: Option 2

→ **Song:** 'The Sowing Seeds little prayers song'. Words © Sharon Moughtin.
→ **Tune:** 'Frère Jacques' (traditional).

[Musical score: For our food, For our food, thank you, God. thank you, God. For our teachers, For our teachers, thank you, God. thank you, God. For Rachel's Nanny, For Rachel's Nanny, hear our prayer. hear our prayer. For people with no homes, for people with no homes, hear our prayer. hear our prayer.]

These prayers are especially suited to churches that prefer less traditional prayer forms.

Either: choose what you'd like the group to pray for before the session.

Or: ask the children at this point if there is anything or anyone that they'd like to pray for. Ask them or others to suggest actions.

You will need two different 'thank you' suggestions and two different 'hear our prayer' suggestions. Try to encourage at least one prayer for other people outside the group.

Invite the children to sing after you, repeating your words and their actions. Sometimes it might be almost impossible to fit the child's own words in! It's really valuable to do this where possible, resisting the urge to try and 'neaten' their suggestions.

For *our foo-ood,*
For *our foo-ood,*
Thank you, God!
Thank you, God!

Fo-r *our teachers,*
Fo-r *our teachers,*
Thank you, God!
Thank you, God!

For *Rachel's Nanny,*
For *Rachel's Nanny,*
Hear our prayer!
Hear our prayer!

For *people with no homes,*
For *people with no homes,*
Hear our prayer!
Hear our prayer!

Having sung your prayers, you could insert a Prayer Action, repeat the process or move straight on to close with the following (or other words that remain the same each week).

For today,	*Point hands down for 'now'*
For today,	*Point hands down for 'now'*
Thank you, God!	*Open hands upwards to God or hands together in prayer*
Thank you, God!	*Open hands upwards to God or hands together in prayer*
Fo-r your love,	*Cross hands on chest*
Fo-r your love,	*Cross hands on chest*
Thank you, God!	*Open hands upwards to God or hands together in prayer*
Thank you, God!	*Open hands upwards to God or hands together in prayer*

Prayer Actions

You don't need to use a prayer action. For some groups the song will be enough. However, if you would like to, choose from the following options.

Prayer Action: Getting Ready for Baby Jesus: Option 1

→ **Action: placing paper/material/wooden stars on a dark piece of fabric.**

Lay a dark piece of fabric in the centre of the circle.
Show the children one or more baskets/trays filled with stars.

Jesus is the Light of the World!
In a moment, *Name* and *Name*
are going to bring around these stars.
If you like, you could take a star
and hold it up high like this.
Model to the children holding their star up.

You can imagine Jesus' love shining on you
And on the special person you're praying for,
like a star shines in the night sky.

We're going to sing
as we wait in the dark for Jesus,
the Light of the World, to come to us.

Hum the tune together, with the words 'Jesus, hear our prayer!' as a refrain, until all the children and adults who wish to take stars have done so.
Let's give our star prayers to God as we sing.
Let's pray that God's light will shine in every dark place.

Hum the tune together, with the words 'Jesus, hear our prayer!' as a refrain, as you lead the children in placing the stars in the centre of the circle on the dark piece of fabric. Some groups may like to invite two children to go around the circle in opposite directions with trays to collect the responses. The stars can then be placed in the centre. End this time of prayer with the final verse of the Prayer Song you've chosen.

Prayer Action: Getting Ready for Baby Jesus: Option 2

→ **Action: placing paper stars or shiny (safe) Christmas decorations on a small Christmas tree or a picture of a Christmas tree.**

The Prayer Actions Options 1 and 2 for the 'Jesus, Light of the World!' unit below are also relevant to the 'Getting Ready for Baby Jesus' unit.

With young children, it's best to have stars/decorations that can simply be balanced on the branches of the tree rather than decorations that need hanging, unless you have a very small group in which each young child can be helped. Place your Christmas tree in the centre of the circle. Show the children a basket of stars or Christmas decorations.

Jesus is the Light of the World!
At Christmas, whenever we see stars/shiny decorations,
we remember Jesus the Light of the World.

In a moment, *Name* and *Name*
are going to bring round these stars/decorations.
If you like, you could take one
and hold it up high like this.
Model to the children holding their star/decoration up.

You can imagine Jesus' love shining on you
and on the special person you're praying for

> *If using stars:*
> like a star shines in the night sky.

Let's sing as we wait for Jesus,
the Light of the World, to come to us.

Hum the tune together, with the words 'Jesus, hear our prayer!' as a refrain, until all the children and adults who wish to take stars or decorations have done so.
Let's decorate our Christmas tree
with our prayers as we sing.
Let's pray that God's light will shine in every dark place.

Hum the tune together, with the words 'Jesus, hear our prayer!' as a refrain, as you lead the children in placing the stars/decorations on the Christmas tree. End this time of prayer with the final verse of the Prayer Song you've chosen.

Prayer Action: Getting Ready for Baby Jesus: Option 3

→ **Action:** placing paper stars on a world map or a simple world map jigsaw that the children can also explore afterwards.

For a similar action that involves a 3D lit globe rather than a 2D world map see the Prayer Action for the 'Jesus, Light of the World!' unit: Option 2.

Place your world map in the centre of the circle.
This is a map of the world.
Jesus is the Light of the World!

Show the children one or more baskets/trays of stars.

In a moment, *Name* and *Name*
are going to bring round these stars.
If you like, you could take one.
Let's sing as we wait.
Let's hold our hands out gently like this
Model cupped hands
as we wait for Jesus to shine in our world.

Hum the tune together, with the words 'Jesus, hear our prayer!' as a refrain, until all the children and adults who wish to take stars have done so.

> *If appropriate, as leader, you could mention specific places for prayer. You could take these from your church's intercessions or other times of prayer:*
> At the moment, there's fighting in the world
> here and here. *As leader, place a star on these places on the map.*
> *Name the countries or areas if appropriate.*
> There's been *an earthquake [or other disaster]*
> here. *As leader, place a star on the map*
> There are people who *have no homes* here. *As leader, place a star on the map*
> There are people who need our prayers all over the world.

As we sing again, let's put our lights on the world.
You can put your little light anywhere you like.
Let's ask God to see our lights as prayers for the world.

Hum the tune together, with the words 'Jesus, hear our prayer!' as a refrain, as you lead the children in placing the stars on the map. We've found that asking the children to do this in age groups helps, as the older children tend to be more intent on finding a location than the others. We invite babies first, then nursery and reception children, then Year 1 and upwards (including the adults). Some groups may like to invite two children to go around the circle in opposite directions with trays to collect the stars. The trays can then be placed in the centre of the map. End this time of prayer with the final verse of the Prayer Song you've chosen.

Prayer Action: Epiphany: Option 1

→ **Action:** placing star shapes with a Baby Jesus doll, lying in a manger or on white/gold cloth on your focal table.
Show the children one or more baskets/trays with star shapes.

Jesus is the Light of the World!
In a moment, *Name* and *Name*
are going to bring around these stars.

If you like, you could take one
and hold it up like this *Hold the star high above your head*
to show that Jesus, Light of the World, is here!
Imagine Jesus' love shining on you
and on a special person you're praying for.

Hum the tune together, with 'Jesus, hear our prayer!' as a refrain until all the children and adults who wish to take stars have done so.

Jesus is the Light of the World!
Our prayers can be part of sharing Jesus' light.
We're going to sing again.
If you like, you can give your star to Baby Jesus.
Let's promise to shine with God's love in the world.

Lead the children in singing again until all the children and adults who wish to place their stars have done so. End this time of prayer with the final verse from the Prayer Song you've chosen.

Prayer Action: Epiphany: Option 2

→ **Action: placing star shapes around a lit globe.**

For this Prayer Action to work safely, it will need to be possible to plug the electric globe in and stow the cable safely away. Think through how this might work safely in your setting with curious young children present. The children could explore the globe along with an adult afterwards, if they like.

For a similar action that involves a 3D lit globe rather than a 2D world map see the Prayer Action for the 'Jesus, Light of the World' unit: Option 2.

Show the children the lit globe.
This is a 'globe', showing the world.
We live here. *Point to where you live on the globe*
But people live all over the world. *Point all around the globe*

> *If your church or group has a connection with people elsewhere in the world, you could briefly show the children this place here.*
> **Example:** This is Zimbabwe, our link diocese in Africa.
> *Point to Zimbabwe.*
> Our friends from Zimbabwe live here.

Jesus is the Light of the World!
Look at the light lighting this globe up from the inside.

Show the children one or more baskets/trays with stars.

In a moment, *Name* and *Name*
are going to bring around these stars.
If you like, you could take one
and hold it up high. *Model holding one up high*

Let's ask God to help us
be part of shining Jesus' light in the world.

Hum the tune together, with 'Jesus, hear our prayer!' as a refrain until all the children and adults who wish to take stars have done so.
Jesus is the Light of the World!
When we pray, we can be part of shining Jesus' light!

Let's sing again.
If you like, you can come and put your little light around the world.
Let's ask God to see our star.
as a prayer for a special person and for the world.

Lead the children in singing again as they place their stars around the globe on a focal table. We've found that asking the children to do this in age groups helps. End this time of prayer with the final verse from the Prayer Song you've chosen.

Prayer Action: Epiphany: Option 3

→ **Action: making 'twinkle' hand actions in a circle around a Baby Jesus doll, lying in a manger or on white/gold cloth.**

Place Baby Jesus in the centre of the circle in his manger or on the cloth.
Jesus is the Light of the World!
Our prayers can be part of sharing Jesus' light.
Let's make 'twinkle, twinkle stars'
with our hands in the air
and show them to Baby Jesus.
Lead children in opening and closing hands
to make 'twinkle, twinkle stars'.

We're going to sing the end of our song now.
As we sing, let's show our 'twinkle, twinkle stars' for Baby Jesus.
Let's ask God to hear our stars as prayers.
Let's ask God to help us be part
of Jesus' light, shining in the world.

Lead the children in singing the final verse from the Prayer Song you've chosen as you make 'twinkle, twinkle' signs in the air.

Prayer Action: John the Baptist unit

The Saying Sorry to God Building Block, with its strong echoes of repentance and baptism, works particularly well with the 'John the Baptist' unit. For this reason, saying sorry is an optional part of the storytelling itself for this unit. If your group would still like to use the Prayer Building Block during this unit, you could use a simple introduction as follows.

It's time to bring our prayers to Jesus,
who came to give the whole world a new start.

Thank You, God

Thank You, God: Option 1

→ **Song: 'My hands were made for love'. Words: © Sharon Moughtin.**
→ **Tune: 'Hickory, dickory, dock' (traditional).**

[Musical notation with lyrics:]
My hands were made _ for love. My hands were made _ for love.
Thank you for the love they've shown! My hands were made _ for love.

Invite the children to sit in a circle for a moment of quiet.
It's time to remember all the things we've done this week.
It's time to say 'thank you' to God
for when we've been part of showing God's love.

Let's wiggle our fingers!
I wonder when you've shown love
with your hands this week?

Wiggle fingers as you sing.
My hands were made for love!
My hands were made for love!

Thank you for the love they've shown.
My hands were made for love!

Let's wiggle our feet!
I wonder when you've shown love
with your feet this week?

Wiggle feet as you sing.
My feet were made for love!
My feet were made for love!
Thank you for the love they've shown.
My feet were made for love!

Let's put our hands gently on our neck.
Let's sing 'Ahhh!'
Ahhhhh!
Can you feel your throat vibrating and dancing with your voice?
I wonder when you've shown love
with your voice this week?

Hold neck and feel your voice 'dancing' as you sing.
My voice was made for love!
My voice was made for love!
Thank you for the love it's shown.
My voice was made for love!

Thank You, God: Option 2

→ Song: 'For the love we've shown'. Words: © Sharon Moughtin.
→ Tune: 'All through the night' (traditional).

For the love we've shown with our hands, thank you, God! For the love we've shown with our feet, thank you, God! When we love all those a-round us, it's the same as lov-ing Je-sus. For the love we've shown with our voice, thank you, God!

Invite the children to sit in a circle for a moment of quiet.
It's time to remember all the things we've done this week.
It's time to say 'thank you'
for when we've been part of showing God's love.

>   *Either:* Let's wiggle our fingers.
>   *Or:* Let's hold up our hands.

I wonder when you've shown love
with your hands this week?

Either: Let's wiggle our feet.
Or: Let's show our feet.

I wonder when you've shown love
with your feet this week?

Let's put our hands gently on our neck.
Let's sing 'Ahhh!'
Ahhhhh!
Can you feel your neck vibrating and dancing with your voice?
I wonder when you've shown love
with your voice this week?

Let's sing our 'thank you' song to God
For the times we've been part of sharing God's love.

For the love we've shown with our hands,
Hold hands up or wiggle fingers.
thank you, God!
For the love we've shown with our feet,
Point to feet or wiggle feet.
thank you, God!
When we love all those around us,
Cross hands on chest.
it's the same as loving Jesus!
For the love we've shown with our voice,
Hands on neck or point to singing mouth.
thank you, God!

Thank You, God: Option 3

→ Song: 'We thank you, God, for all that's good'. Words: © Sharon Moughtin.
→ Tune: 'Greensleeves' (traditional).

We thank you, God for all that's good that makes us feel alive today! We thank you, God for all that's good that makes us want to sing! Thank you for love and life we praise your name for e-ver! Thank you for love and life we praise your name al-ways!

This option has been created for use in contexts that include adults as well as children of different ages. Groups that only include children up to the age of 7 may prefer to use one of the other 'Thank You, God' options.

Invite the group to sit in a circle for a moment of quiet.

If your time together is held during a communion service, you might like to start with these words:
Our service today is called a 'Eucharist'.
Eucharist means thank you!

It's time to remember all the things that we want to say thank you to God for.

> *Optional:*
>
> *Invite two children to give out a wooden or paper heart to everyone who would like one.*
> *Name* and *Name* are going to bring round some hearts.
> If you like, you can take a heart and hold it in the air to say thank you to God.

Lead the group in singing. If your group is not handing out hearts you might like to use the following actions.

We thank you, God *Heart shape with fingers* **for all that's good**
that makes us feel alive today! *Jazz hands*
We thank you, God *Heart shape with fingers* **for all that's good**
that makes us want to sing! *Twirl finger up from lips to show singing*

> *If your group is giving out wooden or paper hearts, repeat as necessary. Once all the children and adults who wish to take a heart have done so:*

Let's close our eyes for a moment.

Let's remember the times we felt most alive this week!
It might have been spending time with someone special
or doing something you love to do
or seeing something that made you think 'Wow!'

What made you feel most alive this week?
What made you want to sing?

> *Either: if your group has given out hearts:*
> Let's bring all our thankyous into our circle.
> *Name* is going to bring this basket around.
> If you like, you can put your heart in the basket
> and give it to God as a thank you.

> *While all the children and adults who wish to place their hearts in the basket do so, lead the group in singing.*

> *Or: if your group has not given out hearts:*
> Let's remember those moments now and thank God for them.
> *Lead the group in singing:*

Thank you for love and life! *Heart shape with fingers*
We praise your name for ever! *Jazz hands*
Thank you for love and life! *Heart shape with fingers*
We praise your name always! *Jazz hands*

Repeat the whole song or the second part as appropriate until all hearts that have been given out are gathered and given to the leader or placed on a focal table (see p. 208).

> **Tip**
>
> In whole church or all-age worship, this song can also be adapted to be used as a prayer at the end of the service, including as a post-communion prayer as follows.

We thank you God for this time today, *Open hands upwards or heart shape with fingers*
for being here with us, *Place hands downwards*
for loving us. *Cross arms on chest*
We thank you, God for this time today. *Open hands upwards or heart shape with fingers*
It makes us want to sing! *Twirl finger up from lips to show singing*

Thank you for love and life! *Open hands upwards or heart shape with fingers*
We praise your name for ever! *Jazz hands*
Thank you for love and life! *Open hands upwards or heart shape with fingers*
We praise your name always! *Jazz hands*

Creative Response

See the Creative Response starter ideas in Part 3 of the book.

Sharing God's Peace

This Building Block is particularly designed for children's groups that join the adult congregation to share communion but can also be used to end any session or Service of the Word.

Sharing God's Peace: Option 1

→ Isaiah 66.12, NIV
→ Song: 'I've got peace like a river' (traditional).
→ Tune: traditional.

> **Tip: Peace cloth**
>
> Groups that choose to use a peace cloth for the 'Sharing God's Peace' Building Block will need a long piece of blue fabric. The fabric needs to be long enough for all the adults and children to stand around it, and to allow each child to hold a section of the fabric with both hands. It helps to have an adult or older and experienced child standing at each end.
>
> Either: hold one end of the peace cloth and ask one of the older children or an adult to hold the other end. Start singing the Peace Song. As the children begin to gather, invite them to join in holding a small section of the cloth, raising and lowering it so it 'flows' like a river as you sing together.
> Or: invite the children to sit in a circle in the worship space. Start singing the Peace Song. As the children begin to gather, invite them to join in raising and lowering their hands like the waters of a flowing river.

I've got peace like a river,
I've got peace like a river,
I've got peace like a river in my soul.
I've got peace like a river,
I've got peace like a river,
I've got peace like a river in my soul.

If your group is about to rejoin the adults for communion: when all the children are gathered, continue with the words of the Peace, below.

Sharing God's Peace: Option 2

→ Isaiah 66.12, NIV
→ Song: 'Peace is flowing like a river' (traditional).
→ Tune: traditional.

> Either: hold one end of the peace cloth and ask one of the older children or an adult to hold the other end. Start singing the Peace Song. As the children begin to gather, invite them to join in holding a small section of the cloth, raising and lowering it so it 'flows' like a river as you sing together.
> Or: invite the children to sit in a circle in the worship space. Start singing the Peace Song. As the children begin to gather, invite them to join in raising and lowering their hands like the waters of a flowing river.

Peace is flowing like a river,
flowing out through you and me.
Spreading out into the desert,
setting all the captives free.

If your group is about to rejoin the adults for communion: when all the children are gathered, continue with the words of the Peace, below.

Sharing God's Peace: Option 3

→ Song: 'I've got peace in my fingers'. Words: © 1995 Susan Salidor ASCAP.
→ Tune: © 1995 Susan Salidor ASCAP.
→ The words and music can be found on the album *Little Voices in My Head* by Susan Salidor © 2003 Peach Head. They can also be found on iTunes or YouTube, or at <www.susansalidor.com>.

If your group is about to rejoin the adults for communion: when all the children are gathered, continue with the words of the Peace, below.

Sharing God's Peace: Option 4: Getting Ready for Baby Jesus

During Advent and Christmas, you might like to keep to your normal option for Sharing God's Peace. Alternatively, if you have a peace cloth of blue sparkly fabric, you could use this special Peace for Advent and Christmas that uses the carol 'Silent night' (Option 4).

> *Before Christmas:*
> We're getting ready for Baby Jesus,
> the Prince of Peace, to be born.
> Let's sing our Peace Song and imagine
> Baby Jesus' peace spreading through the whole world.
>
> *After Christmas, or on Christmas Day:*
> Baby Jesus, the Prince of Peace, is here!
> Let's sing our Peace Song and imagine
> Baby Jesus' peace spreading through the whole world.
>
> *Either: lay the peace cloth (see p. 207) on the floor and invite the children to come and sit around it, and find a sparkle and look at it.*
> *Or: invite the children to lie on the floor and ask two adults to hold either end of the peace cloth at waist height over the children.*

Invite the children to imagine the peacefulness of the night sky on the night that Jesus was born. I wonder what it was like to be there? Sing or play a CD of 'Silent night' (by Joseph Mohr, translated by John Freeman Young) as the children look at their star.

Silent night, holy night,
all is calm, all is bright
round yon virgin mother and child.
Holy infant, so tender and mild,
sleep in heavenly peace,
sleep in heavenly peace.

If your group is about to rejoin the adults for communion, when all the children are gathered, continue with the words of the Peace below.

The Peace

→ 2 Thessalonians 3.16; 1 Peter 5.14

Once you have finished singing . . .
The peace of the Lord be always with you.
Hold hands open to the children.
And also with you.

Invite the children to open their hands towards you.
Let's shake hands or hug each other
and say, 'Peace be with you' *Or whatever is said on sharing the Peace in your church*
as a sign of God's peace.

Lead the children in giving and receiving the Peace. If your group is meeting during a communion service, this is a good time to then lead the children back to join the rest of the congregation to continue worship with the Eucharistic Prayer. Or you might like first to sing the 'Around a table' song with them (see below).

Around a Table

→ Song: 'Around a table'. Words © Sharon Moughtin.
→ Tune: 'On top of Old Smokey' (traditional).

A-round a ta-ble with God's gifts to share as sis-ters and bro-thers, we lift up our prayer. And bread is bro-ken, and wine is poured. And Je-sus is with us and bless-es us all. The Spi-rit is poured out a-gain and a-gain and all of God's peo-ple will shout A-men!

This Building Block is particularly designed for groups that are held during a communion service, either when the children are present throughout, or when the children will be returning to join the rest of the congregation to receive communion.

Around a table *Hold arms out, palms up*
with God's gifts to share
as sisters and brothers *Hold hands, or stretch hands out wide towards each other*
we lift up our prayer. *Swing hands to and fro then lift them in prayer*
And bread is broken, *Mime breaking*
and wine is poured. *Mime pouring*
And Jesus is with us *Hold arms out, palms up*
and blesses us all. *Mime placing a hand on a row of heads*
The Spirit is poured out *Palms down above head, moving down*
again and again *Palms down above head, moving down*
and all of God's people *Point around group and beyond*
will shout 'AMEN!' *Cup hands around mouth to shout*

Taking God's Love into the World

→ Song: 'This little light of mine' (traditional).
→ Tune: traditional.

This Building Block is particularly designed for groups that are not held at the same time as a communion service. Alternatively, you could use one of the Peace Songs above to end your worship.

Our time together is coming to an end.
Invite the children to sit in a circle for a moment of quiet.

God has lit a little light of love inside all of us.
Trace a circle on your heart.

Let's make our finger into a candle.

Bring your finger from your heart and hold it out.
Let's be God and light our little light of love together, after 3.
Lead the children in lighting their finger candle by striking an imaginary match in the air on 3 and pretending to light your finger.
1, 2, 3 . . . Tssss!
Let's imagine God's love shining and dancing like light in us.

Wave your finger in front of you.
This little light of mine, I'm gonna let it shine!
This little light of mine, I'm gonna let it shine!
This little light of mine, I'm gonna let it shine!
Let it shine, let it shine, let it shine!

Blow on your finger as if blowing out a candle on 'puff'. Then hold it up high.
Won't let no one *Puff* **it out! I'm gonna let it shine!**
Won't let no one *Puff* **it out! I'm gonna let it shine!**
Won't let no one *Puff* **it out! I'm gonna let it shine!**
Let it shine, let it shine, let it shine!

Hold your finger behind a cupped hand, then take your cupped hand away to reveal the 'candle' and hold it high!
Hide it under a bushel? No! I'm gonna let it shine!
Hide it under a bushel? No! I'm gonna let it shine!
Hide it under a bushel? No! I'm gonna let it shine!
Let it shine, let it shine, let it shine!

Lead the children in placing your finger back on your heart.
Now let's put our little light of love
back in our hearts, where it belongs.
Let's remember to let our little light shine
in all our playing and working today . . .

If you're building a Service of the Word and this is your final Building Block, you may like to close with a familiar blessing, the Peace and/or one of the following.

    Either: Praise the Lord! *Both hands to self*
                  Alleluia! *Both arms upwards in 'V' shape*

    Or: Let us bless the Lord. *Both hands to self*
               Thanks be to God. *Both arms upwards in 'V' shape*

    Or: And all the people said . . . *Both hands to self*
               Amen! *Both arms upwards in 'V' shape*

Go in Peace to Love and Serve!

→ **Song:** 'Go in peace to love and serve!' © Sharon Moughtin.
→ **Tune:** Bobby Shaftoe (traditional), the same tune as 'I am going to follow Jesus' (p. 100).

Go in peace to love and serve! Go in peace to love and serve!
Go in peace to love and serve! To serve God here! A - men!

This Building Block is particularly designed for groups that are held within a communion service. Alternatively, you could use one of the Peace Songs above to end your worship.

It's time for us to go out into the world!
Go *Point* in peace *Wiggle fingers to show a river*
to love *Cross arms* and serve *Open hands out*

Let's sing that and point to each other to send each other out to serve God here in our place!

Go *Point* **in peace** *Wiggle fingers*
to love *Cross arms* **and serve** *Open hands out*
Go *Point* **in peace** *Wiggle fingers*
to love *Cross arms* **and serve** *Open hands out*
Go *Point* **in peace** *Wiggle fingers*
to love *Cross arms* **and serve** *Open hands out*
to serve God *Open hands out* **here** *Point down*
Amen. *Clap softly twice*

Sowing Seeds resources

Introduction

Sowing Seeds is designed to be sustainable. We aim to use what's already around us rather than buying in lots of new resources. As a starting point, however, we've found the following helpful.

Imaginative aids

Sowing Seeds encourages the use of imaginative aids during the Gathering Song to send a strong signal that this is an environment where imagination is celebrated. Imaginative aids can be anything that the children can use to make shapes and show feelings.

Why use imaginative aids?

- to fire up imaginations
- to familiarize children with active participation
- to present opportunities for worshipping God in ways beyond words
- to give babies the opportunity to explore their bodies and bring them into worship
- to give toddlers and children the confidence to use their whole bodies in worship
- to open up opportunities for babies, toddlers and children to become lost in the moment
- to cut down on preparation time: imaginative aids can become whatever you want them to be!

We tend to use the following imaginative aids but your choice will depend on your space, numbers, imagination and budget. For instance, we've also used fallen autumn leaves to wave during the autumn season.

- hand scarves
- yellow ribbons threaded on to rings
- green streamers on sticks.

For examples of places to purchase these, see the Setting Up page on the website.

If your group is related to a church that uses liturgical colours, you may wish to use imaginative aids that correspond to the season's colour. If your church doesn't use liturgical colours, it may still be worth using only one colour at a time, to prevent upset about which colour each child is given. This will help to keep the emphasis on the children's imagination and how they use the aids rather than on the choice set before them.

The use of imaginative aids during the Gathering Song provides a wonderful opportunity to include any babies who are present and encourage them to take a leading role. Many babies when handed a streamer or dance scarf will instinctively shake it, hide behind it or make some really interesting shapes. We've found that the older children really enjoy copying a baby in her or his innovative actions. They seem to love to discover that babies are individuals, and it's always wonderful to see the reaction of small babies as they realize that everyone is looking to them and following their lead. It can also be a great time to encourage a newcomer or child who may be feeling a little shy to take a lead, where appropriate

Peace cloth

Your group might like to use a peace cloth for the 'Sharing God's Peace' Building Block. Either find a blue piece of fabric that's long and wide enough for all the adults and children to stand around, holding a section with both hands to wave 'the river' up and down as the group sings. (It helps to have an adult or older and experienced child standing at each end.) Alternatively, you could find a long and thin piece of blue fabric or ribbon and stand in a circle, each holding a section with both hands to wave 'the river' up and down as you sing.

Focal table

Your group might like to have a focal table to place objects on during your time together, as indicated in the material. If your church is one that follows liturgical colours, you could place a cloth matching the colour of the season on the table.

Creative Response resources

Sowing Seeds books provide a wide range of creative 'starter ideas' that aim to spark the children's imaginations as well as one or more 'print-and-go' options for each week.

This time of Creative Response is optional but for those groups who choose it, these materials will come in helpful on a weekly basis:

- white paper (different-coloured paper is a nice addition)
- coloured pencils (it's worth getting good-quality pencils that need sharpening less often)
- chunky crayons (for younger children)
- white card (not essential but useful)
- child-safe scissors
- PVA glue kept in small lidded pots with spatulas (for younger children)
- sticks from outside, wooden lollipop sticks or wooden coffee stirrers
- string or wool.

For further ideas for more creative resources, take a look below.

Collage materials

These aren't essential, but will always be useful. Many younger children will not spend long with crayons/pencils and are more likely to enjoy glueing and sticking to make a collage. Most units have suggestions for collaging, which requires little preparation if you have suitable materials to hand.

Gathering a range of textures and patterns as well as colours is ideal. Useful items include:

- scraps of coloured paper discarded by the children when cutting out in the sessions;
- coloured envelopes from birthday cards;
- felt (you can buy offcuts of felt from eBay);
- scrap material;
- offcuts from people who sew;
- ends of wool from people who knit;
- paper napkins;
- string bags used to hold courgettes or satsumas (depending on the type; some fall apart);
- ribbons snipped into small pieces (Christmas and birthdays are good times to keep an eye out for these);
- tinfoil and cotton wool;
- newspapers;
- broken gift bags or wrapping and tissue paper from presents;
- sweet wrappers or gold chocolate-coin wrappers;
- packaging from postal parcels;
- leftovers from art-and-craft sets;
- bark or leaves;
- sandpaper.

Interesting media

While pencils and crayons are adequate for many Creative Responses, we've found that encouraging the children to explore using different media can be inspirational. When introducing a different medium, make it available during the whole unit to give the children the opportunity to develop their use of it, while also saving time on planning and preparation.

Ideas of the different media that might be useful include:

- pastels
- chalks
- watercolour paints
- ready mixed paints (using these with shaving brushes can work well for very young children)
- watercolour pencils (for older children, if you have time to show them how they work)
- charcoal
- dyed string or coloured wool soaked in PVA glue
- sticks and mud
- sponges or rollers and paint
- edible cornflour finger paints (see p. 210)
- dyed cooked spaghetti (see p. 210)
- dyed uncooked pasta (see p. 210).

We also encourage the children to draw or paint on different media as well as paper. These might include:

- thick brown or white card
- cardboard from recycling
- stones
- graph paper, lined paper
- pieces of wood (ensure these are free of splinters)
- shells
- fabric, especially pale fabric
- tracing paper or baking parchment
- coloured or textured paper
- patterned wallpaper
- newspaper or magazine cuttings (check these are appropriate before use)
- long rolls of paper taped to the floor with masking tape.

Exploring the possibilities of 'ephemeral' or 'transient' art can give children the opportunity to discover that beautiful things can be fleeting and last only a moment. We don't need to be afraid of the idea that things may not last: we can still celebrate their beauty. Suitable items include:

- things from the natural world, depending on the season: pressed flowers, leaves, grasses, blossom, bark, twigs, sand, berries, stones, shells (check all these for safety)
- buttons
- milk bottle tops of various colours
- dyed cooked spaghetti, or uncooked rice or pasta (see p. 210);
- salt dyed with paint or food colouring
- edible cornflour paint (see p. 210);
- coloured paper in different shapes: squares, circles, triangles, diamonds, rectangles, hexagons, octagons, etc.

Creative materials from home:

- wooden mosaic shapes
- Etch-a-Sketch
- 'Cordz' sets
- felt sets and boards
- magnetic boards and shapes
- ink pads and stamps
- Post-it pads
- Spirograph
- stencils to use with paint or pencils.

Recipes

How to make salt dough

Mix 2 cups of flour with 1 cup of salt and 1 cup of water. If you'd like coloured salt dough, add a few drops of food colouring to the water before mixing. If it's too sticky, add more flour; if it's too dry, add a drop more water. If you're making the dough in advance, it can become sticky when stored, so make sure you take extra flour with you and check the dough before use. The shapes that are made with the salt dough will air-dry in time (unless they're very thick). The dough can also be dried in an oven (on a low heat for around 3 hours) or in a microwave (check every few seconds).

How to dye cooked spaghetti

Cook the spaghetti according to the packet instructions with a little oil, drain it, then immediately run cold water over it in a colander or sieve to stop the cooking. Divide the cooked spaghetti up into bowls according to how many different colours you would like, add food colouring and mix well. Let the spaghetti dry (this takes an hour or so).

How to dye uncooked pasta

Place the uncooked pasta in a bowl. Mix food colouring with ½–1 teaspoon of vinegar. Pour the vinegar dye mix over the pasta and stir well. Once the pasta is fully coated, spread it out in a single layer on a baking tray to dry.

How to dye uncooked rice

Place the uncooked rice in a bowl. Mix food colouring with ½–1 teaspoon of vinegar. Pour the vinegar dye mix over the rice and stir well. Once the rice is fully coated, spread it out in a single layer on a baking tray to dry.

> **Tip**
>
> If you'd like to make dyed pasta or rice with children, you could use sealed food bags or plastic boxes for the mixing: invite a child to shake them until the pasta or rice is fully coated.

How to make edible cornflour paint

This paint is completely edible, but its neutral taste means that babies and toddlers aren't encouraged to eat it.

Mix 4 tablespoons of cornflour in a pan with enough cold water to make a medium-thick paste. Pour in 1 cup of boiling water slowly and stir until there are no lumps. Heat the mixture gently on a hob, stirring continually. Once you see clear streaks in the mixture, turn off the heat but continue stirring as the mixture thickens. Divide the mixture up into separate pots according to how many different colours you're planning, add food colouring and mix well. If you place it in the fridge (where it will keep for a couple of weeks), make sure you take it out and let it reach room temperature before use. If the paint needs thinning to use, add boiling water a drop at a time.

Photocopiable templates

The templates on the following pages are for use with the Creative Response starter ideas.

They are listed here.

Angel (p. 213)

Paper angel (p. 214)

Baby (p. 215)

Bird (p. 216)

Bodies (p. 217)

Body (p. 218)

Candle (p. 219)

Circle (p. 220)

Crown (p. 221)

Face (p. 222)

Finger puppet (p. 223)

Font (p. 224)

Lantern (p. 225)

Large heart (p. 226)

Postcard (p. 227)

Sheep (p. 228)

Stained-glass window (p. 229)

Star (p. 230)

Suitcase (p. 231)

Treasure chest (p. 232)

Instructions for finger-puppet template

1. Cut the finger puppets out along the thick lines.
2. Fold the flaps along the dotted lines, folding away from you.
3. Again folding away from you, fold the puppet in the middle where the arrow is.
4. Tape the flaps to the other half of the puppet.

Instructions for crown template

1. Cut along zigzag line.
2. Sellotape the two halves together with 1 cm overlap so that you have one long strip.
3. Put the strip round your head so that you can measure where to sellotape the ends.
4. Sellotape the ends together to make a crown.

Instructions for the hatband

1. Fold a sheet of A4 paper in half or thirds lengthways.
2. Open it out and then cut into strips along the folds.
3. Tape or glue the ends together to the required length.

Instructions for paper angels template

1. Cut along the line marked with the scissor symbol.
2. Fold each piece of paper into four along the lines marked 'Fold'. Make sure the angel figure is at the front.
3. Cut round the angel figure, but do not cut where the line is broken at the top of the wings. Be careful not to cut the folds.
4. Unfold the paper. You should have four angels linked together at the top of their wings.

Instructions for the lantern template

1. Optional. If you want to decorate the lantern, you need to do so before folding and cutting it.
2. Fold along the dotted line. Fold away from you so that the solid lines are on the outside.
3. Starting at the fold, cut along the solid lines, being careful not to cut into the white space at the edge of the paper.
4. Open the paper out. Curl the paper into a cylinder shape with the short edges touching, making sure the fold sticks outwards rather than inwards. Tape or glue the short edges together.
5. Optional. To make a handle, cut a strip of paper and glue or tape each end to the top of the lantern.

Julia (6) drew this angel. What can you make from it? Or would you like to draw your own?

Sowing Seeds actively encourages peer-led learning by children. All our templates are created by children or child-leaders.
Copyright © Sharon Moughtin 2017, 2025. From Sharon Moughtin, *Sowing Seeds Book 1: Bible storytelling and worship with children, includes Advent, Christmas and Epiphany.*

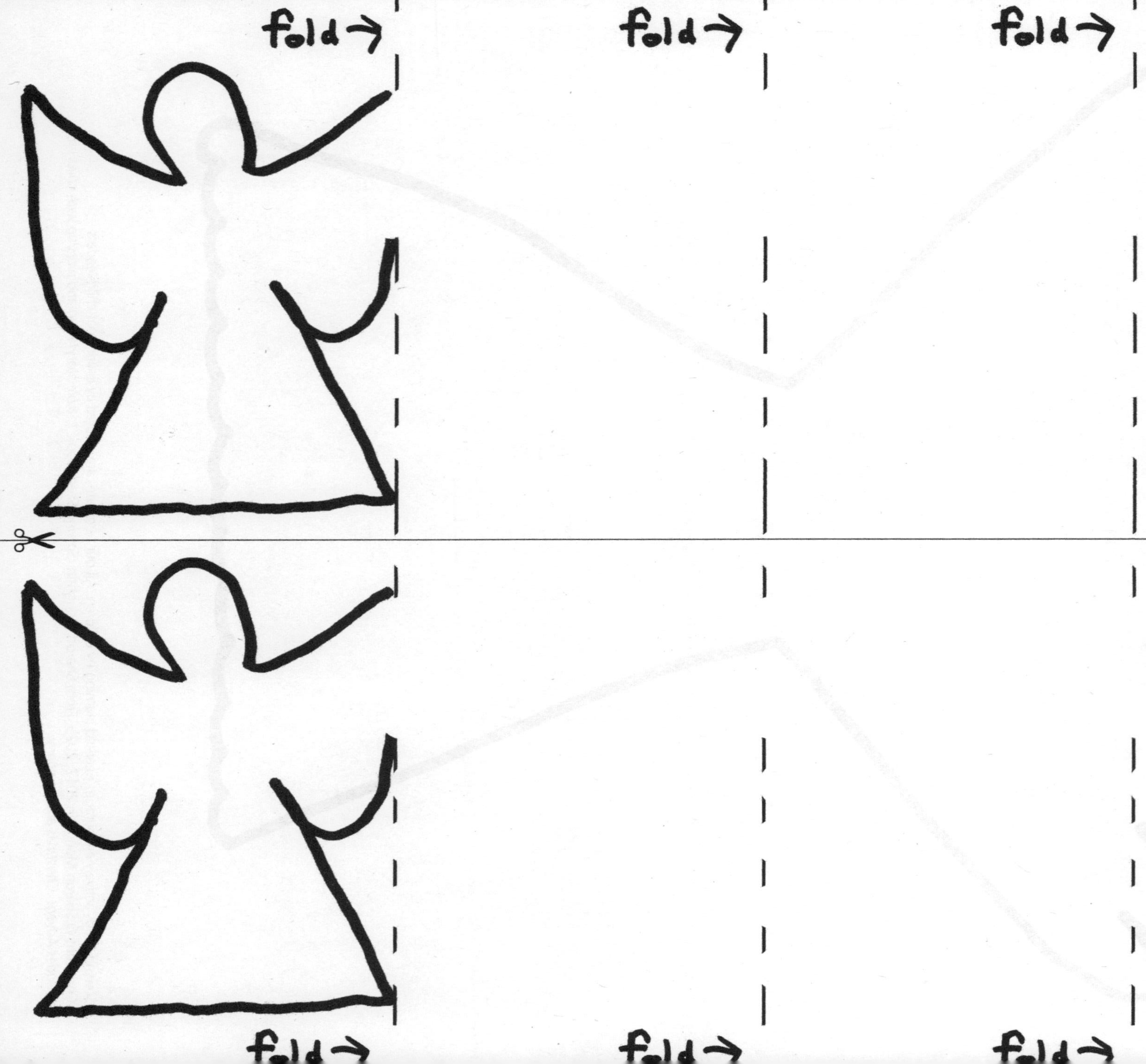

Joy (8) drew these angels. Can you fold the paper at the arrows, then cut round the angels and open them out to make a chain of 'paper angels'? Or would you like to make your own? *Full instructions on p. 212.*

fold →

fold →

fold →

fold →

fold →

fold →

Sowing Seeds actively encourages peer-led learning by children. All our templates are created by children or child-leaders.

Copyright © Sharon Moughtin 2017, 2025. From Sharon Moughtin, *Sowing Seeds Book 1: Bible storytelling and worship with children*, includes *Advent, Christmas and Epiphany*.

Zoe M.-M. (8) drew this baby wrapped in cloth. What can you make from it? Or would you like to draw your own?

Sowing Seeds actively encourages peer-led learning by children. All our templates are created by children or child-leaders. Copyright © Sharon Moughtin 2017, 2025. From Sharon Moughtin, *Sowing Seeds Book 1: Bible storytelling and worship with children, includes Advent, Christmas and Epiphany*.

Joy (9) drew this bird. What can you make from it? Or would you like to draw your own?

Sowing Seeds actively encourages peer-led learning by children. All our templates are created by children or child-leaders. Copyright © Sharon Moughtin, *Sowing Seeds Book 1: Bible storytelling and worship with children, includes Advent, Christmas and Epiphany.* Copyright © Sharon Moughtin 2017, 2025. From Sharon Moughtin,

Julia (6) drew these bodies. What can you make from them? Or would you like to draw your own? *A larger body template is available on the following page.*

Sowing Seeds actively encourages peer-led learning by children. All our templates are created by children or child-leaders. Copyright © Sharon Moughtin, 2017, 2025. From Sharon Moughtin, *Sowing Seeds Book 1: Bible storytelling and worship with children*, includes *Advent, Christmas and Epiphany*.

Julia (6) drew this body. What can you make from it? Or would you like to draw your own?

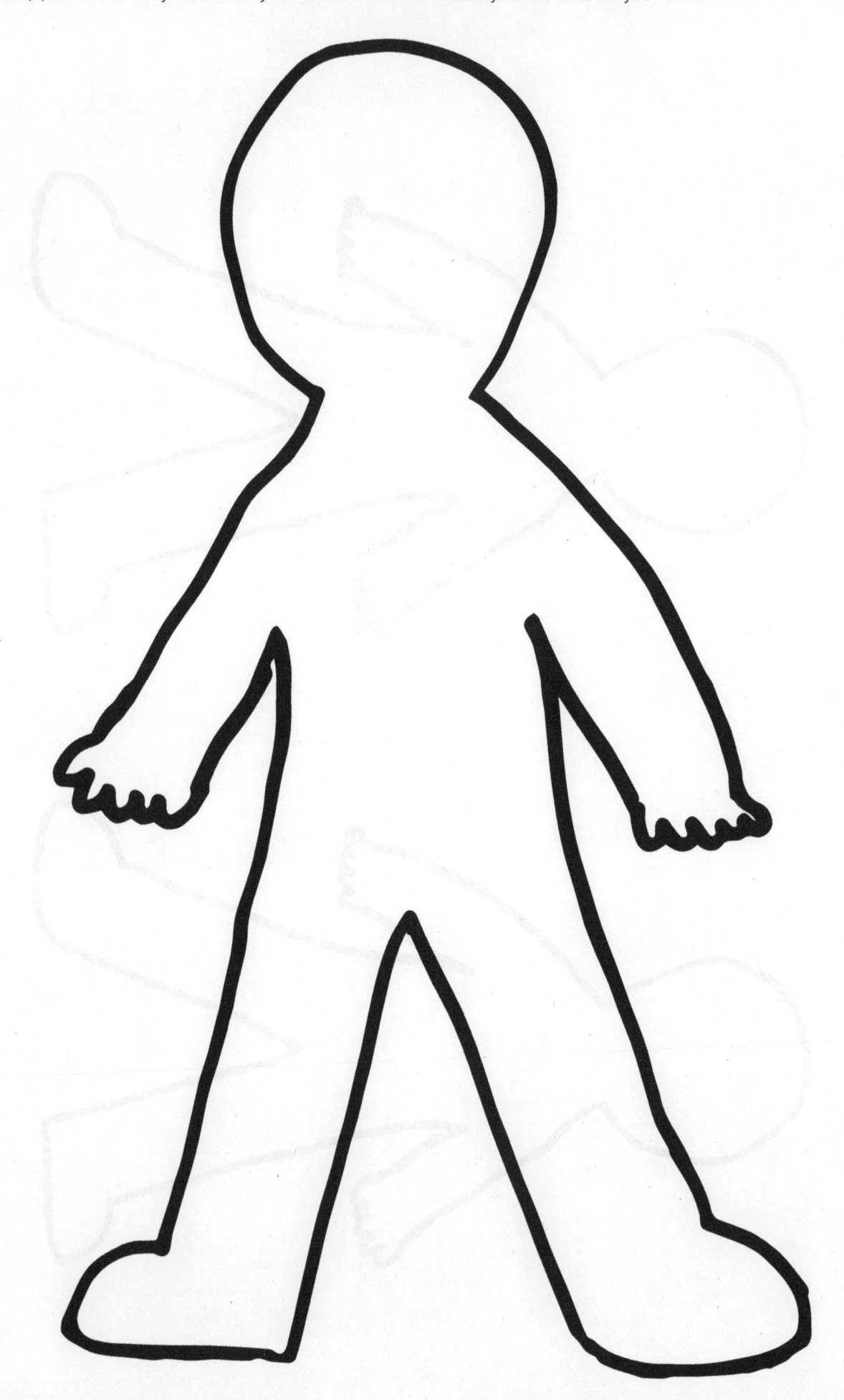

Sowing Seeds actively encourages peer-led learning by children. All our templates are created by children or child-leaders.
Copyright © Sharon Moughtin 2017, 2025. From Sharon Moughtin, *Sowing Seeds Book 1: Bible storytelling and worship with children, includes Advent, Christmas and Epiphany.*

Anastasia (8) and Gavin (6) drew these candles. What can you make from them? Or would you like to draw your own?

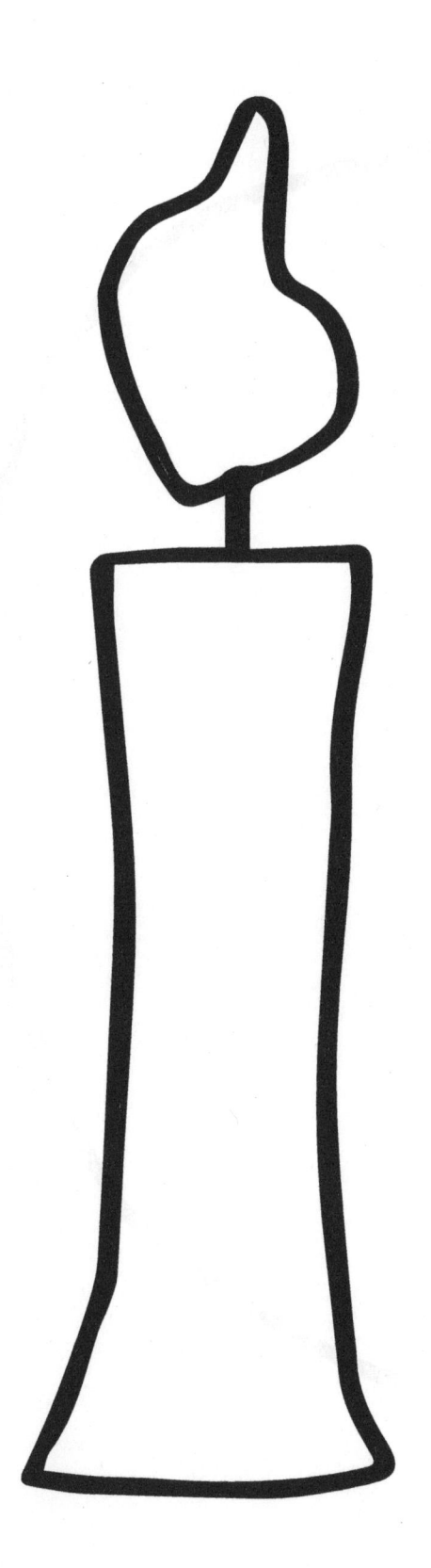

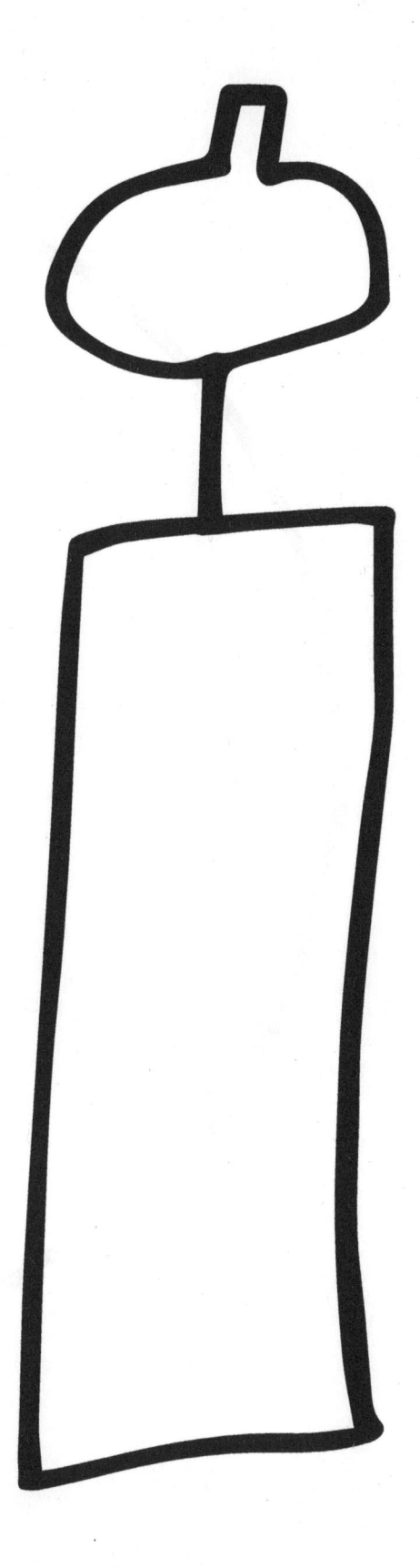

Sowing Seeds actively encourages peer-led learning by children. All our templates are created by children or child-leaders.
Copyright © Sharon Moughtin 2017, 2025. From Sharon Moughtin, *Sowing Seeds Book 1: Bible storytelling and worship with children, includes Advent, Christmas and Epiphany*.

Abigail (6) drew around a plate to make this circle. What can you make from it? Or would you like to draw your own?

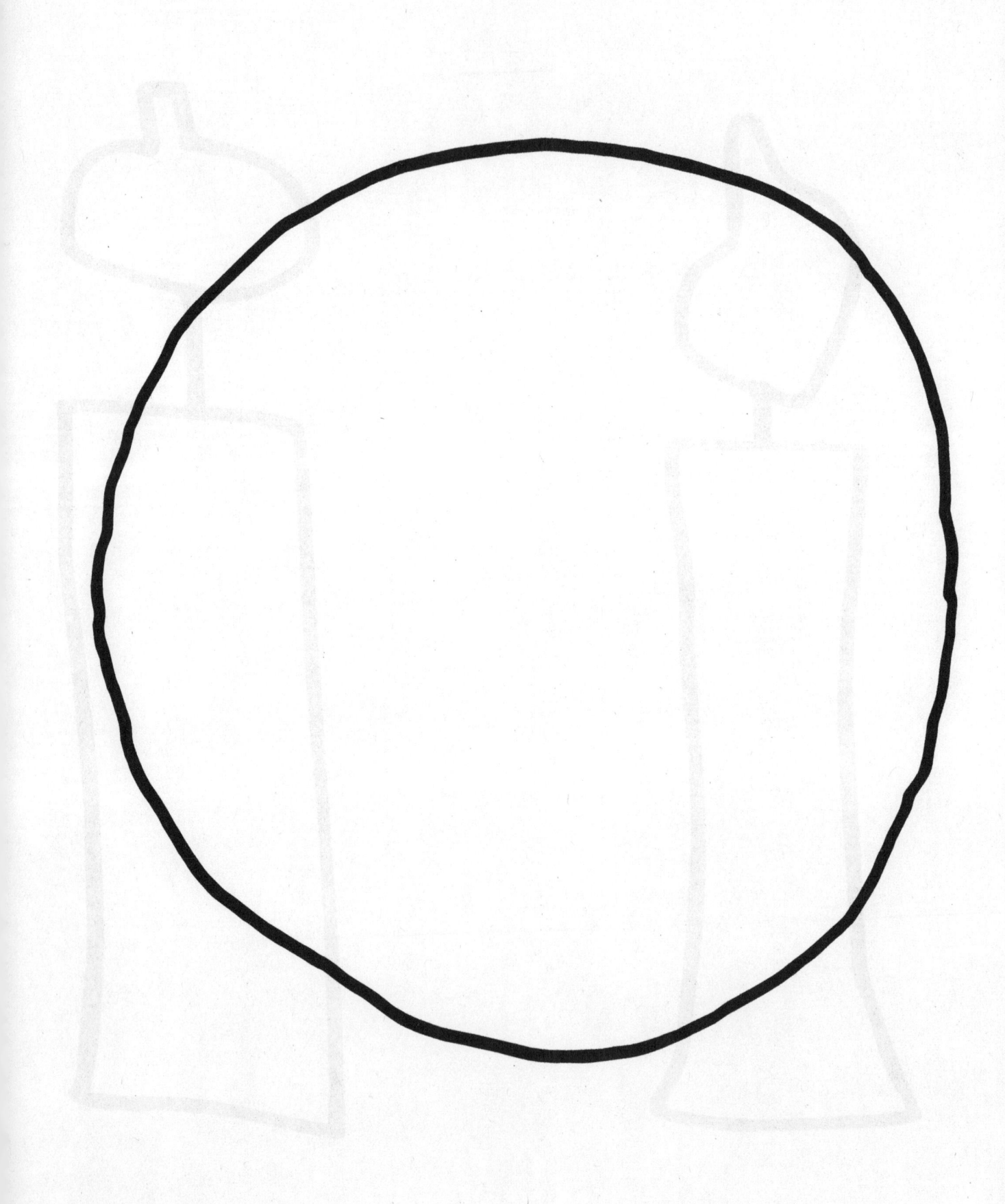

Sowing Seeds actively encourages peer-led learning by children. All our templates are created by children or child-leaders.
Copyright © Sharon Moughtin 2017, 2025. From Sharon Moughtin, *Sowing Seeds Book 1: Bible storytelling and worship with children, includes Advent, Christmas and Epiphany.*

Philip (6) drew this zigzag line. Can you cut down it to make a crown?

Sowing Seeds actively encourages peer-led learning by children. All our templates are created by children or child-leaders. Copyright © Sharon Moughtin 2017, 2025. From Sharon Moughtin, *Sowing Seeds Book 1: Bible storytelling and worship with children*, includes Advent, Christmas and Epiphany. Or would you like to make your own crown?

Elijah (6) drew this face. What can you make from it? Or would you like to draw your own?

Sowing Seeds actively encourages peer-led learning by children. All our templates are created by children or child-leaders.
Copyright © Sharon Moughtin 2017, 2025. From Sharon Moughtin, *Sowing Seeds Book 1: Bible storytelling and worship with children, includes Advent, Christmas and Epiphany.*

Isabella (7) drew these finger puppets. Would you like to make them into people? Or would you like to make your own?

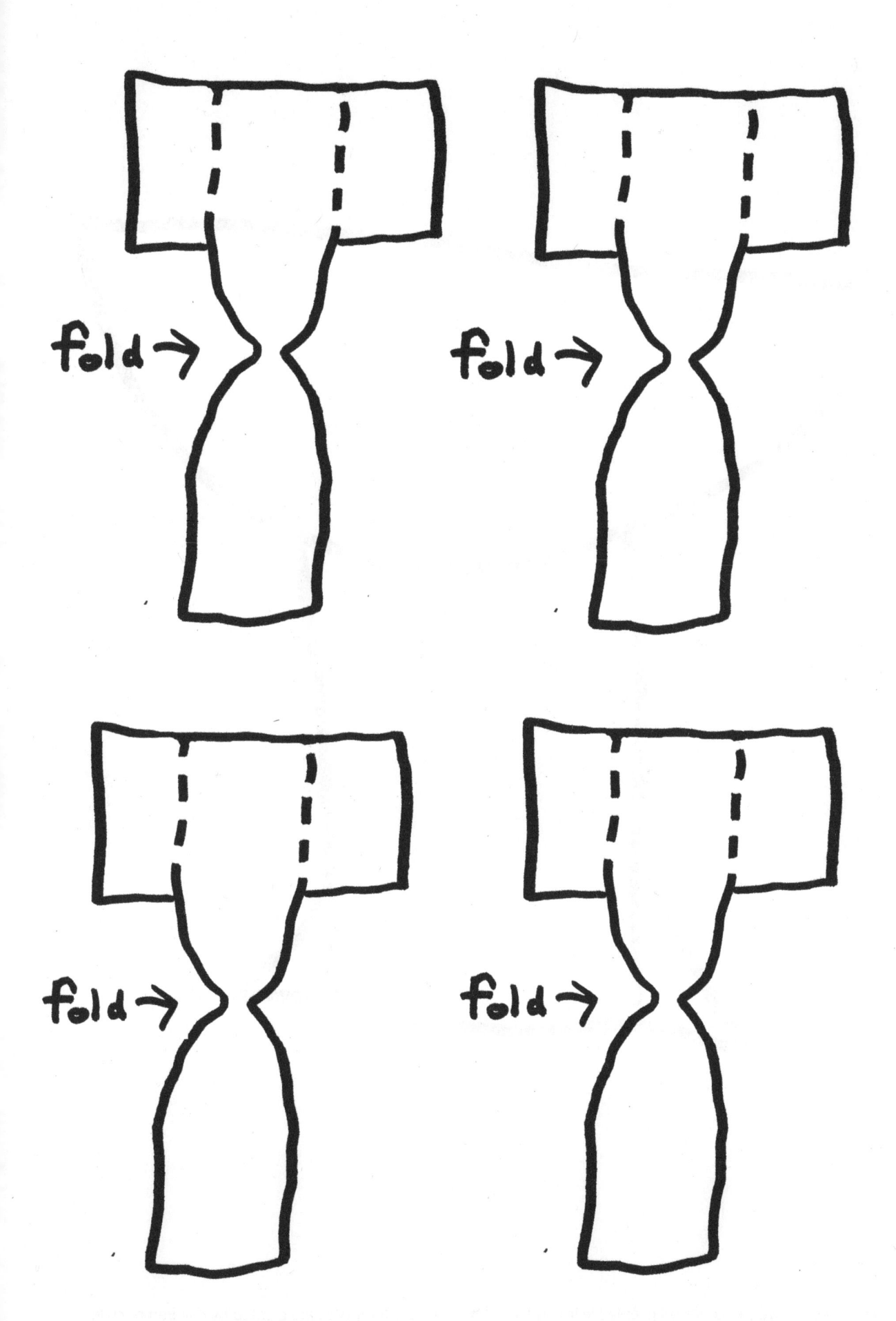

fold →

fold →

fold →

fold →

Sowing Seeds actively encourages peer-led learning by children. All our templates are created by children or child-leaders.
Copyright © Sharon Moughtin 2017, 2025. From Sharon Moughtin, *Sowing Seeds Book 1: Bible storytelling and worship with children, includes Advent, Christmas and Epiphany*.

Elijah (7) drew this font. What will you do with it? Or would you like to draw your own?

Sowing Seeds actively encourages peer-led learning by children. All our templates are created by children or child-leaders. Copyright © Sharon Moughtin 2017, 2025. From Sharon Moughtin, *Sowing Seeds Book 1: Bible storytelling and worship with children, includes Advent, Christmas and Epiphany*.

Anastasia (9) created this template for you to make a lantern. Or would you like to make your own? *See p. 194 for instructions.*

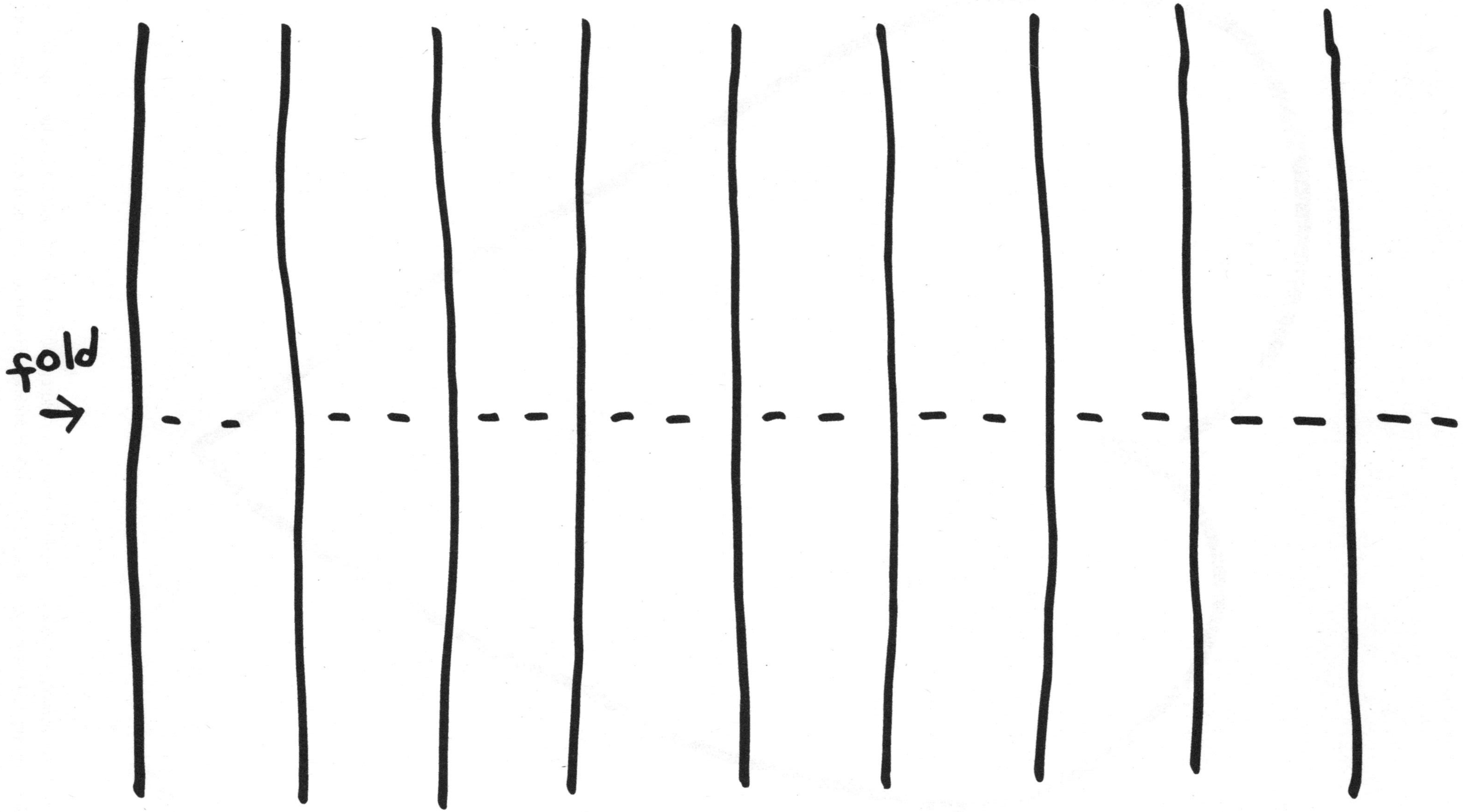

← fold

Sowing Seeds actively encourages peer-led learning by children. All our templates are created by children or child-leaders. Copyright © Sharon Moughtin, *Sowing Seeds Book 1: Bible storytelling and worship with children*, includes *Advent, Christmas and Epiphany*.

Amy (6) drew this heart. What can you make from it? Or would you like to draw your own? *An alternative heart shape is available in Book 2 (p. 209).*

Sowing Seeds actively encourages peer-led learning by children. All our templates are created by children or child-leaders. Copyright © Sharon Moughtin 2017, 2025. From Sharon Moughtin, *Sowing Seeds Book 1: Bible storytelling and worship with children, includes Advent, Christmas and Epiphany.*

Anastasia (8) drew this postcard. What can you write or draw on it? Or would you like to draw your own?

Sowing Seeds actively encourages peer-led learning by children. All our templates are created by children or child-leaders.
Copyright © Sharon Moughtin 2017, 2025. From Sharon Moughtin, *Sowing Seeds Book 1: Bible storytelling and worship with children, includes Advent, Christmas and Epiphany.*

Anastasia (8) drew this sheep. What can you make from it? Or would you like to draw your own?

Sowing Seeds actively encourages peer-led learning by children. All our templates are created by children or child-leaders. Copyright © Sharon Moughtin 2017, 2025. From Sharon Moughtin, *Sowing Seeds Book 1: Bible storytelling and worship with children, includes Advent, Christmas and Epiphany.*

Zoe drew this stained-glass window.

Sowing Seeds actively encourages peer-led learning by children. All our templates are created by children or child-leaders.
Copyright © Sharon Moughtin 2017, 2025. From Sharon Moughtin, *Sowing Seeds Book 1: Bible storytelling and worship with children, includes Advent, Christmas and Epiphany*.

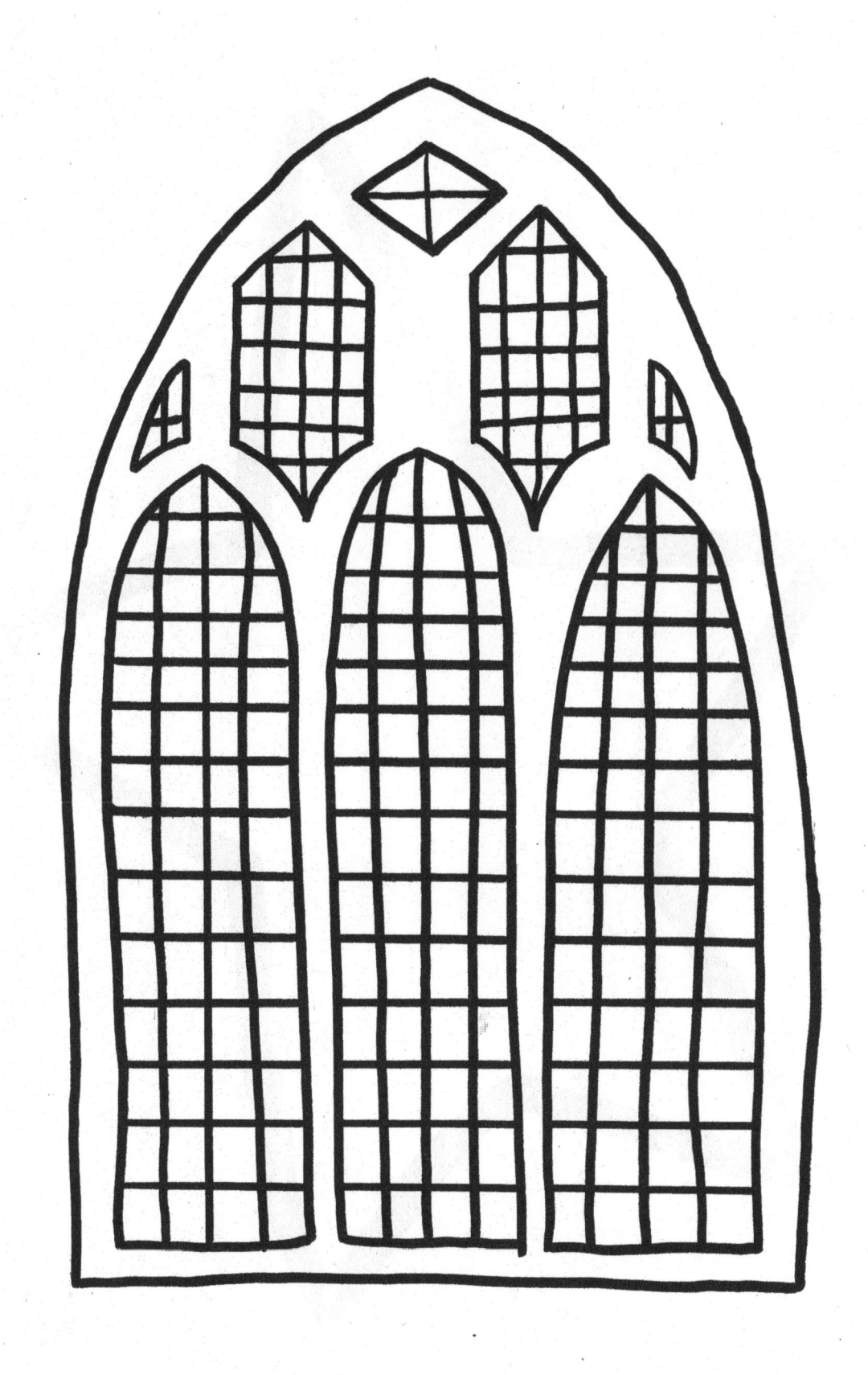

Kayleigh (7) drew round a star shape to make this star. What can you make from it? Or would you like to draw your own?

Sowing Seeds actively encourages peer-led learning by children. All our templates are created by children or child-leaders. Copyright © Sharon Moughtin 2017, 2025. From Sharon Moughtin, *Sowing Seeds Book 1: Bible storytelling and worship with children, includes Advent, Christmas and Epiphany*.

Amelia (7) created this suitcase. What will you pack inside it? Or would you like to draw your own?

Sowing Seeds actively encourages peer-led learning by children. All our templates are created by children or child-leaders. Copyright © Sharon Moughtin 2017, 2025. From Sharon Moughtin, *Sowing Seeds Book 1: Bible storytelling and worship with children, includes Advent, Christmas and Epiphany*.

Anastasia (9) drew this treasure chest. What will you make from it? Or would you like to draw your own?

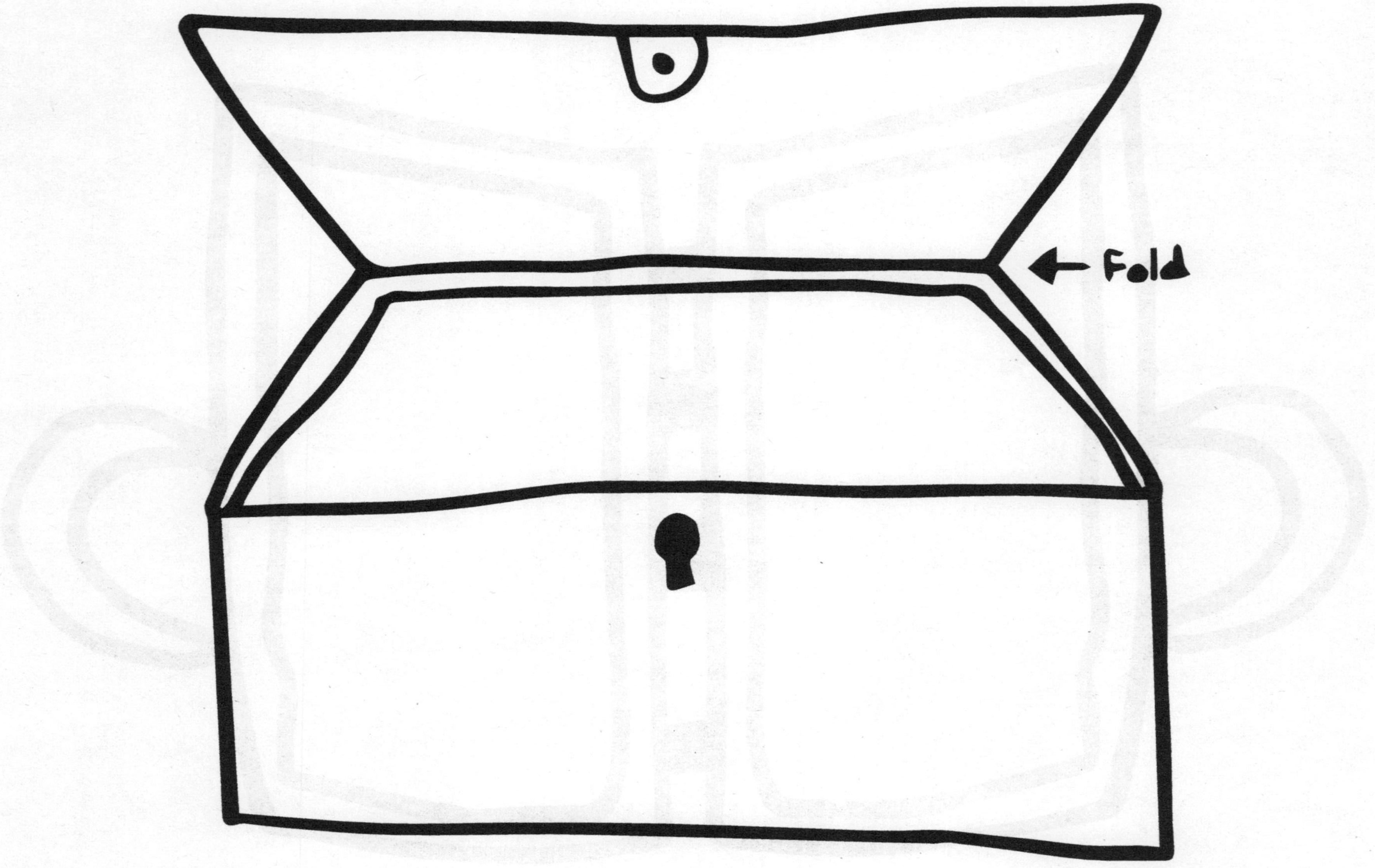

← Fold

Sowing Seeds actively encourages peer-led learning by children. All our templates are created by children or child-leaders. Copyright © Sharon Moughtin 2017, 2025. From Sharon Moughtin, *Sowing Seeds Book 1: Bible storytelling and worship with children*, includes Advent, Christmas and Epiphany.

NOTES

Introduction

1 Søren Kierkegaard, *Three Discourses on Imagined Occasions* (1845).
2 See Rebecca Nye, *Children's Spirituality: What It Is and Why It Matters* (London: Church House Publishing, 2009).

Part 1 Interactive Bible storytelling

1 Observant participants may notice that Jesus also turns the order of the opposites upside down! According to the structure of Mary's song, we would expect 'the last will be first and the first will be last' but Jesus' words are 'the first will be last and the last will be first'. Jesus really is the one who turns absolutely everything upside down!
2 Think of David and Rachel in the Old Testament. What is striking about this is that it makes sense of how the news then spreads through the whole community at the end of the story. This may not have happened easily if the shepherds were people on the outskirts of society (as art and tradition have suggested). However, it is not hard to imagine if the community's children carried the good news. See A. L. Allen, 'A sign for you: A child savior revealed to child shepherds', *Biblical Interpretation* 29 (2), pp. 229–55.
3 At this point in the story, Abraham is strictly called 'Abram' and Sarah is 'Sarai'. You can use these names throughout this story, if you prefer. However, as Abraham and Sarah are the version of the names that the children will hear most often in the church and in the Bible, we will use them from the beginning.